CONRAD'S MODELS OF MIND

► The publication of this book

was assisted by the ATKINSON FUND.

# CONRAD'S
# MODELS OF MIND

*Bruce Johnson*

UNIVERSITY OF MINNESOTA PRESS, Minneapolis

*Library of Congress Catalog Card Number:* 73-150125
*ISBN* 0-8166-0615-3

For MRS. BOODLE

# Acknowledgments

Sections of this book have appeared in *Conradiana*, Summer 1968 (Chapter 8) and *Texas Studies in Literature and Language*, Winter 1971 (part of Chapter 5), and one part is forthcoming in *Studies in Short Fiction* (a small segment of Chapter 5 included in a quite different discussion of *Heart of Darkness*). My thanks to *Conradiana*, the University of Texas Press, and Newberry College for permission to reprint. I have used Bruce Harkness's edition of *Heart of Darkness*. This edition of the story — a collation of all important editions — is from *Conrad's "Heart of Darkness" and the Critics*, copyright 1960 by Bruce Harkness, and is reprinted by special permission of Professor Harkness and the publisher, Wadsworth Publishing Company, Inc., Belmont, California 94002. The Trustees of the Joseph Conrad Estate have kindly given me permission to reprint part of the manuscript of "Falk," as has the Yale University Library, owner of the manuscript.

As for people who have helped me with this book, Richard Ellmann's name must come first for many early contributions to my study of English literature. William Rueckert and George Ford read the manuscript and encouraged me in substantial ways. To all of these friends, my heartfelt thanks. To the many Conradians whose earlier work has made most of my thinking possible, I owe a debt too complex to be expressed in mere footnotes. Finally, Associate Dean Ralph Raimi of the University of Rochester, who is a "secret sharer" of enthusiasm for Conrad, made available a grant to cover the cost of indexing this book.

# Contents

# CONRAD'S MODELS OF MIND

With three exceptions, all page references to the novels and short stories of Conrad are to Dent's *Collected Edition of the Works of Joseph Conrad* (London: J. W. Dent and Sons, 1946–1955). Pagination is identical with the Dent Uniform Edition (1923, 1926) and with the Doubleday, Page and Company Canterbury Edition (1924). For *Lord Jim*, however, I have used the authoritative Norton Critical Edition, edited by Thomas Moser (New York, 1958). For *Heart of Darkness*, Bruce Harkness's *Conrad's "Heart of Darkness" and the Critics* (San Francisco: Wadsworth Publishing Company, 1960) offers the same advantages as Moser: an authoritative text, textual history, and collation. My edition of *Nostromo* is the Modern Library Edition (New York, 1951), simply because it is based, as Claire Rosenfield notes in her book on Conrad, upon the text published in 1904 by Doubleday and Company. This edition contains interesting passages that were apparently deleted in later editions.

# Introduction:
# The Idea of
# Psychological Models

E very writer makes assumptions about the nature of mind, whether they be elaborate theories, metaphors that seem simple but imply a great deal, downright beliefs, or vague gestalten. And such assumptions color his whole creation, the way his characters think and feel and react, possibly even his choice of subject matter. M. H. Abrams has shown how a large part of the history of literary criticism was guided by the seemingly innocuous metaphors of the mirror and the lamp.[1] Similarly, though we may not usually be speaking of metaphors, a writer's whole creation may be guided by fundamental models, shall we say, that allow him to organize and come to grips with the ultimately mysterious phenomenon of mind. If metaphors are involved, usually they are not the ones that turn up from line to line — not the ones that Carolyn Spurgeon was interested in charting. They are, rather, tentative comparisons that dodge behind textual evidence or are deeply submerged, that may not be recognized by the author as models or metaphors at all. To quote Abrams:

The endemic disease of analogical thinking, however, is hardening of the categories. For as Coleridge said, "No simile runs on all four legs"; analogues are by their very nature only partial parallels, and

3

the very sharpness of focus afforded by a happily chosen archetype [metaphor, as I use the term] makes marginal and elusive those qualities of an object which fall outside its primitive categories. While a work of art, for instance, is very like a mirror, it is also, in important respects, quite different, and not many critics have been able to keep the derived aesthetic categories flexible, and sufficiently responsive to data outside their immediate scope. The history of modern criticism . . . may in some part be told as the search for alternative parallels — a heterocosm or "second nature," the overflow from a fountain, the music of a wind-harp, a growing plant — which would avoid some of the troublesome implications of the mirror, and better comprehend those aspects and relations of an aesthetic object which this archetype leaves marginal or omits.[2]

When John Locke suggests that the original mind is an empty room or an unmarked tablet of wax, we may be certain that he knows he is speaking metaphorically or figuratively. When Newton, as Colin Turbayne points out, speaks of bodies "attracting" one another, or a modern engineer speaks of "metal fatigue," we are much less sure that either Newton or the engineer knows that he is speaking analogically or metaphorically.[3] The truth is, of course, that the line between metaphor and identity is no line at all but much more like a fog. Joseph Conrad's first two novels — *Almayer's Folly* and *An Outcast of the Islands* — work with the conception of "paralyzed will," and it is relatively easy to show that he shares that idea (whatever validity it may already have had in his own private experience) with French writers of the late nineteenth century. Whether he recognized that "will" as he used the conception was a notorious part of what Turbayne, and Gilbert Ryle in *The Concept of Mind*,[4] think of as the myth of volitions, we can only guess. But it seems to me Conrad instinctively knew that his assumptions about the human mind were by way of being tentative models and in a few important instances, actually metaphors. The point of this study is, however, that Conrad, unlike many artists, did not suffer from "hardening of the categories." His art continually undercuts — while nonetheless exploiting — his conception of the mind. He is no philosopher, but the general effect of Conrad's redefining the whole idea of a faculty called will is not unlike that of Ryle's attempt (described by Turbayne) to achieve a "correct ontology of the mind":

> He notices that in the official or mistaken theory such entities as the will, volition, vanity, and the mind are regarded as mental existents, some of which cause effects in the physical realm. Thus the impulse of vanity causes acts of boasting, while the mind itself exists to house impulses, volitions, and other incidents. These entities Ryle exposes as myths or occult qualities on a parity with phlogiston, vital force, etc. . . . Part of Ryle's re-allocation consists in replacing causal explanations by explanations in terms of reasons and incidents; the reasons being expressed as hypothetical or law-like statements in which such terms as "volition," "vanity" etc., are eliminated because they denote no observables; and the incidents being treated innocuously as cues. Hamlet's remark, "Had he the *motive* and the *cue* for passion that I have, he would drown the stage with tears," characterizes this kind of explanation. Thus, instead of occult forces causing occurrences we have the streamlined procedure of premises entailing conclusions.[5]

Such "streamlined procedure" would have pleased Conrad even less than the old idea of will; but it is nonetheless true that in his own way — the imaginative way of a novelist concerned first with seeing and feeling — Conrad moves steadily and impressively away from deductive psychology, involving "faculties" or entities such as will, passion, ego, or sympathy, toward a flexible and — for the period — new psychology that has implications for his entire development as a writer. To call this new psychology one of "self-image" is to court all the clichés surrounding that useful cliché. Yet during Conrad's life the conception and the phrase were nothing short of revolutionary, and Conrad must be given credit for his part in this fundamental shift of gestalt.

While writing this study it has occasionally been suggested to me that what I call models and, rarely, metaphors of mind are in fact simply Conrad's beliefs. Conrad would have said at various times in his life that they were beliefs, that such categories as will and passion, ego and sympathy, were aspects of the mind that could hardly be denied and were obviously primary. In his practice, however, he seems aware that it is more appropriate to say that "the metaphor [or model, or simply concept] creates the similarity than to say that it formulates some similarity antecedently existing." [6] Had Lord Jim's leap from the *Patna* existed in the imaginative context of Conrad's first two novels, it would almost certainly have been presented to us in terms, however complex, of paralyzed will. By the time he writes *Lord Jim*, however, Conrad has become aware that the earlier conception has beclouded some aspects of experience, and he searches for a new pair of glasses that will allow a wider spectrum of light, or that will in any event allow a different angle of vision.

It may, furthermore, seem likely to some readers as they proceed through this study that Conrad did not change his conceptions of mind but adjusted those models to changed subjects. Thus, it may be said that will and passion are useful "faculties" when creating Conrad's colonial men and native women, but not so useful when, say, creating the masculine company of the *Narcissus*. And is it not possible that Conrad entertained two or three of these models simultaneously? Some of them are not, after all, mutually exclusive. Granting all this, it is nonetheless true that a pattern of genuine change emerges and that a root conception of mind has a habit of persisting despite a change in subject, *if* the author really likes it and wants it. I can easily imagine an analysis of the *Narcissus* in terms of will and passion, had Conrad felt that emphasis continuing to be useful. There are, after all, many kinds of passion. It is as fair to say that a change of subject is often the result of an author's desire to see mind differently as it is to make a change in subject the cause of altered root conceptions.

Throughout the argument that follows I will be talking about affinities between Conrad's models and those of certain other writers — Schopenhauer, Sartre, Pascal, and so on. It does not really matter to me whether these affinities are "influences," though I shall say so when it seems likely. My point throughout is, however, that we can better grasp Conrad's models by comparing them with conceptions from areas where they are habitually taken as unalterable reality. The difference between Conrad's ultimately flexible use of them and this other kind of use — their use, let us say, in the text of Schopenhauer — is precisely my emphasis.

One more self-justification. I have had little or nothing to say in this study about some of Conrad's novels and stories: *Chance, The Secret Agent, The Shadow Line,* and many others. Still, I have followed the line of Conrad's developing root conceptions where it has led, and it has not, for instance, led to *Chance.* The novels and stories I have skipped seem to me usually based rather comfortably upon key models that Conrad is not, on those occasions, interested in stretching or challenging. Often there is nothing "wrong" with these fictions; some of them, like *The Secret Agent,* are quite remarkable achievements. But they are invariably achievements that, given my special interest in this study, should be called "conservative." No doubt if I were clever enough every one of them would reveal to me its true revolutionary stripe.

# 1

# The Paralysis
of Will:
*Almayer's Folly* and
*An Outcast of the Islands*

Let me at the outset reassure the reader that I
have no intention of even sketching the history of key metaphors
for the mind as they become important to the English novel. Ian
Watt has suggested just such a basic shift in epistemology at its
origins.[1] Furthermore, it has occasionally been observed that several of the great early novels — *Clarissa* and *Tristram Shandy*, for
example — show clearly the tensions between two seemingly in-
compatible visions of the human mind, the Lockean and the sentimental, and that even the sentimental and gothic views of the human mind and spirit demonstrate a great number of important
variations. The Brontës, for instance, do to the old gothic models
what Conrad does to certain *fin-de-siècle* assumptions: stretch them
and test them instinctively until something quite different emerges.
Nor is the so-called Victorian novel easily summarized in this regard, as Mark Spilka's remarkable comparison of Dickens and Kafka shows.[2]

Even when the novelist offers a fairly exact metaphor for the
mind we cannot be sure it is really the one that guides his imagination in practice. Richardson's Pamela talks about "little minds like
wax" while she becomes expert in Locke's theory of education —

8

yet how characteristic of Richardson's work is this model? Tristram Shandy tosses off plump metaphors on every other page (the mind at one point is a "chair" that some people, Locke included, try to use without a part called "wit"). Yet how do the sentimental and the Lockean perspectives coalesce in his imagination?

The most important of such models never appear in convenient images but are doubly influential and extensive for being submerged. The author himself may not be able to describe his assumptions in these fundamental matters or to say when he has most directly challenged them through the unfettered power of his imagination; but great novelists do seem invariably to challenge their own models. We are accustomed to thinking of artists doing so with earlier models of artistic form — with, say, an earlier form of the sonnet or of prose narrative or with earlier ideas. But seldom do we observe how a novelist, needing a particular moral-psychological model of the human spirit, nonetheless turns upon that very conception and tests it in the fire of his own talent and in the act of using it.

There seems to be general agreement among critics that in his first two novels Conrad is particularly interested in a late-nineteenth-century phenomenon often called the *mal du siècle*: the paralysis of will or, as Paul L. Wiley describes it, the "division between mind and will." [3] Such paralysis took many forms, ranging all the way from a loss of the will to live to the disdain for ordinary, bourgeois life found in Flaubert, Huysmans, and Baudelaire, an attitude that included among its detestations the goals of the ordinary will and substituted for them the perfect will-lessness of art or of life lived as art. Generally, the forms of such paralysis or abulia took a tendency toward negation from Schopenhauer. [4] In a sense that can best be explained by their common debt to Schopenhauer, all three of these men and many other decadents and Symbolists found something radically wrong with the world of ordinary, middle-class aspirations and achievements. And for such striving they all substituted a condition that appeared will-less, dreamlike in its reverie of ideal perfection.

Conrad in his first two novels focuses on withdrawal in a manner that shows both his interest in the *fin-de-siècle* metaphor of the paralyzed will and yet his desire to make psychological sense out of it, to strip it of its characteristic mystery and to examine forms of it that covet bourgeois satisfactions rather than despise them. There can in any event be no doubt that at this point in his career his principal psychological interests pivot on the role of the will in human behavior and on its apparent widespread failure at the turn of the century. The withdrawal of the decadents and Symbolists was, far from being merely a chapter in the history of art, characteristic of a general spiritual crisis. If the old sanctions and imperatives had failed, a man's will either to live without them or to create new ones became the vital issue; the apparent enfeeblement of such will was an ominous failure, whether seen in Willems or, as a desirable quality, in the aesthete's imitation of art's own alleged willessness. The whole idea of a faculty that might be called will would ultimately have to be revised by Conrad, but its apparent paralysis was his starting point, his first and indeed most characteristically late-nineteenth-century model of the human mind.

Although "paralyzed will" is apparently unlike such obviously metaphoric statements as "the mind in creation is like a wind-harp," it has all the analogical force of Newton's bodies "attracting" one another. Arms and legs may be paralyzed, but will is an abstraction — Ryle would argue — that does not exist as an entity causing acts of volition. I am not choosing Ryle's analysis over Conrad's or putting the wrinkled hand of philosophy on the dimpled knee of art, but simply suggesting that Conrad is really saying that Willems's betrayal of Lingard is an instance of a man who knows what is right but is *as though* paralyzed, prevented in some way (he believes not of his own responsibility) from behaving morally. The most interesting feature of all metaphors of paralyzed will is that they enable the free agent to avoid responsibility for failing to act correctly. One does not take responsibility when one's hand has "fallen asleep" (of course hands do not "sleep" at all) and is thus unable to support a falling friend. "Paralysis of will" is not only pregnantly metaphoric but seemingly designed to put the believer in what Sartre would call "bad faith," to allow him to obscure his own responsibility.

It is also clear that although Conrad had begun with the metaphor of paralyzed will he instinctively began to challenge its validity, to introduce problems of identity and subjectivity that tend to expand beyond the manageable limits of the original model. He cannot think about the paralyzed will without evaluating Almayer's and Willems's illusions, the cause of that paralysis; no sooner has he done so than the whole metaphor of inquiry has shifted away from absolute faculties such as will and passion and toward the more relativistic and supple conception of self-image. My point is perhaps elementary: in trying to understand and use the original metaphor, Conrad inevitably challenges and changes it.

The conception of will developed in the first two novels undoubtedly comes in part from the nineteenth-century French writers he knew so well, especially Flaubert and Villiers de L'Isle-Adam, whose *Axël*, published in 1890, has been called a *fin-de-siècle* Faust. Although it is not until *Victory* and the character of Axel Heyst that Conrad clearly reveals his apparently lifelong interest in Schopenhauerian "escape," Villiers's *Axël* constitutes important background for Almayer and Willems as surely as it does for Marlow in his Buddha posture during the narration of *Heart of Darkness*.[5] I shall need to say more about Villiers later, but if *Axël* is a Faust it is only in the sense that the Romantic willfulness of Faust, the Romantic self that seems Byronic or Shelleyan in its energy, has given way to a retreat from the world of action into dreams where will is a useless conception. As Edmund Wilson has said in *Axel's Castle*:

And whereas the Romantic, in his individualism, had usually revolted against or defied that society with which he felt himself at odds, the Symbolist has detached himself from society and schools himself in indifference to it: he will cultivate his unique personal sensibility even beyond the points to which the Romantics did, but he will not assert his individual will — he will end by shifting the field of literature altogether, as his spokesman Axel had done the arena of life, from an objective to a subjective world, from an experience shared with society to an experience savored in solitude.[6]

Without denying Conrad's originality, it is not too much to claim that Almayer and Willems are a variation on Flaubert's description of the character destroyed by illusions, Villiers's and Huysman's peculiar isolattoes, and the familiar late-nineteenth-century pattern of the disintegrating colonial.

By emphasizing these late-nineteenth-century influences, however, I do not mean to deny Conrad his place in an ancient tradition that must go back at least as far as Saint Paul and the famous "incapacity" passage in the seventh chapter of Romans. It is usually difficult in talking about Conrad to determine which of his traditions is at that moment most important. In something like *Chance*, for instance, his background in English novelists and especially in Charles Dickens's *Bleak House* will leap to the fore. Just when one has settled down comfortably with that idea, however, Shakespearean echoes will suggest that his exposure to an English tradition was rather more extensive than we ordinarily suppose. A story such as "Falk" may even suggest Coleridge and the *Ancient Mariner*, though we do not usually look for an interest in poetry in Conrad. Of course the nineteenth-century French background often blends with a still relatively obscure Polish literary inheritance, and on the whole we must continually remind ourselves that we could hardly expect less of so cosmopolitan a sensibility. But one thing we must never forget; indeed, we are continually reminded of it by such critics as Paul Wiley, Walter F. Wright, Adam Gillon, and Eloise Knapp Hay: Conrad instinctively placed himself in the main current of Western literary tradition. Even his Polish heritage, he was careful to note, was distinctly Western. Denying his "Slavonism," he says:

Racially I belong to a group which has historically a political past, with a Western Roman culture derived at first from Italy and then from France; and a rather Southern temperament; an outpost of Westernism with a Roman tradition, situated between Slavo-Tartar Byzantine barbarism on one side and the German tribes on the other; resisting both influences desperately and still remaining true to itself to this very day. I went out into the world before I was seventeen, to France and England, and in neither country did I

feel myself a stranger for a moment: neither as regards ideas, sentiments, nor institutions.[7]

He goes on to say that he was as a boy "fed on French and English literature" and "steeped in classicism to the lips." The classical
and biblical echoes are there almost without his attending to them,
as, for instance, the long series of critical articles on classical echoes
in *Heart of Darkness* and Paul Wiley's or Claire Rosenfield's analysis of the "fall" would imply. We are, with Conrad's interest in the
paralyzed will and the corruption of will by passion, in the presence of Saint Paul, Thomas Aquinas, Pascal, some of the French
and English Romantics, and indeed of a whole Western tradition
that begins with Socratic philosophers who associate will with reason or speak, as does Aquinas, of will as the "rational appetite."

The enfeeblement of will is never better described than by Saint
Paul, who is too early even to use the key terms of Western faculty
psychology: reason, will, passion, imagination, and so on. His terms
are "heart," "body," "flesh," and "spirit," words with a Hebrew
rather than a Greek background. What he says, however, describes
better than most the psychological focus of Conrad's first two novels.

For we know that the law is spiritual: but I am carnal, sold under
sin. For that which I do I allow not: for what I would, that do I
not; but what I hate, that I do. If then I do that which I would not,
I consent unto the law that it is good. Now then it is no more I
that do it, but sin that dwelleth in me. For I know that in me (that
is, in my flesh) dwelleth no good thing: for to will is present with
me; but how to perform that which is good I find not. For the
good that I would I do not: but the evil which I would not, that I
do. Now if I do that I would not, it is no more I that do it, but sin
that dwelleth in me.
I find then a law, that, when I would do good, evil is present with
me. For I delight in the law of God after the inward man: But I
see another law in my members, warring against the law of my
mind, and bringing me into captivity to the law of sin which is in
my members. (Romans 7: 14–23)

No one need claim any direct influence from Saint Paul to Conrad to assert that the deracination of the above passage and that of

Dain and Willems are remarkably similar. Of course Conrad was moving in the core of a tradition without needing to know that its grain went at least as far back as Saint Paul. As Paul Wiley says of Willems: "Yet throughout all his fits of craving and disgust, his intelligence remains clear and detached in the knowledge of its separation from the debased will." [8] This all-too-credible sense of a lucid intelligence watching, as though behind glass, its debased will surrender to passion is central to the passage from Romans, though not nearly so important as the sense in both Saint Paul and Conrad's characters that it is somehow not *they* who execute the betrayal. That line of Saint Paul's, "it is no more I that do it," rings with particular resonance for these first two novels and for stories such as "Karain" and "The Lagoon." It is not simply that the Conradian hero does something terrible (murders his best friend or his brother, betrays his patron, deserts his ship, plays God, and so on) but that he is unable to feel it is *he* who has done so. The action usually precipitates a crisis of identity which brings into question the very faculty psychology that lies behind the conception of the crisis.

The second sentence of the foregoing quotation from Romans really suggests a mind beginning to question the very scheme it proposes: that volition is rational, that human willing has nothing to do with the "law of sin which is in my members." To externalize the transgression, to place it beyond the "self" and in some almost impersonal "sin," is, to my way of thinking, not far from Willems's contention that the sin was not in him but in Aïssa's savage eyes. Conrad, however he came by it, is well aware of the tradition; what he does not apparently like is the way it handles problems of responsibility and identity. Indeed, it is really only with Schopenhauer that the will is extended beyond the rational or reasonable faculty toward the evidence of action and feeling. Schopenhauer, in fact, implies that the will cannot be understood if we are going to associate it only with the rational and the conscious. More of this later. Suffice it to say here that Conrad's roots go deep, that they are typically Western, and that when I mention his most recent analogues or his most perfect analogues I do not mean to limit his incredible resonance.

Both Almayer and Willems have conventional, complacent notions of economic, bourgeois self: they are weak men who see a role as nearly the entire substance of self. Their principal talent is for denying responsibility, for attributing their misfortune to anything rather than to their own failure of will, their own actions or inertia. Ultimately both men create from their enforced isolation a dream of identity requiring no power of will to sustain it, an identity based largely on the faith that there are certain ingrained white qualities deserving success simply because of their moral superiority to native surroundings.

The influence from Schopenhauer on what Paul Wiley has called the hermit figure in nineteenth-century French writers — especially Flaubert in *The Temptation of St. Anthony* and *Saint Julien* — seems to have been a taste for the escape from insatiable, unsatisfying will, an escape Schopenhauer found possible through art or asceticism. Axël, as an heir to this influence from Schopenhauer, prefers his aesthetically satisfying dreams precisely because the world as an object of insatiable will *must* be forever disappointing, possibly tragic. The quality Wiley senses in the hermit figure that Conrad shared with these French writers is not of course a taste for aesthetically perfect dreams or even a refinement of sensuous taste designed to satisfy as the outside world never can. Though both Almayer and Willems live in dreams, their vision is, first, of gross material success and pleasures — a dream nearly opposite to Axël's aristocratic aestheticism — and then of a saving remnant of whiteness within the innermost self. They share with Axël and his ilk, however, the sense that their isolation involves a transcendence of the rigors and disappointments of will. The same, oddly enough, may be said of certain kinds of colonial experience in which the white man falls back on his role as sahib or tuan for all sense of identity, for authority, for moderate success — for all the things he would have to accomplish laboriously among his white peers. There is an entire genre of nineteenth-century literature dedicated to describing the dangers to the will in a colonial situation: Stevenson, Haggard, Louis Becke, and especially Kipling have all come close to realizing that the colonial may not have been inviting a great test of will (seeing whether he could kindle the flame of civilization among the intractable savages) so much as escaping from the more mundane test of will going on daily in London or Brussels.

Almayer and Willems both think they have been adopted and guaranteed by a man who has will enough for all — by Lingard. The essential quality of both their positions is not only vaguely colonial but also familial: they have been adopted by a father who has given them more than the "opportunity" Stein tenders Lord Jim — given Almayer the vision of an orgiastic future, and Willems an escape from the conspicuous miscarriages of his own will. Both Axël and these two early Conradian antiheroes discover an isolation they hope will be an escape from the context in which will is normally tested, although when we see Willems before his retreat to Sambir, he seems already to have a sense of identity requiring not an act of will but the mere fact of whiteness. Although he has stolen money, this immorality seems to him incapable of affecting his identity: "He fancied that nothing would be changed, that he would be able as heretofore to tyrannize good-humouredly over his half-caste wife, to notice with tender contempt his pale yellow child, to patronize loftily his dark-skinned brother-in-law, who loved pink neckties and wore patent-leather boots on his little feet, and was so humble before the white husband of the lucky sister" (p. 3).

The marvelous rhythm of racial and color adjectives in this passage declares the source of our antihero's identity: it is not something achieved but merely a function of his whiteness, adjusted to shades of "tender" contempt, noblesse oblige, accommodation, and anything but the outright hostility which might drive away the dark skins so necessary to establish his whiteness.

It is at least partly this desire to escape the necessity for will that disturbs Conrad in both the aesthetic, Symbolist isolation and that of Almayer and Willems. For one thing, such isolation undercuts and finally destroys the sense of responsibility, and thus of morality. The alleged decadence of the Symbolist retreat had become a cliché by 1895; and the decay brought about by colonial isolation had become equally commonplace in the literature of Empire long before Conrad used it and put it perhaps unwittingly into a Schopenhauerian context. There are of course many ways to attempt living will-lessly, some of them conspicuous for their seeming willfulness; Willems seems quite correctly to associate will with morality, as Conrad does, but then to rise above both. The passage already quoted about the delights of his racial identity continues: "Those were the delights of his life, and he was unable to conceive that the moral significance of an act of his could interfere with the very nature of things, could dim the light of the sun, could destroy the perfume of the flowers, the submission of his wife, the smile of his child, the awe-struck respect of Leonard da Souza and of all the Da Souza family" (p. 3).

He assumes that his identity is part of the "nature of things," as inevitable as the sun's light and the flower's perfume, and that the activities of his will, whatever they may be and whatever their morality, exist on an inferior plane. Of course the passage is ironic because of the great Conradian assumptions dictating the rhythm and tone of the entire résumé: first, that identity, sense of self, must be created continuously by will; second, that the realm of will is also that of morality. Identity does not exist as a given natural fact that can afford to be disdainful of morality. If identity were part of established natural certainties, man would indeed be godlike. In assuming this natural sense of identity, Willems has become a kind of Axel Heyst or Axël, withdrawing from the struggle of will — a struggle within will itself, between wills, and especially with the sense of responsibility that Heyst discovers so painfully in his retreat. Of course Almayer and Willems do not want to escape gross forms of desire, as Axël does, and as Marlow in *Heart of Darkness* presumably does while he increasingly resembles Buddha. But Conrad is suggesting that Almayer and Willems develop an attitude toward the exercise of will that I find remarkably Axël-like despite the growing intensity and crudity of their desires; in fact the stories focus on just this paradox — that their increasing passions diminish their understanding of will and intensify their claims of will-lessness. One does not need to imitate Buddha or Axël's idealized sensuousness to reach a state of will-lessness characteristic of both. And clearly it is not *Axël* but the generalized *mal du siècle* for which Axël was to serve as an epitome that Conrad has continually in mind in these first two novels.

Most of the earlier activities that Willems sees as evidence for his own willful success have been given to him, he finally discovers, as a matter of charity from Lingard and Hudig. His position in Hudig and Co., his wife, his house, his "success" — all are merely Hudig's attempt to secure for a half-caste daughter the life of a white woman. All the pride Willems has taken in the success of his will in trading ventures and opium intrigues, in overcoming the bizarre will of a local rajah — all these successes he now sees (not quite correctly) as part of the grand scheme to make him "succeed" so that Hudig's daughter might have a proper white husband. When Willems loses his position and Joanna turns violently upon him, half-caste Leonard comes running from beneath the house and says, ironically enough, "Do not hurt her, Mr. Willems. You are a savage. Not at all like we, whites" (p. 28). Both Joanna and Leonard now emphasize Willems's loss of identity: "You are nobody now." "Man from nowhere; a vagabond!" Leonard still seeks passionately his own white identity, and is willing only for appearance's sake to allow Willems some remnants of his: "'Do not be brutal, Mr. Willems,' said Leonard, hurriedly. 'It is unbecoming between white men with all those natives looking on'" (p. 29). Willems considers, with some justice, that Hudig "had stolen his very self from him" (p. 36).

There are some striking parallels suggested when Lingard agrees, almost as father to wayward son, to take Willems away from the scene of his loss of self. Lingard has used Almayer much as Hudig has Willems: to supply a white husband for an adopted native "daughter." Thus Almayer's perpetual expectation of reward, his will-less wallowing in Lingard's necessarily unsatisfactory benevolence, becomes allusive to Willems's past and future. Almayer, even though he sees daily the enormous difficulties of will through which his own half-caste daughter must go in search for identity, shares Willems's assumption of a natural, white self.

Only Paul Wiley has discussed with any sense of the French background the idea of will in these two novels. Speaking of the hermit figure, he says:

With the French the character had come to stand, either in a serious or a semicomic light, for a pose of contempt toward bourgeois life which expressed a peculiarity of modern temperament. Conrad likewise stressed at times the temperamental peculiarities of the type. Many of his hermits — Almayer, Willems, Wait, Jim, Kurtz — are men whose mental or spiritual aberrations cause them to deviate from a norm of conduct. But for Conrad . . . the anchorite is not an agent of anti-bourgeois satire but a figure who, in his retreat, offers a challenge to a ruling principle of order. By a system of contrasts — setting Willems against Lingard, Wait against Allistoun, Jim against the fraternity of seamen — Conrad gave dramatic expression to moral and social tendencies in his age which, because unresolved, allowed for a play of reciprocal irony. But in this balance of forces the weight of the irony lies heaviest upon the hermit as a departure from the implied norm of limited man in an ordered society. In his withdrawal the anchorite becomes a victim of extremes, of the division which ensues when man tries to cast off the trammels of his middle state. He envisions paradise at the moment when he sinks deepest into the toils of the wilderness. Once again, therefore, Conrad engages in an ironical reversal of an image from a Christian background with the apparent intention of a gibe at Providence for the disorderly state of creation. Retirement to a wilderness for ascetic or contemplative purposes can be justified only on the premise that God dwells in solitary places. When, instead, the wilderness is left abandoned to the strife of savage instincts, the ascetic ideal becomes absurd and the hermit himself a prey to the evils which he seeks to reject.[9]

Even this subtle analysis, however, attributes to Conrad an interest mainly in the "division between mind and will" in men like Willems and Almayer and fails to stretch the psychological metaphor as Conrad had begun to. If Conrad seemed to be interested in that paralysis of will, he had, even while exercising the model, begun to experiment with a new vocabulary and new answers to the question, What's it like? What, after all, was this "will" that had failed so conspicuously to sustain the isolated man? Even when understood as "the severance of conscious mind from the unconscious powers that it should control," [10] the process had perhaps not yet been seen clearly. Conrad had already begun to suggest that rather than a failure of the will because of passion, Almayer and Willems had partly tried to avoid will's exercise by a belief in the paternal powers of Lingard and in an ordained "self." "Passion" was not so easily to be made the culprit.

While Conrad officially might have accepted the near allegory of will corrupted by the serpent of passion, he provides materials within *An Outcast* for a different explanation of Willems's fall. Willems tries to adapt the conception of a natural self to explain what he views as his reduction by the empty, savage eyes of Aïssa: in short, refusing to acknowledge the error of any such assumption of natural identity, he sees his decline as the result of a conflict between two great natural identities, between the "savage" and the white. At no point does he understand his reduction as genuinely a problem of free choices. He explains himself to Lingard in terms of the savage "stealing" his white identity; and Lingard listens, as if to a "fairy tale": "She took away with her something of me which I had to get back. . . . Look at them [her eyes]! You can see nothing in them. They are big, menacing — empty. The eyes of a savage; of a damned mongrel, half-Arab, half-Malay. They hurt me! I am white! I swear to you I can't stand this! Take me away. I am white! All white!" (pp. 269, 271).

This is the cry of the "natural" identity, the preordained self. Conrad is careful to indicate through Willems's description of Aïssa's eyes that the emptiness is in Willems and probably in any man who fancies himself possessed of a naturally ordained self. Such a man is peculiarly vulnerable, as Nina Almayer, forced to choose and will identity, is not. Willems does at least come to realize that moral choices can affect his identity; but he sees the "evil" which has unmade him coming from outside, from Aïssa: "Willems said hurriedly: 'It wasn't me. The evil was not in me, Captain Lingard.' 'And where else — confound you! Where else?' interrupted Lingard, raising his voice" (p. 273).

Lingard never dodges responsibility (although we shall have to examine his idealism once again in a later chapter); yet he cannot hope to awaken Willems's sense of the operation of will in a single comment or in a whole course of what might be called will-therapy. Conrad shows the consequence of one particularly dangerous mode of establishing identity and is content to end the novel, to end both these novels, without effectively penetrating our heroes' pathetic armor.

What interests me most in these first two novels, however, are the faint but unmistakable signs of Conrad's dissatisfaction with the idea of a paralyzed will. The focus of his uneasiness with this metaphor seems to be its habit of equating choice with the rational mind. Will, then, almost becomes an aspect of the rational mind. If we do something other than what our reason says we want to do, we adopt the linguistic dodge of saying that our faculty of choice has been overcome and we have been "swept away" — or some such image — by passion. We should not think of saying that choice is not exclusively the function of the conscious or rational mind or that we may harbor wishes unconsciously that are in conflict with conscious or rational wishes but *are nonetheless chosen by us.*

What, really, is the content of that "chosen"? Conrad is struggling with the problem that bothered Schopenhauer as he probed the same area: are we responsible for what we have not rationally or even consciously chosen? As Willems never tires of reminding us, it is as though another person had "done it"; so in what sense can he hold himself responsible? This is Almayer's state of mind as well. It is, so far as he can see, always Lingard who holds his fate in his hands, or, later, Dain, or finally his daughter. And Almayer is never, he believes, responsible for the wishes and choices of these people — much in the sense that Willems feels he is not responsible for being overcome by passion. For both Willems and Almayer, the role of passion is remarkably similar to the role of people in whose hands they put themselves: just as passion is somehow beyond them rather than "theirs," so they suspend the operation of will in flaccid deference to powers over which they have little or no control and for which they bear no responsibility.

Yet Conrad's point is that Almayer has chosen Lingard's proposition and has, through his own behavior, thrust his daughter into an explosive dilemma between cultures, where, disgusted by the disdain of a convent school and by the grossness of her "traditionless" (p. 43) father, she is of course going to choose the savage splendor of Dain. Almayer regards her choice much as Willems regards his passion — something beyond his choice or control for which he consequently bears no responsibility. The fundamental gestalt of both men is the same, and the key figure is Lingard, who in playing his godlike role for both thereby satisfies their deep need to imagine forces that are beyond them — rewarding, controlling, and finally victimizing them. The key moral note of both novels is responsibility and a peculiar mode of dodging it, no less in Willems's description of his passion or in the alleged "theft" of his identity than in Almayer's reaction to Nina's choice. Certainly Lingard and Hudig provide the initial encouragement for our heroes' need to be adopted and fathered. Given this impetus, their natural inclinations lead them to a strong sense that their wills have been paralyzed by something beyond their control. Almayer would say that Lingard's and Dain's "broken promises" and above all his daughter's choice have led him to Jim-Eng's opium pipe — Willems, that Aïssa and an intractable passion which somehow is not "his" have brought him down. Conrad's analysis, however, suggests that both men have deliberately disguised their own choices and consequent responsibilities — and, finally, that their metaphors are intuitively built to allow these deceptions.

Conrad is by no means simply prepared to suggest that our passions are "chosen" and consequently something we must be responsible for. Nor is he quite clear as to whether unconscious wishes are related to the passions we are aware of, that we can at least view with the rational mind. He has the first of these questions in focus, but will worry it imaginatively for many years. Perhaps what he really needs at this point is a new perspective on it, a new viewing glass, a new metaphor for its comprehension. After all, these first two novels are in many ways repetitious, especially in their use of Lingard, the bribed marriage to a native or half-caste woman, the colonial "letting-go," and so on.

What we may be sure of, however, is Conrad's tendency in both novels to look past their *mal-du-siècle* atmosphere for a series of free choices that had brought about the ultimate sense of hopelessness and paralysis in both men, and to note how their sense of identity was somehow a more useful device for imaginative moral analysis than any conception of a mysteriously enfeebled will.

*The Nigger of the Narcissus* would take Conrad a long way from Almayer's opium and Willems's passionate paralysis. He was about to experiment with a fresh way of imagining the psychology of moral choice, but a way which nonetheless used two of the oldest terms in the moral lexicon, *sympathy* and *egoism*. Anyone who had read Conrad's first two novels when they appeared might have felt his discontent with the fashionable metaphor, but it would have been extremely difficult to predict his new direction unless the pervasiveness of Schopenhauer in the period had been duly noted. Conrad cannot be said to have "borrowed" from Schopenhauer—but as his friend John Galsworthy was to say, "Of philosophy he [Conrad] had read a good deal, but on the whole spoke little. Schopenhauer used to give him satisfaction twenty years and more ago." [11] That phrase "[gave] him satisfaction" is a clue to the whole question of influence here: Conrad apparently found in Schopenhauer support for his own attitudes and dispositions. The fact that his work sometimes implicitly criticizes certain Schopenhauerian recommendations only confirms the importance of his general sense of satisfaction. To quote Conrad quoting Novalis in the motto for *Lord Jim*: "It is certain my conviction gains infinitely, the moment another soul will believe in it."

# 2

# Ego and Sympathy:
# The Nigger
# of the Narcissus

*The Nigger of the Narcissus* is, in an almost in-
calculable number of ways, a break with much of Conrad's earlier
work. His first masterpiece, *The Nigger* is also his first sustained
view of empathy and sympathetic identification. Even the narrator
is involved in questions of distancing that are reminiscent of the
narrator in "Karain" and, ultimately, of Marlow in *Lord Jim*. What
have usually been seen as flaws in Conrad's manipulation of this
narrator are — flaws or not — unmistakable signs that Conrad had
begun in earnest a rendering of sympathetic identification that was
to beckon him on for many years. Neither of his first two novels
takes sympathetic identification as a major formal or thematic issue, though both of these novels share with *The Nigger* and such
short stories as "The Lagoon" and "Karain" the tentative idea that
man's greatest moral struggle may be to suppress "passion" for the
sake of various masculine, hierarchical values. In this model, of
course, "will" is all-important; and it is clear that when Willems,
for example, reaches a moment when "abruptly, came a relaxation
of his muscles, the giving way of his will" (p. 78), we have in Conrad's eyes also reached a moment of great moral significance. Both
*Almayer's Folly* and *An Outcast of the Islands* pivot on the idea

of will even while the whole rubric is being challenged in ways that eventually reveal to Conrad, as I suspect they do to many readers, that the collapse of Willems's volition is a moment of very little moral significance, and, further, that his betrayal of Lingard carries little moral weight. If we take the obvious path into the moral complexities of *An Outcast* — instead of, as I have suggested, the more oblique approach that leads through various conceptions of self — the novel strongly resembles "The Lagoon" and "Karain" in their portraits of will seduced by passionate love for a woman. Who can say how much of this popular formula Conrad simply borrowed from the exotic adventure stories, full of white traders and the seductive daughters of native chieftains, which provide an almost forgotten context for his early work; how much from a traditional Christian background that can never forget the seduction of the first man; and how much from the depths of his own mind where, as Thomas Moser and Dr. Bernard Meyer have suggested,[1] women seem always to have been a threat to his masculinity?

In any event, if we avoid the path suggested by the rubric of erotic passion seducing will, if we play down the highly advertised drama of will in these first two novels, both novels reveal moral significance that somehow eludes the psychological model that Conrad intended us to use. Especially *An Outcast* comes alive in passages far from the well-beaten track of Willems's will-oriented melodramatics. What seems to him the explanation of his fall is not, of course, the explanation Conrad intends us to accept. For example, we are obviously not intended to accept his description of Aïssa's responsibility for all that has happened. When he says, "The evil was not in me," we are to side with Lingard's demand that Willems accept responsibility for his failure of will. All this is obvious. Yet the moral center of *An Outcast* does not even lie where Conrad apparently thinks it does, much less where Willems thinks it does. Although the novel does not entirely provide the means for challenging what might be called the Lagoon-Karain psychological model, I hope my previous chapter has suggested that Conrad instinctively undercuts it in the very act of exploiting its ancient advantages. And, as I have noted in my introduction, he characteristically avoids that "hardening of the categories" that M. H. Abrams warned of in all analogical thinking.

A close examination of stories written about the time of Conrad's painful transition from the Malayan vein to *The Nigger* reveals his growing sense that the psychological model permeating the first two novels, "The Lagoon," "Karain," and the manuscript of *The Rescue* — not to mention *The Sisters* — was failing to enrich his perceptions and his experience in the way really successful metaphors always have. Surely there is nothing intrinsically inferior in the answer Conrad had given in all these stories to the question, What is the psychology of important moral struggles like? I am not even sure that my emphasis on will adequately describes the peculiarity of the model behind these stories. What I am sure of, however, is that all this early work uses roughly the same model and that in the manuscript of *The Rescue*, more than anywhere else, it apparently broke down entirely and was replaced, in a flurry of relatively easy and inspired writing, by something rather new in *The Nigger*. Many years later when *The Rescue* was finished, the difficulties of Conrad's return to a manuscript predicated on the old model are all too clear. There are of course many possible explanations for Conrad's pain with the manuscripts of *The Sisters* and *The Rescue*. It seems to me probable that the fear of writing about love for a woman from his own culture and class (rather than the exotic native girls of his love stories before *The Rescue*) accounts at least in part for the neurotic symptoms he experienced with that novel. It is probable that his own emotional state had something to do with the psychological model he predicated for his characters. But whether it is partly the cause or the effect of his own emotional life, that model changes in *The Nigger*, and this new novel seems to come as a release after what may be seen as the nervous breakdown of the old conception in the manuscript of *The Rescue*. Such new channels of thinking may indeed provide as genuine a release as — it is often claimed — the exclusively masculine company of the *Narcissus* did after the suffocatingly erotic and civilized Mrs. Travers.

As the old model is exercised in "The Lagoon" and "Karain," it shows more clearly than in either of the first two novels its inability to cope with the very experience it is designed to handle. Conrad is interested in those moments when, as Saint Paul says, we know the right but are powerless to will it. Arsat flees with his love when he ought to turn back and aid his brother, whose rearguard action is making the whole escape possible. To save a girl he will never touch and really knows only in his own imagination, Karain kills his best friend. The ability of Conrad to persuade any reader of the passion possessing both these natives, and Willems as well, has often been called into question; all these stories subscribe to the theory that saying something three times makes it so. There is, in fact, a rhetoric of passion here that grows into one of the most offensive stylistic peculiarities in all Conrad's work. At one point Willems says: " 'Look!' and he bared an arm covered with fresh scars. 'I have been biting myself to forget in that pain the fire that hurts me there!' He struck his breast violently with his fist, reeled under his own blow, fell into a chair that stood near and closed his eyes slowly" (p. 91). If there is any believable passion at all in these stories it lies — strangely — not at all where Conrad thought he was putting it. There is a good deal of credible passion when Willems feels that he has been robbed of his identity, very little when he pants for Aïssa.

We are, in short, asked to believe that the moral significance of these stories lies in the struggle of will with passion, even though we cannot believe in the passion and the will seems oddly out of focus, strangely on the periphery of events that are allegedly centered on it. We need only compare the allegedly involuntary moments of failure in "The Lagoon" and *An Outcast* (where Conrad seems unable to cope with the character's own implication that he has not really *chosen* his alienating action) with the treatment such an "involuntary" action receives in *Lord Jim*. There, Jim's own contention that he had not really chosen to jump ("I had jumped . . . it seems" [p. 68]) is subject not only to Conrad's ironic disbelief but to the most intense scrutiny from every vantage the complex narrative technique makes available. In *Lord Jim* the means are available for such a crucial investigation. In "The Lagoon," although Arsat's sense that he has done something involuntary is not so strong as in "Karain" and *An Outcast*, the rubric of will and passion is not supple enough to accomplish the imaginative task at hand. Although the precise chronology of the composition of these stories is not important (no one suggests that an old metaphor dies precisely in one story while a new one is born precisely in another), it is significant that when Conrad returns to the familiar pattern of will seduced and paralyzed by passion in "Karain" (immediately after he had finished *The Nigger* with — as I shall demonstrate — a new model) he seems to feel the necessity of refurbishing the old pattern with an ending to the story that immensely complicates the implications of Karain's alienating action. We would do well to examine this ending in order to see what effect it has on action that might have been nearly indistinguishable from Arsat's betrayal of his brother in "The Lagoon," a story finished immediately before Conrad began *The Nigger*. Conrad was simply incapable of returning, after finishing *The Nigger*, to the kind of central action seen in *An Outcast* and "The Lagoon" without seriously changing the conceptions through which he perceived it.

After betraying and killing Pata Matara for the love of a woman, Karain is haunted by the "ghost" of his friend until temporarily relieved by an old shaman. We are never sure (as presumably Conrad was not) just what the nature of this cure is, except that we know Karain is not haunted when the shaman is around and that the old holy man has given him a "charm." One of the complicating and enriching devices in "Karain" is the involved narrator, an early anticipation — as everyone agrees — of Marlow. The narrator is one of a crew of Englishmen who have traded guns to Karain in the past and are now confronted with his request that they give him some kind of charm to ward off the ghost, now returned at the death of the holy man. They are so different from him, he feels, so cool and objective, that surely they must have a potent Western cure for ghosts — no less efficient than the rifles they have always sold him. Finally one of the young men, with a peculiar mixture of cynicism and sympathy, ceremoniously confers a Jubilee sixpence upon Karain, placing it in a small sack or pouch and hanging it around his neck, persuading Karain that the image of the great Queen Victoria has sovereign power over all ghosts. The pouch and ribbon are fashioned from the white man's own amulets, souvenirs of his own love for a woman.

The charm, despite its partly comic value to the Englishmen and to the reader, works perfectly. Karain is freed from his ghost, and the story ends by having the narrator — who is not the man conferring the charm — wonder whether illusions are not as powerful as reality, whatever that may be. He recognizes, however, a certain danger in such solipsism.

It seems to me that in writing "Karain," Conrad had added an important new psychological dimension to the central betrayal of will by passion. The focus of the story is not on either of those faculties but on what is for Conrad at this moment a relatively new way of imagining the human mind and spirit. The moral interest of the story lies very little in the killing and very much in the moral quality of a world where images of the fat Queen cure tormented consciences only through the power of belief. Karain is reborn too easily; the rebirth has nothing to do with any increased moral or psychological perceptiveness on his part. Yet — Conrad implies — the world is what we think it is and the power of events and things lies in the authority we are prepared to confer upon them. The image of the mind suggested by the end of the story has little to do with such categories as will and passion (there is, in "Karain," no crescendo of the word "will" as there is in *An Outcast*); in fact, the image suggested is less topographical, less suggestive of areas of mind or categories of force, than it is broadly subjective and prior to any such ordering. We can see, I think, that Conrad is about to probe the key issues of impressionism that lie at the heart of the entire Marlow technique. From "Karain" on it is not at all misleading to say that Conrad is never far from the implications of Schopenhauer's *The World as Will and Idea*, at least insofar as that work contends that the world is my idea of the world.

Criticism of *The Nigger* since Vernon Young's psychoanalytic study of the novel in 1952 has often been persuaded that consciously or not Conrad operates here with a model of the mind not unlike Freud's or Jung's.[2] The rescue scene, James Wait trapped in his newly painted shrine, the crew trying desperately to batter through the side of his cabin (which because of the ship's angle has become their floor, his ceiling), the layer of nails they must dig through — all these details and many others have proved irresistible. I shall suggest, however, that it is probably not Freud but Schopenhauer who proves most useful in explaining what is clearly a major change in root conceptions as we move from *An Outcast* to *The Nigger*. It ought scarcely to be surprising that in some of his insights Schopenhauer can resemble the most basic Freudian or even Jungian orientation. Freud himself recognized the similarity.

Recently Lawrence Graver has argued in detail that *The Nigger* is best understood as Conrad's exploration of the intricate relations between egoism and altruism.[3] Graver analyzes all Conrad's short fiction in terms of five basic kinds of egoism and a number of forms of altruism; and he suggests — as by now seems unavoidable — that one can hardly ignore the presence of Schopenhauer somewhere in the background. Zabel and Guerard, without suggesting the affinities with Schopenhauer, had long ago pointed out Conrad's overt interest in these relations between egoism and altruism as they pivot on the crew's reaction to Wait and on the Captain's final control of the near-mutiny.[4] Graver, however, feels that Conrad works with this basic scheme all his life, while it seems to me that it does not become crucial — though some of its implications are certainly present in the first two novels — until *The Nigger*, and does not continue in anything like its form there without fundamental revisions and trials beginning almost at once in *Lord Jim* and *Heart of Darkness*. Conrad was not the sort of writer who exploits in relative ethical comfort a single model all his life. I disagree with Graver, finally, as to whether the ship is saved by the subtle altruism of Captain Allistoun. Allistoun's action needs a rather different interpretation, as does the whole idea of altruism and sympathy in the story. Though Graver's definition of Conrad's altruistic ideal rings true, it does not seem to me the crucial moral perspective in his changing metaphors. I would no more analyze all Conrad's work in terms of this fundamental and often subtle dichotomy than I would suggest it is not often present in fictions where Conrad is, apparently, experimenting with other conceptions that are more important to the creative energy of the work. Egoism and altruism are everywhere in Conrad — but the perspective they suggest is not everywhere crucial or even important.

When James Wait becomes obviously ill, nearly the whole crew falls into a trance of sympathetic identification. The first signs of this are touching and we are all reminded of the universal truth that sympathy has at least something to do with all morality. Even Christ, however, counted not on sympathy but on self-love as the *measure* of our concern: love thy neighbor as thyself. James Wait knows that he is touching nothing but self-love in any of the crew: "He had found the secret of keeping for ever on the run the fundamental imbecility of mankind; he had the secret of life, that confounded dying man, and he made himself master of every moment of our existence" (p. 37). Wait's appeal has nothing altruistic about it; there is no implication of abstract standards or imperatives. He is so purely selfish that his dying reminds every man of his own unavoidable death. They identify with Wait and draw slowly but easily into their individual circles of self-love, largely because the appeal is so simple and unabashed. Rarely do we find an instance of self-love so direct as to be completely disarming, reminding us that it is only through great effort that we modify even temporarily this disposition. When during the storm he is finally saved with excruciating effort, that rescue serves as a tribute to the authenticity of Wait's appeal.

As each member of the crew bows down to this fetish of self-love, acknowledging his own guilt and moved by that sense of guilt to serve Wait, only Donkin (who has nothing to discover about self-love — hence no guilt and only mock servitude) and the cook dissent. The cook, fanatically loyal to pseudo-Christian imperatives, cannot acknowledge the sin within himself — though he talks about sin constantly — and indeed is not even tempted to. Wait becomes a fetish only to the ordinary man who, though he might like to honor what Hemingway would call "the big words," will confess to his guilty love when faced down with a Wait.

As the apparent charity and care for Wait increase, the crew's sense of loyalty and hierarchy diminishes — and this is of course puzzling. Why should an access of sympathy, and conspiracy in Wait's own delusion that he will not die, dilute those qualities which hold a crew loyal to its duty and captain? It should by all logic be the other way around, and might, except that Conrad believes this noble quality sometimes arises from the most endur- ing, animal force in man — his self-love. Ego is often at the bottom of sympathy: "Falsehood triumphed. It triumphed through doubt, through stupidity, through pity, through sentimentalism. . . . The latent egoism of tenderness to suffering appeared in the developing anxiety not to see him die" (p. 138).

Although ego here disguises itself within identification, Conrad is by no means saying that this basic process is always immoral. But such identification can degenerate into sentimentalism and pity, and at its best is always a danger to duty and hierarchy. If loosed under the guise of benevolence, self-love comes into inevitable conflict with those communal standards — in this case maritime — which above all demand the compromise of self-love. Eventually in *The Nigger* self-love and self-congratulation (after the storm) become so inimicable to authority that Wait is used as the excuse for near mutiny. There is no doubt in Conrad's mind that Wait has nearly become an animal, feeling only his own desperate existence. All the civilized claims on the transformations of that ego — the hundred different ways ego can be civilized — are now beside the point for him:

Jimmy sat high in the bunk, clasping his drawn-up legs. The tassel of the blue night-cap almost imperceptibly trembled over his knees. They gazed astonished at his long, curved back, while the white corner of one eye gleamed blindly at them. He was afraid to turn his head, he shrank within himself; and there was an aspect astound- ing and animal-like in the perfection of his expectant immobility. A thing of instinct — the unthinking stillness of a scared brute. (P. 118)

A self-loving, brutalized Narcissus he is — and his single emotion is at the root of identification and appears with increasing intensity as sympathy degenerates into sentimentalism and pity. The basic paradox: only with the root of primitive self-love are apparently civilized forms of empathy grown.

It is an act of sympathy on the part of Captain Allistoun that brings the crew's orgy of self-pity to a head. After the cook's frantic attempt to convert him, Wait stumbles forward and declares that he is now well and had intended to stand to the following day. Such is his own deception; he is obviously dying. Yet so attuned to him has the crew become that they are equally able to deceive themselves that he has recovered. The simple fact that they are able to do so, to shout, " 'D'ye mean to say, sir,' he [an elderly seaman] asked, ominously, 'that a sick chap ain't allowed to get well in this 'ere hooker?' " (p. 120) is extraordinary testimony to the identification that has occurred. Apparently (though Conrad is by no means lucid on this point) the crewmen present actually deceive themselves — are not merely speaking out, claiming Wait should be allowed to stand to, in order to sustain Wait's own self-deception. At best there is a fine line between their superficially benevolent desire to agree with Jimmy (thereby helping him to believe he has recovered some of his health) and really believing that he can stand to. The important event here is Allistoun's lie, his sentimental lie. The corruption has begun to affect even the top of the hierarchy.

The captain refuses on the spot to allow Wait's return to duty, but not for the obvious reason that he is nearly dead. Rather: " 'You have been shamming sick,' retorted Captain Allistoun with severity; 'Why . . .' he hesitated for less than half a second. 'Why, anybody can see that. There's nothing the matter with you, but you choose to lie-up to please yourself — and now you shall lie-up to please me. Mr. Baker, my orders are that this man is not to be allowed on deck to the end of the passage' " (p. 120). Like the others, Allistoun helps sustain Wait's self-deception, though he nearly understands the symbolic importance that deception has assumed. With results that are both logical and symbolic, his action

brings the near-mutiny which follows. Allistoun himself is embar-
rassed at what he has done, and does not quite understand what
caused him to do it: "When I saw him standing there, three parts
dead and so scared — black amongst that gaping lot — no grit to
face what's coming to us all — the notion came to me all at once,
before I could think. Sorry for him — like you would be for a sick
brute. . . . H'm! Stand to it now — of course" (p. 127).

Only Singleton realizes in his primitive wisdom that Wait is so
potent an influence he must be told to die and shut up about it. The
captain's sympathy — really a kind of sentimental pity — has created
a dangerous situation. It really makes no difference whether any
given member of the crew only sympathizes with Wait's desire to
stand to, or actually feels he has been malingering. The whole
structure of discipline, loyalty, and hierarchy has been shaken from
bottom to top.

The captain, however, is not likely to go far toward being corrupted by overcivilized feelings. He pulls himself together, reminded of the real devils he once commanded, and the ship awaits
the freedom granted by Wait's death. The paradox has been faith-
fully imagined. Civilization demands we control self-love; but this
is best accomplished through means other than an access of sympathy. Far from despising sympathy, however, Conrad has simply
recognized its enormous potency and several forms of its decadence. Paradoxically, one of the great civilizing forces, man's ability to identify imaginatively with another (as the crew does with
Wait), often serves only to intensify ego and to challenge the order
which makes life more than a survival of the fittest. For Conrad at
this stage in his career, the issue is not how man can be prevented
from being Narcissus but how he can use that unavoidable identification to his moral advantage. Later in his life, as we shall see,
Conrad was no longer to regard self-love as an almost ineluctable
human essence; but even then, sympathy, and its culmination in
some ideal of human solidarity, was still the compelling mystery of
his art. What he had begun in Lingard but more particularly in the
crew of the *Narcissus* was an understanding of sympathy's evolution toward decadent forms of pity and sentimentalism and away

from the primitive appreciation of ego that might be its only real salvation. (It is interesting that Axel Heyst, whom Conrad presents in the late *Victory* as one of the last creatures of a decadent society, has been schooled by his father to feel not sympathy but "pity" for mankind.) From this moment on in his work Conrad will spend a great deal of his energy trying to grasp the moral significance of sympathy, but always from the vantage point established in *The Nigger*, with the knowledge that sympathy must somehow be purified by a recognition of its complex involvement with ego.

In "An Outpost of Progress" (finished in July, 1896), a story which preceded *The Nigger* and prepared for it, we find sympathy once more under close inspection. The sense in which this story anticipates *Heart of Darkness* has often been mentioned, but its affinities with *The Nigger* are equally important in understanding the development of Conrad's models. The threat to Kayerts and Carlier is the lure of primitive, unrestrained ego — very similar to the appeal of James Wait. The "primitive and unfamiliar" *initially* drives them into an unnatural comradery: "Before they reached the verandah of their house they called one another 'my dear fellow'" (p. 70). The threat of James Wait to the *Narcissus* is revealed in a reversal of terms: the apparently civilized is seen to be primitive, the primitive (Singleton's attitude, for instance), civilized in a healthy rather than decadent way. Such a reversal also determines the movement of "An Outpost of Progress."

As Kayerts and Carlier are drawn closer together despite great differences in background and personality (the one is a plodding civil servant, the other a fashionable wastrel of an army officer), it appears that the threat of the primitive may create community where none could conceivably have grown under more ordinary circumstances. Kayerts and Carlier are not likely to sympathize with one another in civilized surroundings. So too the crew of the *Narcissus* is bound into an unnatural community under the irresistible appeal of Wait's self-love. Such is the initial result of the primitive coming into contact with civilization; there had, after all, been the testimony of colonial life to the same effect. To the colonial,

the "primitive" surrounding him would be equivalent to that threat
from another world which Robert Maynard Hutchins some years
ago saw as the only hope for a truly United Nations. (The Victorians were interested in this kind of threat, as H. G. Wells illus-
trates with disturbing clarity.)

The unnatural community in both stories continues and seems to
grow while the reversal of terms occurs. In *The Nigger*, of course,
the apparently civilized sympathy begins to look more and more
primitive and leads nearly to anarchy (presumably one definition
of "primitive"). The apparently primitive denial or restraint of
sympathy — Singleton is tattooed like a savage chief — paradoxically sustains civilized order. Even the captain's sentimental decision
has ultimately enough of the primitive fiber in it to be civilizing
and settling for the crew.

In "An Outpost of Progress" it is the local native chief who,
after several of his people are sold into slavery (one is murdered)
partly through the ignorance of Kayerts and Carlier, shows great
restraint and foresight in his attitude toward these mysterious and,
he believes, immortal white men. In a number of superficial details
this chief, Gobila, is a simple native ("and he knew that they
[white men] were all brothers" — pp. 95–96) and is so regarded by
the two white men. ("They . . . recklessly struck off matches
for his amusement. Kayerts was always ready to let him have a
sniff at the ammonia bottle" — p. 96.)

But after his people have been kidnapped by the slavers, he dis-
suades his warriors from violence: "Who could foresee the woe
those mysterious creatures, if irritated, might bring? They should
be left alone. Perhaps in time they would disappear into the earth
as the first one had disappeared. [Gobila assumes he has done so as
some mysterious strategy to rejoin his own people.] His people
must keep away from them, and hope for the best" (p. 107). His
moderation contrasts with the increasingly ominous implications
of the false bond between the two Europeans. They enforce one
another's growing disposition to accept the ivory obtained through
their native manager's deal with slavers. Step by step the acceptance by either of them of the horrors committed supports a similar

acquiescence in the other. Makola's deal with the slavers has, after all, given them several choice tusks of ivory. In a number of scenes the actions of one man help to trigger and justify those of the other; the unnatural bond works subtly for their equal damnation until both have managed to accept the idea of slavery and murder as a means of getting such fine ivory.

In *Heart of Darkness* the reversal of terms is allowed to go much farther than in "An Outpost of Progress." To suggest only one instance: the cannibals show more restraint during their hungry journey upriver than Kurtz does. Although no one pretends that Conrad is offering either the chief Gobila or the cannibals as models of proper behavior, he is in both stories subjecting the idea of "civilization" to the cold scrutiny of a Victorian accustomed to finding a grim phylogeny behind the grand conception, even while accepting in broad outline the idea of slow cultural evolution. The most frighteningly "civilized" moment in "An Outpost" comes when sympathetic identification has, in a sense, run to its limits. In the strange passage quoted below, Kayerts is obsessed by the most savage insight he or perhaps any of us is capable of at the very moment when, ironically, his sympathetic imagination is at a nearly insane pitch. He has just shot Carlier (who has, though unarmed, come after him):

Incidentally he reflected that the fellow dead there had been a noxious beast anyway; that men died every day in thousands; perhaps in hundreds of thousands — who could tell? — and that in the number, that one death could not possibly make any difference; couldn't have any importance, at least to a thinking creature. He had been all his life, till that moment, a believer in a lot of nonsense like the rest of mankind — who are fools; but now he thought! He knew! He was at peace; he was familiar with the highest wisdom! Then he tried to imagine himself dead, and Carlier sitting in his chair watching him; and his attempts met with such unexpected success that in a very few moments he became not at all sure who was dead and who was alive. This extraordinary achievement of his fancy startled him, however, and by a clever and timely effort of mind he saved himself just in time from becoming Carlier. (P. 115)

Surely this is one of the most amazing passages in all Conrad's
work. The peak of the ability to identify with the dead "beast"
coincides with the height of savagery, the "highest wisdom," that
the individual means nothing. This is the danger from the false
sympathy imposed on Kayerts and Carlier by the wilderness, just
as the community formed by the attraction and threat of James
Wait on the crew of the *Narcissus* creates and guarantees progress
toward a disguised egomania. In both stories an unnatural sense of
community is seen to encourage an approach toward savagery.

Kayerts's ability to identify with the dead Carlier is genuine. He
kills himself a short while later not from any great sense of guilt
(though he is shocked to discover that Carlier has come after him
without a gun), but rather as a man under the unbearable pressure
of that "highest wisdom": that neither Carlier's nor his own life
now means anything. The fact that he hangs himself from the cross
on their predecessor's grave suggests an ironic parallel to Christ's
powers of sympathy, epitomized in Milton's "Account mee man."
In "An Outpost" Conrad has reduced the idea of sympathy to an
evil sharing of nature's disdain for the individual life. The story is
to be taken as a metaphysical parable. The self-love which allows
both men to accept the slaving and murder disappears in Kayerts
when he accepts the almost mathematical premise that makes possible the most grotesque of all sympathy: the meaninglessness of
all individual life before the indifferent statistical process of nature.

One can only ask at this point what a true sense of community
would be. Presumably it ought to be based on the pursuit of an
"idea" constantly regulated by a sense of identity, of individual
ego and self-love. Ironically, unrestrained self-love destroys identity. Kurtz seems desperately to maintain his, but the individual
members of the *Narcissus* who come under Wait's influence talk
and think remarkably alike; Kayerts's self-love results in a total
loss of identity when it seeks justification in a grotesque empathy
with Carlier.

Conrad's analysis of sympathy in "An Outpost" and *The Nigger*
has the authentic late-nineteenth-century flavor. There is something of the idea — present in one branch of Darwinian ethics —

that sympathy was peculiarly vulnerable to assorted forms of decadence. In its crudest form this idea was used to defend ruthless social and economic laissez-faire: nothing ought to interfere with the survival of the fittest. Conrad conceived of a time when society had been somehow more virile, had produced Singletons rather than Donkins and James Waits. One suspects that he associated Wait with a brand of ersatz humanitarianism that often attracted the kind of egomaniacs seen in *The Secret Agent*. The self-confident civilization that emblazons "progress" on its every excrescence and seeks to rationalize economic greed with a parade of benevolence and uplifting sympathy partakes of that same decadent softness observed in Wait and his effect on the crew of the *Narcissus*. Conrad does not propose or even conceive of a "healthy" Darwinian struggle; but he does call some modern life incredibly softened and consequently brutalized by impossible humanitarian boasts, false ideals of community proposed on every hand, grand attempts to be like the angels which only reduce man to a bestiality more subtly corrupt than the animal quality any fool already acknowledges in himself.

Any such reading of *The Nigger*, it must be observed, offends many students of Conrad, largely because they want to emphasize the heights of courage and solidarity achieved by the crew during the storm and especially in the rescue of Jimmy. Guerard feels that the major structural task of *The Nigger* is to avoid making two stories which simply cancel one another out, one of the crew's "solidarity, courage, and endurance," as the storm evokes these fine qualities, the other of the crew's "egoism, solitude, laziness, anarchy, fear," as Jimmy evokes these dark qualities.[5] The two stories, he feels, must finally both be remembered in a complex portrait of human capacity. Yet are there really two stories being told? Certainly the storm evokes a remarkable performance in the men, but their greatest courage and solidarity is nonetheless due to the same old appeal radiating from Jimmy, an appeal which under circumstances created by the storm now demands extraordinary physical courage and cooperation. Nowhere in *The Nigger* does the crew show a courage and solidarity commensurate with the

real threat: not the storm, but the subtlest mask of self-love. Allistoun does and Singleton does — but the crew as a whole has not
risen to the challenge that most fundamentally disturbs Conrad in
this novel. They have indeed transcended their grubby limitations
ashore; as creatures of the sea and of the craft they are worth far
more than any of them seem as they flounder among the docks.
And they are in many senses entitled to the "flood of sunshine" in
which they finally disappear. But that same sunlight graces even
the most unlikely and ungraceable things: "The sunshine of heaven
fell like a gift of grace on the mud of the earth, on the remembering and mute stones [of the Tower], on greed, selfishness; on the
anxious faces of forgetful men. And to the right of the dark group
the stained front of the Mint, cleansed by the flood of light, stood
out for a moment dazzling and white like a marble palace in a fairy
tale. The crew of the *Narcissus* drifted out of sight" (p. 172).

   This is a marvelously visual means of elevating them when most
they need it, of acknowledging their accomplishments during the
storm and in the craft, yet of reminding the reader that if the same
sunshine can grace the agonies of the Tower and remove the stains
from that bastion and symbol of commercial selfishness, the Mint,
it can make us forget that the crew could not handle Jimmy Wait
and is in no sense ultimately successful. We may join in the speaker's enthusiasm for the craft and salute them, but they are no better
than we when confronted not with physical storm but the complexity of relations between egoism and sympathy or altruism —
when confronted, in short, by the quiet certitude of their own mortality.

# 3

# A Source for the Ego-Sympathy Model: Schopenhauer

The problem of sympathy had become a passionate interest, indeed almost a compulsion for Conrad, one whose intensity demands rather precise explanation. What was there in Conrad's background that made this issue supplant that of the failure of will, which had so characteristically marked the first two novels? The explanation, it seems to me, lies in the fact that both metaphors derive from the more basic orientation Conrad had inherited from Schopenhauer and his often unwitting followers. Thus it is probably not correct to speak of analysis in terms of ego and sympathy *supplanting* the earlier concern; aside from a slight evolutionary bias in the ego-sympathy metaphor, it is as much Schopenhauerian as the idea of paralyzed will. And both, it need hardly be said, must have appealed strongly to Conrad's sense of his own emotional problems. A man who had been as much of an outsider as Conrad, between nations and between careers, might well have turned to his experience with the crew of a ship in order to understand the true conditions of human solidarity. By the time he wrote *The Nigger* Conrad had become very much an Englishman and presumably very much interested in speaking about relations between the individual and society. He was a writer who had

41

now made commitments toward various kinds of human solidarity (he had just married an English girl and, despite great fears, must have anticipated raising English children). We need not look far to discover good reasons for Conrad's interest in sympathy and ego, for the tensions and doubts in a man who now found himself, after years of anguished search for an identity, at once a father, an Englishman, and an English novelist sufficiently well established to foresee a career of writing. To say that his key terms in *The Nigger* are ego and sympathy is perhaps only to point out that Conrad is trying to name the two forces determining human association. It is interesting, however, that "will" as a term and concept has dropped from sight, as has "passion," and not merely because we have changed situations and story. It is true that ego and sympathy are much more useful conceptions and feelings for imagining problems of human association than are will and passion. Yet the shift of subject matter will not begin to account for Conrad's alteration of model between the first two novels and early short stories and *The Nigger.* Conrad has somehow begun to feel that ego and sympathy are prior to the psychological bench marks used in the earlier work, more basic and comprehensive, capable of describing both the action on the *Narcissus* and, say, Willems's relations with Aïssa and Lingard.

If we ask where Conrad got this ego-sympathy model, surely the simplest and most economical answer is that some such spectrum is obvious in human nature. But for Conrad the flavor of ego and sympathy was rather more precise than the above explanation would allow. As I have suggested, he appears to have gotten support from his reading of French nineteenth-century writers, especially from Flaubert and Villiers, for just the sense of ego we have seen. The French took it from that German Francophile, Schopenhauer, for whom the life will, on the one hand, and sympathy, on the other, were the only two characteristic impulses in man and the only conceptions he needed for psychological and moral analysis. Schopenhauer's will was an irrational plunge toward life, not a will at all in the sense of rational free choice. The will was at once in every living thing individually and in life monolithically. It deals, insofar as man embodied it, with what one translator of Schopenhauer has called "representation" rather than reality, with what Conrad called "illusions" or, as in *Nostromo*, "ideas" in proper Schopenhauerian language. Even identity was an illusion that might profitably be lost in two ways: temporarily, in art, or permanently in the transcendence of maya, appearance, by ascetic discipline. From this bizarre combination of neo-Kantianism and Eastern religion the French writers producing in the last forty years of the century (and probably some of the English decadents in the nineties) borrowed, as I have said earlier, the idea of Axël, who refuses a world which can never satisfy his ideal conception of love, adventure, and taste. Because the world was appearance, maya, it was unworthy of the sensitive man who could only find it tragically inadequate to his ideal conceptions. The connections between Conrad, the French *fin-de-siècle* spirit, and, ultimately, Schopenhauer are extensive and almost completely unexplored. But what interests me here is Schopenhauer's assertion that the irrational will toward life inevitably feeds on maya, on the world as "idea"; it is this thought that helps to connect the key model of Conrad's first two novels with *The Nigger*'s model.

Conrad's "ego" and Schopenhauer's "will" are very similar, just as Conrad's use of the word "idea" to represent a man's projected and idealized illusion, and Schopenhauer's use of that concept in *The World as Will and Idea* are too close to be accidental. (I of course keep in mind here the problem of translating "Vorstellung" into English, but the resemblance is nonetheless striking.[1]) The whole suggestion that life is unworthy of the dream, at least as that idea appears in French writers such as Villiers, Laforgue, Mallarmé, Rimbaud, and Huysmans, derives from Schopenhauer. To quote Edmund Wilson in *Axel's Castle* again, "The heroes of the Symbolists would rather drop out of the common life than have to struggle to make themselves a place in it—they forego their mistresses, preferring dreams." And, one might add, intensifying dreams of a perfection that is not inherent in the world of maya, the "real" world.

A contemporary Catholic philosopher has summarized this ego-sympathy ambiance as found in Schopenhauer's broad conception of will:

The Will, the macrocosm, is objectified in each individual, the microcosm, and the inner nature of the individual is shown in his fundamental egoism: because he is the objectification of the Will, indeed *is* the Will, he acts as if he alone mattered. . . . Now, when a man "sees through" the principle of individuation, realizes that all individuation is phenomenon, Maya, he realizes too that he suffers in all, that the suffering of all is *his* suffering, and he attains to love, the essential of which is sympathy. Knowing that the sufferings of others are, metaphysically, his own sufferings, he will do what he can to alleviate those sufferings. Sympathy then, is an essential grade of morality, but it is not the highest stage: the complete penetration of the principle of individuation, the complete lifting of the veil of Maya, which reveals the whole world as one and all suffering as one suffering, consequent on life itself, will lead a man, no longer to assert this life through the constant acts of the will and ever-renewed desire, but to deny the will to live, to turn away from life by voluntary renunciation, chastity and asceticism (*not*, as we might expect, by suicide). Beyond and above the ethic of sympathy there stands, therefore, the ideal of "holiness," exemplified in the lives of Christian, Hindu and Buddhist saints.[2]

In its concern with the relation of ego and sympathetic identification, *The Nigger of the Narcissus* may be read as a critique of Schopenhauerian ideas that had become fashionable by the time a young Francophile Pole reached Marseilles in 1874. French skepticism had seized Schopenhauer's oversimplification of human psychology and had taken it seriously. But the important point for this discussion of Conrad's fascination with man's conceit is that the will was inevitably trafficking in illusion. Only the renunciation of that will, first toward sympathy and ultimately toward "holiness," enabled an individual to see through such illusions as ego and identity. Thus the conceit which so fascinated Conrad inevitably — and this is also Schopenhauer's doctrine on the subject — manifested itself in and was itself a collection of illusions. In one sense, the will — that irrational thrust — was the refusal of the organism to see through its own identity to a sympathy which might be debilitating in the struggle for existence. Man's will to live may depend on illusion; and Kayerts's grotesque sympathy at the conclusion of "An Outpost of Progress" may be read as a parody of the penetration of maya recommended by Schopenhauer. Seeing "the whole world as one" clearly did not mean to Conrad what it did to Schopenhauer.

Much of Conrad's work (in *Victory*, "Falk," *The Nigger*) is at once a criticism of Schopenhauerian skepticism and a tribute to its influence. But the hints at asceticism as some sort of final solution in *Heart of Darkness* have been exaggerated by at least one critic. Marlow's lotus posture in *Heart of Darkness*, it is alleged, was meant to suggest that he had, through his experience with Kurtz, attained a triumph over self and maya. The essay continues: "Although qualified to enter nirvana, like the true Bodhisattva, Marlow remains in the world to work for the salvation of all people. In his stage of enlightenment he teaches what his descent into the imperfections of the human soul has taught him — egoless compassion. Cancelling out all personal desire and fear, he has made available to humanity the gift of complete renunciation." [3]

Though there may be readers, thinking perhaps of Marlow's role in *Chance*, who will immediately and impolitely snicker at the idea of Marlow in his new-found role of "true Bodhisattva," this whole article ought to be read as a further indication not of Conrad's commitment to Buddhism but of his sharply critical interest in certain key Schopenhauerian ideas. *Heart of Darkness* is, of course, a deliberate exercise in sympathetic identification, as is in general the entire Marlow technique. But the result of such journeys, far from being selflessness and an ascetic renunciation of the world, is for Conrad an intensification of the need for sustaining ego. The purification of sympathy that Conrad envisions in so many of his characters involves their learning more about ego and coming to terms with it (often tragically) rather than fleeing toward nirvana. If anything is as sacred to Conrad as the protean idea of human solidarity, it is the value of the individual ego. In my discussion of Schopenhauer I shall have more to say about Conrad's reaction to Buddhism and to the idea of selflessness.

Schopenhauer, as he is important to Conrad, is best seen in the context of what had become one of the liveliest nineteenth-century issues. In response to a contest topic assigned by the Royal Danish Academy of Sciences, Schopenhauer early in his career submitted an essay on "The Basis of Morality," an attempt to establish morality without recourse to any conception of god or, indeed, of the supernatural.[4] The essay criticizes Kant's attempt to found morality in the categorical imperative as really only supernaturalism disguised. Schopenhauer purports, in effect, to do a more thoroughly mundane job of locating the basis for morality in man's behavior. Having claimed the two forces, ego and sympathy or compassion, which must be crucial to any discussion of Conrad, Schopenhauer goes on to derive most of the standards we think of as morality from compassion, from the only force in man which — he claims — mitigates otherwise incessant ego.

Conrad was faced with a similar problem in founding morality without divine sanctions. And at least since the eighteenth century, English thought had been familiar with the search for a peculiarly human well of morality; "sensibility" had become the most popular if not convincing answer to that quest in the eighteenth century as utilitarianism was to be in the nineteenth. Where Schopenhauer got his dichotomy of will and sympathy it would be difficult to say, since he is especially careful to claim that it comes only from common-sense observation. He discourages any attempt we might make to see philosophic "influences" behind his tools of analysis. Nonetheless, Schopenhauer, Conrad and many others were looking for the same thing: values which did not depend on sanctions transcending man.

In *The Nigger* Conrad suggests that if sympathy is to be used as an ethical sense it must be cultivated with critical understanding. His analysis of ego's role in sympathetic identification is very much unlike one that Schopenhauer too is careful to refute in the eighteenth-century Italian philosopher Cassina:

His view is that compassion arises from a sudden hallucination, which makes us put ourselves in the place of the sufferer, and then imagine that we were undergoing his pain in our own person. This is not in the least the case. The conviction never leaves us for the moment that he is the sufferer, not we; and it is precisely in his person, not in ours, that we feel the distress which afflicts us. We suffer with him, and therefore in him; we feel his trouble as his, and are not under the delusion that it is ours; indeed the happier we are, the greater the contrasts between our state and his, the more we are open to the promptings of Compassion. The explanation of the possibility of this extraordinary phenomenon is, however, not so easy; nor is it to be reached by the path of pure psychology, as Cassina supposed [this is a very important claim]. The key can be furnished by Metaphysics alone.[5]

Conrad, like Schopenhauer, would claim that we know full well who the sufferer is, but he might remind Schopenhauer that at least in the affair of James Wait a common mortality was enough to generate the "latent egoism of tenderness toward suffering."

Schopenhauer's metaphysical explanation of compassion is a crux at which Conrad insistently disagrees with the sentiment that the brotherhood of man is achieved by the denial of ego. Compassion, says Schopenhauer, is the natural, instinctive recognition of the "identity of man, so far as he is noumenal, with the transcendental Reality behind phenomena."

The crude threats of punishment and promises of reward, the stern Moral Law, poised in mid-air — these hypotheses, and all their varieties (whose function is in reality nothing else but to check Egoism), are seen to be due to the intellect's imperfect comprehension of, or rather its vague groping after, the transcendental unity of life, however individualized and differentiated as a phenomenon in Time and Space.[6]

And this rather technical but shrewd bit of metaphysics had a popular counterpart in the widespread Victorian appeal to the unity of man rather than to anything supernatural as a basis for morality. If humanity was one, whether the assumption behind this claim was evolutionary or metaphysical, compassion was only recognizing the truth. At nearly the same time as Schopenhauer, Comte had proposed his religion of humanity. If God was dead, the Victorian and early nineteenth-century conscience set about relocating spiritual authority with a fervor that might have pleased a primitive Christian.

What really disturbed Conrad, however, were attempts to found morality on selflessness, a state of heart and mind that Conrad knew too well to bandy about as a foundation for the brotherhood of man. Selflessness was terrifyingly possible for some men — as Conrad was to experience many times in his life, perhaps first in 1888, in Bangkok — but it was more often a mask for ego and self-love. In its authentic form it was anything but productive of compassion. His anger had most often been provoked by political schemes for such universal brotherhood. He wrote with bitterness to Spiridion Kliszczewski on December 19, 1885:

By this time, you, I and the rest of the "right thinking" have been grievously disappointed by the result of the General Election. The newly enfranchised idiots have satisfied the yearnings of Mr. Chamberlain's herd by cooking the national goose according to receipt. The next culinary operation will be a pretty kettle of fish of an international character. Joy reigns in St. Petersburg, no doubt, and profound disgust in Berlin: the International Socialist Association are triumphant, and every disreputable ragamuffin in Europe feels that the day of universal brotherhood, despoliation and disorder is coming apace, and nurses daydreams of well-plenished pockets amongst the ruin of all that is respectable, venerable and holy. The great British Empire went over the edge, and yet on to the inclined place of social progress and radical reform. The downward movement is hardly perceptible yet, and the clever men who started it may flatter themselves with the progress; but they will soon find that the fate of the nation is out of their hands now! The Alpine avalanche rolls quicker and quicker as it nears the abyss.
. . .
Where's man to stop the rush of social-democratic ideas? The opportunity and the day have come and are gone! . . . England was the only barrier to the pressure of infernal doctrines born in continental back-slums. . . . The destiny of this nation and of all nations is to be accomplished in darkness amidst much weeping and gnashing of teeth, to pass through robbery, equality, anarchy and misery under the iron rule of a military despotism! Such is the lesson of common-sense logic.
    Socialism must inevitably end in Caesarism.
    . . . Disestablishment, Land Reform, Universal Brotherhood are but like milestones on the road to ruin.[7]

Though perhaps only an aristocratic Pole would have been quite so suspicious of a British general election, Conrad's bias is unmistakably that of *The Nigger*. By a not unjust extension, "Socialism must inevitably end in Caesarism" might be the political motto of that not overtly political story. Universal brotherhood, like sympathy aboard the *Narcissus*, serves to cover and extend ego; hence that familiar progression mentioned in the letter: "equality, anarchy and misery under the iron rule of a military despotism." Excessive and corrupt sympathy begets false "equality" which then slips imperceptibly, and finally, into a brutal despotism analogous to Wait's dominion and the antithesis of Allistoun's rule.

Conrad proposes hierarchy rather than an anarchy of thinly disguised self-love, and a confrontation with ego rather than destructive dreams of selflessness. It is no accident that he spells out the conditions of mankind's solidarity in the Preface to *The Nigger*. As an Author's Note appended to the story's last installment in the *New Review*, it was not only an aesthetics but a direct comment on the theme of *The Nigger*, suggesting that the true solidarity of mankind lay in a tragic awareness of our position in nature, in knowing that we are, as Stein in *Lord Jim* suggests, imperfect creatures with dreams of perfection. There is of course much more to the solidarity this Preface describes, including the aesthetic "sympathy" Conrad intends to evoke through his attention to the universal senses, especially to sight; but the implication clearly is that whatever may bind mankind together is not to be found in the illusion of selfless brotherhood or in transcending maya. In one sense, the Preface is the most telling defense of maya ever written.

If sympathy is thus continually probed in Conrad's work and ego is the unavoidable companion subject, Schopenhauer's escape from ego is Conrad's principal objection to him. Paul Wiley has, as I mentioned earlier, seen the metaphysical pessimism of Schopenhauer in Flaubert's *The Temptation of St. Anthony*, in the precise quality of the hermit's detachment. Since the will was an irrational and insatiable desire, life could not possibly satisfy it; tragedy was built into the nature of will in its relation to the world of other people and physical things. It has been argued that "Schopenhauer's system was thus a system of *metaphysical* pessimism, for his pessimism does not consist simply in an empirical observation (whether true or false) that human life contains more pain than joy, more suffering than happiness, but is based on a metaphysical doctrine concerning the ultimate nature of Reality, a doctrine that is radically pessimistic in character." [8]

Thus when Axël (and the "hermits" Wiley speaks of so often in nineteenth-century French literature and in Conrad) withdraws from the world, when Axël says of the exotic travels and experiences he had proposed to Sara, "Why realize them?" we detect the Schopenhauerian disdain for a contest with reality that can never be won. The will can never be satisfied in reality as it is in the idealizing dreams of an Axël. I have discussed all this earlier in connection with the escape from will in Conrad's first two novels. But for Schopenhauer and for many French and English writers who were, knowingly or not, under his influence, art was the principal means of escaping will, and this aspect of the tension between Conrad and the whole Schopenhauerian influence needs further discussion.

The aesthetic experience is, Schopenhauer says, will-less and self-less:

If raised by the power of the mind, a man relinquishes the common way of looking at things . . . if he thus ceases to consider the where, the when, the why, and the whither of things, and looks simply and solely at the *what*; if, further, he does not allow abstract thought, the concepts of the reason, to take possession of his consciousness, but instead of all this, gives the whole power of his mind to perception, sinks himself entirely in this, and lets his whole consciousness be filled with the quiet contemplation of the natural object actually present, whether a landscape, a tree, a mountain, a building or whatever it may be . . . if thus the object has to such an extent passed out of all relation to the will, then that which is so known is no longer the particular thing as such; but it is the *Idea*, the eternal form, the immediate objectivity of the will at this grade; and therefore, he who is sunk in this perception is no longer individual, for in such perception the individual has lost himself; but he is *pure*, will-less, painless, timeless *subject of knowledge*. [9]

I have quoted this passage in full because there is much in it that

Conrad can agree with; but its feeling is, as one critic has said, one "of escape from reality, a flight from objects in their concrete, unimpeachable meanings and significance." [10] To this spirit Conrad would never submit, as the Preface to *The Nigger* precisely states. Further, Schopenhauer's aesthetic experience is valued because it leads away from life — Conrad's, because it allows a dialogue between what Conrad also called "ideal" value and the world of sensation and imperfection.

The above passage describes the aesthetic experience of low-grade objectified will ("a landscape, a tree, a mountain"); in a higher grade of objectification, in man or in man's poems or music, the perception of an "eternal form" is just as important as the release from will. But in all aesthetic experience, the quality of escape is essential — or so Schopenhauer insists. When one of the foremost students of Schopenhauer's aesthetics says of this spirit that "it is a passing from the compulsions of every-day things and experience to the ivory tower, to the 'golden dream' of essences, of iridescent Ideas of a 'disembodied joy,' " [11] he is perhaps unwittingly suggesting connections with the "yellow" nineties and with the Symbolist movement that I should like to insist on.

It may be nearly impossible to distinguish the rather late influence of Schopenhauer on French *l'art pour l'art* (and on related but by no means identical Symbolist theory) from that of Kant, whose elusive idea of aesthetic "purposiveness without purpose," expressed in the *Critique of Judgement*, had affected a number of French popularizers of German aesthetics as early as 1815. (The phrase *l'art pour l'art* was apparently first used in 1804 by a Frenchman, Benjamin Constant, who had come under the influence of some Kantian aesthetics while in Germany.[12]) By the 1820s, nearly ten years before Théophile Gautier seized the banner, what might be called a movement was under way in Paris. The irony in even trying to sort out these threads of influence is that in any event Schopenhauer himself probably derived a good part of his aesthetics from Kant, providing a late reshaping of ideas that had, though only crudely grasped, been very much a part of French literature, especially of the so-called Decadence, for years before Schopen-

hauer's thought became influential. The contribution of Schopenhauer to French aesthetics and subsequently to the English was
nonetheless potent and in some important respects unique and unlike Kant, especially in its use of art for the ultimately "moral"
purpose of escaping will (this despite the fact that he shared with
Kant the sense that aesthetic perception had to be "disinterested").
It is in the late Symbolist aesthetic that this unique disdain for the
realm of will is principally found.

In summary: Conrad was not about to use his art as a means of
escaping will, especially not in the sense of climbing into an ivory
tower. I suspect his objections, however, would not have been quite
so intense to Schopenhauer's original suggestions as to the so-called
decadent versions of those suggestions. Conrad, like Schopenhauer,
would not have thought art ought to create desires or direct desires; he might have accepted Kant's term, *disinterested*. But his art
would always imply an aesthetic coming-to-terms with ego. For
Conrad, losing a sense of unique identity — far from creating value
by allowing one to see through maya to the unity of mankind —
meant losing the only force that can sustain one against the "scientific" knowledge of his place in the universe, or at least against intimations of meaninglessness that come in many forms.

Thus, the individuation of will is a crucial source of value; on
self-knowledge depends the quality of the sympathy one can muster for another human being and for human solidarity. The cheap-
est, most unenlightened sympathy is based on ego largely ignorant
of itself. Nowhere is Conrad's sense of ego revealed with more bril-
liance and complexity than in *Lord Jim*. In "Falk," completed in
May 1901, he offers an egoism that is almost orthodox Schopenhauerian will. For the young captain of "Falk" to share this life-
force (an energy that allows Falk himself to survive even the guilt
he feels at cannibalism) is unquestionably good — the sharing is
supposed to produce in our captain a kind of purified compassion
or sympathy, not one that denies ego but one that comprehends its
full nature and role. "Falk" proposes a view of sympathy antithetical to Schopenhauer's and does so with a tenacity that suggests
Schopenhauer was kept firmly in mind throughout the story. *Lord*

*Jim* and *Heart of Darkness*, however, have the inestimable Marlow at their service for the exploration of ego and sympathy, and both use a more powerful fable than either Falk's melodramatic cannibalism or his romantic-sexual "hunger" for the speechless girl aboard the *Diana*.

# 4

# The Psychology of Self-Image: *Lord Jim*

Insofar as Conrad tried to transfer the imperative solidarity of a crew at sea to the nation, to the community of Patusan, or even to individual loyalties, he was immediately in trouble. Such conceptions are not all-purpose appliances to be shifted around at will, and most critics make far too much of the profundity of *The Nigger* for issues of human solidarity.

In beginning to write "Tuan Jim: A Sketch," Conrad was very close to the relativism suggested in "Karain." Nonetheless, the seaman's career appeared to suggest imperatives, and the basic structural principle of *Lord Jim* represents an attempt to imagine a young seaman who, having violated such a fixed standard, attempts to transfer it to a human community significantly unlike a voyaging ship, and to decipher what being faithful to it means in such a new situation. Of course the unique structural element in *Lord Jim* is its division into two halves, into *Patna* and Patusan. Conrad at times felt that division to be a flaw, the "plague spot" on the novel; and there has always been some difficulty deciding what aesthetic and moral impulses caused him to add Patusan to *Patna*. I should like to suggest that Conrad intuitively wanted to see whether the fixed standard Jim had violated in his leap from the ship could be

54

applied to the community, as Jim surely thinks it can. Is the con-
figuration of the *Patna* morality useful in discovering the key moral
issues in Patusan? Or are the two situations different enough so
that Jim is victimized by a facile attempt to shift his maritime, craft
morality to a more complex area of human association? I feel that
the latter is true, that Conrad taught himself in writing *Lord Jim*
how the relative ease with which one could believe in the imperatives aboard ship became impossible in the shadowy maze of Patusan. It is, furthermore, only through discussing this issue that we
can discover the precise quality of Jim's egoism and of Conrad's
sense of altruism.

No one asserts that the moral imperatives applying to the *Patna*
are absolutely simple; yet it is clear that had Jim simply stayed with
his ship the demands of a fixed standard would have been satisfied.
Patusan, however, involves a woman and love and at least two hier-
archies of loyalty. There is only one legitimate hierarchy aboard
ship, and should the captain fail to enforce it the fixed standard
soars above him, much as Oliver W. Holmes envisioned the
common law, "a brooding omnipresence in the sky." Jim wants
"another chance," yet there can be no duplication in Patusan of
the rather special circumstances of a ship at sea. In order to satisfy
a pledge to Doramin made in imitation of the fixed standards imposed on a ship, Jim must violate a pledge made to Jewel; further,
he is inflexible in a situation that may require flexibility and the
compromise of glorious fixed standards in order that certain moral
realities emerge. Except the ecstatic marriage with his own self-
image, what does Jim accomplish by sacrificing his life? Even less
in the way of useful solutions, certainly, than he had a right to expect by staying on board the *Patna* with its quaking bulkhead and
few lifeboats. But his remaining on the *Patna* would have satisfied
unequivocally a fixed standard that must obviously remain authoritative for the very existence of the seaman's life. His suicide confirms no fixed standard necessary to the political, economic, or
moral well-being of Patusan; it is more civilized to keep pledges
than not (and Patusan has had no surplus of kept pledges in the
past), but if a pledge must be kept by removing the only source of

political stability the community has known, then we may well
suspect that Jim is thinking of his self-image before any consequences his death may have for the community. It has been pointed
out time and again that Jim's honor is at stake, that Conrad is Polish, and that after the death of Dain Waris Jim's authority is in
any event irretrievable. It is even tempting to imagine that in his
death Jim has idealistically shown Patusan the only real example of
honor and fidelity it has known, and that such a precedent for human solidarity is as imperative on land as on the sea. We must,
however, explore the texture and quality of this landlocked version
of the seamanly imperative.

I am grateful to Mrs. Hay in *The Political Novels of Joseph
Conrad* for believing nearly the opposite of everything I feel the
novel suggests about the authority of a fixed standard. She refers to
the "man-made doubt in the power of a fixed standard of conduct,
which is the ghost Marlow hopes Jim can lay," and contends that
"Jim fails to redeem himself, but he comes as close as humanly possible to redeeming Marlow's belief, in the only way belief can ever
be proven, Conrad seems to say — by his willingness to die for it." [1]
Although belief in a standard may be confirmed by one's willingness to die for it, the fixedness of that standard, the ordained authority of it is not so confirmed: no doubt Karain would be willing
to die for his sixpence.

Mrs. Hay goes on to insist that the "ethical or moral postulate
that sovereign power *can* be enthroned in a fixed standard of conduct is axiomatic in the conduct of the French lieutenant and Stein,
as well as of Marlow and Jim; whereas it is conspicuously absent in
the motives of the 'Patna' officers, Chester, Cornelius, and Brown."
How can Stein, suggesting the same therapeutic relativism found
in the young sailor who gives Karain the sixpence, confirm the absolute authority of any standard? We all agree that Stein is an
idealist and advises determined pursuit of the dream to an end very
likely to be destructive. Because man, unlike butterflies (the precise balance of cosmic forces) is imperfect, idealism will always be
a "destructive element." But it will be so even for someone like
Chester. Surely we are not to agree with Chester's estimate of his

own state of mind, that he is a realist and sees things as they are. He
is one of the serious jokes in the novel, for Chester wants to exploit
a guano island having no water, no anchorage, and subject to the
most violent tropical storms. No one who knows anything about
the area (except senile Captain Robinson) will listen to his incredible plans. So obvious is the chasm between Chester's professed real-
ism and his fatal dreaming that Marlow later calls him "that
strange idealist" who had at once found a practical use for Jim: "It
was enough to make one suspect that, maybe, he [Chester] really
could see the true aspect of things that appeared mysterious or utterly hopeless to less imaginative persons" (p. 105). It is hard to find
in this novel a character who is not in some sense an idealist, and it
is a rare person who tries to reach out of the destructive element, to
see through all dreams, and to drown in the attempt. Even Gentleman Brown's egoism often suggests that lack of practicality which,
in the popular mind at least, marks the idealist. He has fallen in love
with the lonely wife of an island parson, but she is nearly dead
when he brings her aboard and he is romantically distraught when
she dies. He orders the attack on Dain Waris for no practical purpose and, in fact, by this violence loses the food Jim has promised
to deliver downriver. Of Brown Marlow says, "But Jim did not
know the almost inconceivable egotism of the man which made
him, when resisted and foiled in his will, mad with the indignant
and revengeful rage of a thwarted autocrat" (pp. 239–40). The destructive element of which Stein speaks includes more than virtuous, perhaps heroic ideals. There may even be "evil" ideals: idealism for Stein consists of abstracting a standard of conduct which
does not accommodate man's imperfection, measured by any pure
criterion, "good" or "evil," beside, above, or below moral considerations.

Thus Stein is committed to the process, the form of idealism
rather than any specific content. He is no more enthusiastic about
Jim's heroic selflessness than he might be about another less obviously virtuous pursuit. His own heroism, we are told, is unlike
Jim's self-conscious prescription for himself: "this man [Stein]
possessed an intrepidity of spirit and a physical courage that could

have been called reckless had it not been like a natural function of the body — say good digestion, for instance — completely unconscious of itself" (p. 123). Of course Jim, Stein, and anyone else Mrs. Hay wants to nominate for the group that enthrones sovereign power in a fixed standard may be quite unlike one another and yet retain their membership privilege. Nevertheless, it is extraordinary how unlike Jim Stein is shown to be, despite his own feelings of profound sympathy for Jim's romanticism. I think Conrad has arranged these real differences between the two men partly to cast doubt on the moral authority of Jim's peculiar commitments to Doramin and to suggest that Jim's fidelity to the abstract form of idealism no more guarantees its morality than does Chester's to his mad scheme.

Stein and Jim are characterized by opposite sorts of physical action. Jim tries to avoid messy involvement with lifeboats that will not come free of their fastenings and with awkward rescuers who injure the man fallen overboard. After the rescue aboard the training ship Jim persuades himself that he is better off having taken no part in action which falls so far short of the clean, decisive heroism he fancies. But after the crew of the *Patna* has done all the awkward, even comic work on the intractable lifeboat, Jim does after all jump into it, need it and use it just as much as they. In both instances he shows a deep disdain for attempting heroism in the tangle of reality where, unlike boys' adventure stories, heroism is seldom unambiguous and neatly packaged. As Gentleman Brown says in his conversations with Jim: "I've lived — and so did you though you talk as if you were one of those people that should have wings so as to go about without touching the dirty earth. Well — it is dirty. I haven't got any wings. I am here because I was afraid once in my life" (p. 233). The reader can hardly fail to remember Conrad's use of butterflies throughout the novel to suggest the delicate perfection which naturally escapes man. Stein, after all, has captured his rarest, most beautiful specimen while it sits on a "small heap of dirt," although "this species fly high with a strong flight" (p. 128); he has been ambushed, surprised by just the sort of messy reality Jim finds intolerable. Jim, we remember, dislikes surprise and the unfortunate effect it has on his heroic self-image. In an emblematic action Stein pursues the butterfly while carrying his hat in one hand and his gun in the other, thereby suggesting a combination of practical readiness with idealism that manages to cope with reality, that does not require wings "to go about without touching the dirty earth" (p. 233). Conrad depends a good deal upon symbolic objects in this novel (the butterflies, the ring, hats, and so on) and has, I believe, meant to remind us that although Stein feels a romantic kinship with Jim, there are *moral* differences between the two men.

In probing the morality of Jim's death we need to remember the basic differences between the leap from the *Patna* — a leap which drives Jim away from the community of men and from the solidarity of his craft, and makes him talk, as Marlow remarks, like a "hermit" — and the leap into the mud at Patusan, a commitment which leads back to community and, to my way of thinking, a complexity of responsibility requiring the faith that ideals can be captured on a small heap of dirt.

After Dain Waris has been murdered, the Bugis followers of Doramin are furious with Jim. He is rejected not only because their young leader has been killed through what they apparently now regard as Jim's weakness, but because they had thought him infallible, magic, a Lord in more than the secular sense. Jim revels in the fictional quality of all he has done among these people who, as he twice says, resemble characters in an adventure story. Jim, clearly, is playing a role which does not in his eyes include any patchwork job of reconstruction after the murder of Dain Waris, even if one were possible. Jewel, who is no idealist at all, tells him to fight or run; but Lord Jim, as his earlier taste for fictionalized action has indicated, cannot include in his linear self-image such arabesques of compromise or qualification. He has guaranteed one kind of legitimacy for his suicide by earlier pledging his life should anything go wrong in the release of Gentleman Brown. Stein and Doramin, as the ring indicates, also make pledges, but presumably neither would deliberately bind his life, as Jim does, primarily as a gesture required to sustain this fictional role he plays. In imagining that Jim has pursued the ideal *usque ad finem* ("True! true! true!"), Stein praises in Jim a fictional purity of ideal that he himself instinctively modifies with a practical earthiness; he admires Jim without understanding the full import of the advice he himself had earlier tendered. Stein in recommending that we submit ourselves to the destructive yet humanizing element knows that the idealist is striving futilely to make perfect the imperfect; Jim, on the contrary, believes that he *is* a hero even when his own behavior either denies it or invalidates the whole idea of someone being either a hero or not. The difference between Stein's point of view on this idealist and Jim's own view of himself is that Jim, like Almayer and Willems with their self-images, believes he has an ordained identity as hero, a predetermined self which, though experience may temporarily frustrate its appearance, will ultimately shine forth. Stein—who, we are told, is instinctively heroic—ironically believes in the contingent self; Jim, who is contingently cowardly or heroic believes in the ordained self. Like Henry Fleming in *The Red Badge of Courage*, Jim believes that some people are created courageous, others not. What Stein's advice suggests, on the contrary, is that the man who recognizes his contingency, his moment-to-moment formlessness, pursue the ideal as an expression of his humanity. To be human is—if I may be forgiven the apparent absurdity—to be unlike the butterfly, not the precise and peaceful balance of cosmic forces, but the magnificent imbalance of a lust for perfection in a creature aware of his imperfection. To pursue the ideal as one's already innate essence is not to *pursue* it at all.

This novel, then, pivots not on the theme of lost honor so much as on the ironic juxtaposition of different conceptions of self. Stein, who has the least contingent "self" in the novel, gives advice (at least when he is standing in the shadows) to those who must live with their contingency. Jim, on the contrary, conceives of self as an absolute and eventually contrives his reality (pledges his life) so that he can choose a clean death should reality once more conspire to show him the truth.

In order to play on this ironic contrast, Conrad has given special attention to the second jump, from the rajah's compound, and the third, over a stream and into deep mud. Quite early in the novel when Jim is testifying at his trial, attempting to convey his own complex, imaginative explanation to the board of inquiry, Conrad uses the image of a creature held captive in a staked compound:

He wanted to go on talking for truth's sake, perhaps for his own sake also; and while his utterance was deliberate, his mind positively flew round and round the serried circle of facts that had surged up all about him to cut him off from the rest of his kind: it was like a creature that, finding itself imprisoned within an enclosure of high stakes, dashes round and round, distracted in the night, trying to find a weak spot, a crevice, a place to scale, some opening through which it may squeeze itself and escape. (P. 19)

The "stakes" of this fence are the "facts" the board of inquiry demands rather than Jim's imaginative rationalization of his leap. But like Jim's later detention in the rajah's compound, this fence keeps him "from the rest of his kind," and it is necessary to escape in order to make contact with some sort of human community once more.

Interestingly enough, the escape from the rajah's stockade is the beginning of Jim's commitment to Patusan and is at least temporarily a way of transcending the cold facts of his desertion from the *Patna*. No one who has detected the numerous other parallels and pairs between *Patna* and Patusan ought to be surprised at Conrad's suggesting the stockade image early in the novel. Having watched that image develop into Jim's actual detention, we can agree that the third leap becomes even more comprehensible. Jim's reaction to landing deep in the mud of Patusan (significantly, at a spot later used for the meeting between Brown and Jim) is one of agonized disgust for, of course, a number of reasons, some of them practical, some symbolic. To be caught hip-deep in mud is no way to redeem one's reputation; but more important, the sensation of being trapped in mundane reality is shocking to one who, as Brown points out, would like to fly above the earth. The mud symbolically anticipates the detailed, day-to-day involvement with Doramin's people that awaits Jim. Just as Jim's successful struggle with the ooze (followed by a peculiar instant of sleep) suggests to many critics a rebirth, so it is reasonable to see in that rebirth an anticipation of his accepting such total commitment as a means of confirming his self-image. True, it is not entirely or even mainly the active heroism he had earlier dreamed of: it involves a glorious assault on the Arab stronghold but also means settling an old man's quarrel with his wife as some sort of family-court judge might; it is a leap into the mundane as much as a flight in which "the earth seemed fairly to fly backwards under his feet" (p. 155). Jim expands these commitments to the breaking point; he returns to the scene of his third leap in order to include in his embrace of responsibility Gentleman Brown. In doing so, Jim repeats the error of the *Narcissus*: sympathetic identification springing from covert egoism. He bloats his responsibility to include — at least in theory — all men who "act badly sometimes without being much worse than others" (p. 240) and thereby endangers all his more immediate responsibilities despite the rationalization that he is protecting his people from Brown's promised mayhem. It is entirely appropriate that the meeting should be described as though it were a larger concentric circle of responsibility added to the first one drawn on this center: "They met, I should think, not very far from the place, perhaps on the very spot, where Jim took the second desperate leap of his life [I have called it the third, as Marlow does on occasion] — the leap that landed him into the life of Patusan, into the trust, the love, the confidence of the people" (p. 231).

As *The Nigger* suggests, sympathy which seems to be extended infinitely loses its true nature; and as among the crew on the *Narcissus*, Jim shares with Brown "a sickening suggestion of common guilt, of secret knowledge that was like a bond of their minds and of their hearts" (p. 235). In a different context it might be possible to see this shared guilt as a perfectly legitimate, even Christian awareness of man's fallen state. But here as elsewhere in Conrad we must be cautious with such analogues. While Conrad may be willing to admit that it is extremely difficult to say whether allowing Brown to escape is absolutely good or bad, the possible consequences for Jim's most immediate responsibilities are clear to all his native advisers. Conrad does not suggest in *The Nigger* that sympathy for Wait must always be founded in egoistic fear or that when so founded it is in other situations quite so poisonous as on board the *Narcissus*. His perception in both novels is that sympathy is often an oblique expression of egoism, but that even in such form it is not undesirable when brought within manageable limits, where it is blended with a certain amount of selfless love for Jewel, say, rather than artificially extended to most guilty men. In his letters Conrad could not say enough against ideals of universal brotherhood that suffocated more reasonable goals of intimate sacrifice. He is careful to show that the portion of egoism in Jim's sympathy grows as that sympathy expands in irrationally large circles. Of course Jim always uses Patusan for the repair of his self-image, but in allowing Brown to escape he defies the best judgment of Dain Waris and Doramin in order to preserve that ego ideal, and in guaranteeing that release with his life he has (as I have suggested) left himself a clear path to peaceful union with that self-image should reality suddenly become less fictional than he can bear.

In what sense, then, can Jim's death support our belief in the authority of a fixed standard? Jim's standard is the belief that he is naturally heroic, an error immediately clear to anyone who has seen the illusion of ordained self thoroughly undercut in Conrad's first two novels. The "fixed standard" cannot really be honor: what is honorable to Jim is anything confirming his notion of an ordained or natural self. It is certainly true, however, that in this novel Conrad delicately probes the conditions under which human solidarity of some sort is possible. The novel echoes with the phrase "one of us," and the narrative technique itself travels continually the distance between involvement and objectivity, between sympathy and judgment. Marlow at one point calls Jim's sense of honor ("his fine sensibilities, his fine feelings") "a sort of sublimated, idealised selfishness" (pp. 107–8). But it is nonetheless true that in Patusan the satisfaction of that idealized selfishness comes so close to pure benevolence and love that we are inclined to wonder how far Conrad will continue to seek for the egoistic base: "You take a different view of your actions when you come to understand, when you are

*made* to understand every day that your existence is necessary —
you see, absolutely necessary — to another person. I am made to
feel that. Wonderful!" (p. 185).

This is a vital moment in Jim's very slight development as a character. He is speaking of his love for Jewel, and there is a sense in
which the conclusion of *Lord Jim* becomes a choice between Jim's
idealized selfishness and this new feeling of genuine personal sacrifice, of love, that he bears toward Jewel. Some readers tend to
minimize his abandonment of this woman. Yet the novel ends with
her agony, and with her effect upon Stein who "has aged greatly of
late. He feels it himself, and says often that he is 'preparing to leave
all this; preparing to leave . . .' while he waves his hand sadly at
his butterflies" (p. 253).

At the end of the novel Jim must choose between a nearly selfless love for Jewel (selfless because it will ruin the confirmation of
his self-image) and his ego ideal. Having pledged his life to Doramin, Jim must either give his life to Jewel or to that conception of
an ordained self; there can be no compromise. If we are to believe
Marlow that "the real significance of crime is in its being a breach
of faith with the community of mankind" (p. 95), we may wonder
whether faithfulness in one quarter can be built upon betrayal in
another, whether the fictional image of his own perfection that Jim
has elaborated in Patusan (partly by pledging his life to Doramin
and by behaving as though he had always to deal with adolescents)
has not forced him into the final dilemma. Jim's ultimate dilemma —
which he sees as a choice between honor and Jewel — would not
be inherent in a more normal relation between Jim and Patusan.
(Clearly, despite the natives' deification of the man, nothing of the
sort was inherent in Rajah Brooke's involvement with Sarawak.)
He has, through believing in his own *natural* heroism, created a dependence that in a less exaggerated form is common enough between natives and white men; pledging his life to Doramin is just
the sort of theatrical gesture we might expect from someone who
confuses a role with reality.

But, after all, is there any value in *Lord Jim* more potent than
Jim's own illusion? Marlow, writing to the British imperialist about

Jim's last days, remarks: "The point, however, is that of all mankind Jim had no dealings but with himself, and the question is whether at the last he had not confessed to a faith mightier than the laws of order and progress" (p. 206). And, we might add, mightier than love and anything else that was not part of his self-image. In the end *Lord Jim* is about the isolation of a human soul, not human community, not even the love between two people. Further, the novel makes it quite clear that another ideal might have functioned with equal power having found its own Lord Jim. Jim's version of heroism has no special claim, no inherent authority apart from the intensity his imagination confers upon it.

What we are left with is not the authority of fixed standards but the power of human ego and imagination to confer value upon abstractions and to idealize its own desires. Until the individual finds his own peculiar way of idealizing his activities, however, his sense of identity is not strong and certainly cannot provide a sense of value. This impregnation of abstract values with human imagination suggests a far subtler conception of the human mind than either the paralyzed will of the first novels and stories or the ego and altruism of *The Nigger*. Jim, like Karain and Arsat in "The Lagoon," experiences an evil moment when will fails, though of course Jim's will is not paralyzed by passion for a woman. Nonetheless, the failure of will in all three stories means the betrayal of a basically masculine bond and causes great disorder. Like Karain, Jim wanders the East trying to escape a ghost. But in *Lord Jim* the inadequacies Conrad had already begun to see in artificially separating will and passion become part of his most important themes. For the first time in Conrad's work we are carefully led to see that what had been described as more-or-less rational will struggling with irrational passion is more accurately an individual struggling to contain all his behavior as a single identity. The quest is not to master passion for the sake of order — and hence not really to transfer the moral imperatives of a voyaging ship to Patusan — but to understand what one is; not to win a victory for will, but to examine the validity of that model. The way has been opened, in short, for such stories as "The Secret Sharer" in which the irrational is not to be defeated but integrated. Conrad's attempt to assess the authority of a fixed standard has given way to the distinctly modern belief that value arises from a strong sense of identity and possibly in no other way. Jim's importance is not in confirming Marlow's or Stein's belief in a fixed standard, or in redeeming himself, or in having found a fixed "simple value" essential to both *Patna* and Patusan, but in celebrating an orgiastic marriage which is at once physical death and the birth of value in an absurd universe. The limbo of paralyzed will which obsessed the last decades of the century may well have partly been caused by the fact that modern experience had outrun old metaphor; if one does not imagine man defined by a struggle of will and passion then the failure of will is an idea with little substance. In both "Karain" and *Lord Jim* we are invited to see moments of betrayal as a corruption of will; yet Jim and Karain speak as though the metaphor of will and passion does not get either of them or us very far toward understanding what had happened. As in so much literature of the late nineteenth century, the idea of paralyzed or enervated will is intimated by both men to be at best an unsatisfactory explanation for moments when one is unable to admit the frightening array of behavior that can indeed be "chosen."

For many of Conrad's characters before *Lord Jim*, such values as they could muster came from resisting passion, or would have, had they been up to the test. Yet such resistance implied that man was eternally at war with nature and achieved his worth only by denying his kinship with the rest of life. How to come to terms with the unrational, with passions, with instinct (or more precisely how to stop thinking of will as merely rational) became an issue characteristic of the late nineteenth century. Fortunately such men as Freud and Frazer turned their attention to it. Lord Jim himself, though hostile to what he imagines is at best a deceptive Nature, seeks to be totally at one with himself even at the price of his life; but as we are reminded endlessly in that novel, only natural creatures such as the butterfly, unconscious and perfectly complete, exist in this mode. There is throughout Conrad's work a fascination with some kind of natural man, unfragmented, usually unimaginative, who follows his instinct without thereby losing his honor among men. Though Conrad despaired of man finding a satisfactory place in nature, the attempt is not uncommon in his characters and could not have been a settled issue in his own mind.

Significantly enough, *Lord Jim* and the "Youth" volume, containing *Heart of Darkness*, are followed in 1903 by the volume containing "Typhoon" and "Falk," stories which present men who instinctively achieve some kind of harmony with natural forces. Earlier, in *The Nigger*, Singleton had shown the same primitive virtue, the same unselfconsciousness and natural control of sympathy so necessary to the survival of the *Narcissus*. There can be no doubt that these primitive, unimaginative types do have a place in nature denied to Jim except through the peculiar device of his own death. When events are going his way in Patusan, Jim seems to believe that even the moon itself rises precisely between the two hills of his success against the Arab stronghold, in sympathy with his control of Patusan and, seemingly, of his own "fate." But of course we know how Jim reads significance into indifferent nature according to the current success or failure of his self-image.

If Jim were the authoritative consciousness in *Lord Jim*, we might call the novel another manifestation of romantic faith in the power of "self." Through various perspectives on Jim, however, we learn he is not what he thinks he is in the *way* he thinks he is. Conrad suggests that most men can never be at one with their self-image unless they are willing to stop reality from undercutting it, to stop the possibility of failure as Brierly and Jim do. Marlow learns nearly as much as we do about Jim. (I cannot accept those readings of the novel which place between the reader and Marlow some ultimately significant irony.) And so Marlow comes to occupy a position midway between romantic faith in the perhaps revolutionary self and a distinctly modern doubt about the existence of self at all. He sees that men cannot be one with an ego ideal, that even Stein who is instinctively and successfully a romantic hero has in the end done something which makes him want to leave his butterflies, his faith in the tragic pursuit of ideals. But Marlow is a long way from speaking like Samuel Beckett and Ionesco in their despair at man's inability to locate anything that might be called "self"; he is much closer to Lawrence Durrell's amazement and optimism at man's ability to become so involved in the illusion of self that he fails to lift up his eyes to the ultimate absurdity.

Some fifteen years ago Robert Penn Warren gave what has always seemed to me the definitive explanation of Stein's famous image. His reading is so convincing, so much in harmony with the context that it is amazing to see recent articles on the subject that make no mention of that 1951 Introduction to the Modern Library *Nostromo*. Warren suggests that the man who tries to climb out of the "destructive element," out of dreams and ideals of perfection, is one obsessed by his animal nature:

Because man, in one sense, is purely a creature of nature, an animal of black egotism and savage impulses. He should, to follow the metaphor, walk on the dry land of "nature," the real, naturalistic world, and not be dropped into the waters he is so ill-equipped to survive in. Those men who take the purely "natural" view, who try to climb out of the sea, who deny the dream and man's necessity to submit to the idea, to create values that are quite literally "super-natural" and therefore human, are destroyed by the dream. They drown in it, and their agony is the agony of their frustrated humanity. . . .

To conclude the reading of the passage, man, as a natural creature, is not born to swim in the dream, with gills and fins [is not naturally adapted to it], but if he submits in his own imperfect, "natural" way he can learn to swim and keep himself up, however painfully, in the destructive element. To surrender to the incorrigible and ironical necessity of the "idea," that is man's fate and his only triumph.

Which is to say that while Jim has been true to his dream (as Stein later insists) he has not the state of mind of a man who has learned to swim. Like the "natural" man who tries to deny the necessity of the dream and to crawl onto the dry land he conceives of as his natural environment, Jim thinks of the dream and of one particular dream as his natural environment. He behaves as though he had always been meant to swim like a fish. The man who, in Warren's analysis, has learned to survive in the unnatural but inevitable medium of ideals must be something like Stein himself.

Significantly unlike Jim's "sympathy" for Brown, Marlow's sympathy for Jim is slowly schooled in a detailed confrontation with ego, both his own and Jim's. The process is elusive yet painful, and when it is over Conrad has shown us once again what was wrong on board the *Narcissus*: ironically, only by understanding Lord Jim's self-love can we understand his self-destruction.

*The Nigger* had not imagined the birth of value in the human soul with so much freshness as to challenge the very bedrock moral and psychological models of his age. That was the achievement of *Lord Jim*, where will and passion, ego and sympathy are all concepts lost in the drama of self-image and in the superbly delicate analysis of the process rather than content of idealism. Allegedly fixed faculties of mind, such as will, passion, and ego, are as irrelevant to *Lord Jim* as the idea of fixed moral standards. Conrad perhaps would have liked to believe in the innate authority of some such standards, but he was too good a psychologist to do so. Ego, and indeed altruism and sympathy at least as Jim seems to show these qualities, are given so radical a redefinition in *Lord Jim* that they cannot be grasped without our changing the root conception.

# 5

# Existential Models:
## *Heart of Darkness*
## and *Lord Jim*

If ever a story seemed to be about the full spectrum of ego and the "complex altruism" generated in a man who sees the full appeal and corruption of such ego, it must be *Heart of Darkness*. Yet it seems to me that *Heart of Darkness* implies radical changes in Conrad's root conceptions of mind and will not, ultimately, yield to analysis with "ego" and "sympathy," however subtly employed. It shares with *Lord Jim* the tremendous innovative energy that stretches beyond the key conceptions of *The Nigger* and is scarcely equaled again in Conrad's career. To call Kurtz an egoist is surely one of the great understatements of our time. Few people will deny you the right to do so, but no one will quite believe that you have found an adequate term or concept for the analysis.

*Heart of Darkness* presses into implications that are very disturbing to Conrad, as they have been to Marlow and as they are to us and the anonymous first speaker — though not, apparently, to the Lawyer, the Accountant, and the Director of Companies. Conrad and Marlow can barely find words to contain the "unspeakable" implications. Much of Marlow's inability to articulate, however, needs to be put in the proper context. In this story Conrad presses his early taste for the aesthetic use of primitives until it becomes vital in comprehending much of the "unspeakableness" in Marlow's narrative. While Marlow and the other white men — with the possible exception of Kurtz — are outsiders, unable to "read" nature and, at least in the case of Marlow, constantly and uselessly pondering its "inscrutable" intention, the native is one with it, embraced by it, fairly breathed by it: "and the wilderness without a sound took him into its bosom again" (the native who is mistakenly beaten for setting a shed on fire, p. 20); and after Kurtz has quieted his people before he is first carried down to the steamer, "I noticed that the crowd of savages was vanishing without any perceptible movement of retreat, as if the forest that had ejected these beings so suddenly had drawn them in again as the breath is drawn in a long aspiration" (p. 53). I need not provide the full list of phrases suggesting that the native is an organic part of nature, as breath to the living body. Although a modern cultural anthropologist will agree that every primitive society must achieve some kind of harmony with nature, few still subscribe to that small part of the myth of the noble savage which carried over into Conrad, Freud, and a number of other late Victorians: the idea that the savage is one with nature, while the civilized white man has fallen — for better or worse — from the primal unity and now, if he is at all like Marlow, spends a good deal of his time trying to read a message no longer legible: "The woods were unmoved, like a mask — heavy, like the closed door of a prison — they looked with their air of hidden knowledge, of patient expectation, of unapproachable silence" (p. 50). As it does for Melville, nature tantalizes Marlow with symbols that cannot truly be read; it masks not only the hidden natives (whose weapons Marlow cannot even identify: arrows seem "little sticks," a spear, a "long cane") but an intention, an attitude, a personality which only serves to disguise the "truth" of its fundamental indifference. Everything connected with the savages seems to Marlow to have a hidden symbolic value, beginning with the white piece of worsted wrapped around a dying native's neck early in the story ("Was it a badge — an ornament — a charm — a propitiatory act? Was there any idea at all connected with it?" [p. 14]), contin-

uing through the sound of their drums ("and perhaps with as profound a meaning as the sound of bells in a Christian country" [p.
16]; "Whether it meant war, peace, or prayer we could not tell"
[p. 30]), and the restraint of the cannibals ("Restraint! What possible restraint? Was it superstition, disgust, patience, fear — or some
kind of primitive honour?" [p. 36]) to the summary, revealing
comment, "we were cut off from the comprehension of our surroundings" (p. 31). Nature presents the same inscrutability as the
savages, and to rehearse the occasions when Marlow reminds us of
this would be to point out the most offensively portentous diction
in the story: for example, "It was the stillness of an implacable
force brooding over an inscrutable intention" (p. 29). But in one
of these effusive moments, the author appears at Marlow's shoulder
and virtually tells us what nature is: "And outside, the silent wilderness surrounding this cleared speck on the earth struck me as
something great and invincible, like evil or truth . . ." (p. 19).
What may inadvertently be revealed here is something that Marlow as yet perceives only imperfectly: that the universe, apart from
man's heroic will to give it meaning, offers no moral sanctions and
that in any ordinary sense of language this fact, because true, is
"evil." Marlow intends merely to cite evil and truth as examples of
the invincible; but the effect of the sentence is to intimate the indifferent, amoral "knitting machine" universe (as Conrad once
called it) which had been part of the "mystic wound" at least since
Darwin and the rush of scientific activity in the early fifties. If the
savages lie behind a mask which is also the door of a prison, if they
are in some sense imprisoned as well as embraced by nature, they
at least have a ready capacity for worship (though not for the idealization of abstract qualities), a capacity which is perhaps a function
of their organic role in nature. Because the native is at one with nature and feels no sense of alienation, he does not sense the need to
create his own contingent values and sanctions and so can readily
accept what presents itself convincingly as divine sanction; he has
the capacity to create gods and to worship them (as Kurtz is worshiped). The Marlovian white man who has undercut easy notions
of natural moral purpose has little or no capacity for this categori-

cal belief. Hence Kurtz's behavior depends on his being able to perceive the natives' relation to nature through his own godlike effect
on them.

The Malay Babalatchi in *An Outcast* tries to force Tom Lingard
to see the difference between native and white. And his distinction
is precisely that pointed out years ago in Warren's Modern Library
Introduction to *Nostromo*: the men who are always "investing
their activities with spiritual value," and those who do not, perhaps
cannot. Speaking to Babalatchi of his earlier activities in Sambir,
Lingard says:

> "If I ever spoke to Patalolo, like an elder brother, it was for your
> good — for the good of all" . . .
> "This is white man's talk," exclaimed Babalatchi, with bitter ex-
> ultation. "I know you. That is how you all talk while you load
> your guns and sharpen your swords; and when you are ready, then
> to those who are weak you say: 'Obey me and be happy, or die!'
> You are strange, you white men. You think it is only your wisdom
> and your virtue and your happiness that are true. You are stronger
> than the wild beasts, but not so wise. A black tiger knows when he
> is not hungry — you do not. He knows the difference between him-
> self and those that can speak; you do not understand the difference
> between yourselves and us — who are men. You are wise and great
> — and you shall always be fools." (P. 226)

Babalatchi's point is that Lingard feels the typically Western
need to idealize his desires, to the extent that he can no longer read
his own passions accurately. Though the ideal may originally have
been no more than the rationalization of a desire, it gets out of
hand, and the white man can no longer even know — unlike the
*black* tiger — that having fed he is no longer hungry. The ability
to idealize one's activities creates unnatural appetites beyond the
original need. The native is the black tiger in this comment, and
knows when he is hungry and when he has satisfied his appetite.
Further, he recognizes the difference between himself and the
white man, who, in the metaphor of Babalatchi's comment, can
"speak." Without taking the metaphor as in any way a disparage-
ment of the native, it nevertheless suggests that man's ability to talk
is to the beast as the white man's capacity for idealization is to the

native — that the native cannot understand the ideal but at least recognizes its presence and effects. And Conrad is quite serious in intimating through the metaphor that as the ability to talk is an obvious sign of humanity, so this idealization seems to be the essence of the Western mind. While it is true that in *Nostromo* he attributes this talent to "Northern people" rather than to Italian Nostromo, that novel is after all later than *Heart of Darkness*, and its setting and political themes encourage discriminations among types of Western mind that are uncalled for in the more elementary contrast of white and native. Babalatchi's further suggestion that a white man's "greatness" springs from this sometimes fatal idealism is also to be taken as Conrad's own feeling on the subject. The dilemma has been drawn by Warren: without the ability to *invest* activities with spiritual value, some men are unable to "justify" themselves; with it, they are often fools or soon dead or both.

Although they have an acute sense of human loyalty, neither Aïssa nor Jewel has any talent for abstract idealization, which is the key reason Jewel fails utterly to understand Jim's reaction to Gentleman Brown's attack. There are apparently some exceptions to this general characteristic among Conrad's natives (possibly Karain and Arsat), but on the whole the pattern is carried right into *Heart of Darkness* in order to emphasize, I think, a more important issue there: the sense in which Marlow is cut off from any easy acceptance of meaning. Of course this does not mean he can learn from the savages; their harmony with nature is not instructive. For Marlow the steamer is not a river monster (despite the monstrous difficulties he has running it), nor is Kurtz a god. Nor, so far as we can tell, are the savages happier than white men who are outside the mask. All we do know is that for Marlow language is nearly useless in gathering meaning from his surroundings; he senses a predicament thrown into bold relief by the natives, who do not experience it.

The anonymous first narrator is rather comfortable with names: the Director of Companies, the Lawyer, and the Accountant represent the first and perhaps the last secure use of names in the whole story. In using their titles, the narrator apparently feels he has reached the essence of these men, despite the additional fact that they all love the sea; here the name bears some relation to reality, as names from this moment on in *Heart of Darkness* seldom do.

Things are, at the very least, not what they seem. London too has been one of the dark places of the earth. Marlow's narratives, we are told, do not contain meaning like a nut does a kernel but evoke it "as a glow brings out a haze, in the likeness of one of these misty halos that sometimes are made visible by the spectral illumination of moonshine" (p. 3). A tale that contains its meaning in the traditional way might rest content with names, but obviously Marlow's "glow" cannot offer kernels of named essence; it insinuates, rather, the very difficulty of using names: "Kurtz — Kurtz — that means 'short' in German — don't it? Well, the name was as true as everything else in his life — and death. He looked at least seven feet long" (p. 53). Names far from securing meaning often betray it. As James Guetti has suggested, the whole traditional implication that we may in this journey pass from the meaningless outside of things to the meaningful inside or "heart" is deceptive: the "heart," the "essentials of experience remain amoral and, even, alinguistic."[1]

The extent to which this play on names is carried, however, is astonishing. Clearly Conrad has some compelling reason for doing so. Even the "man-of-war" seems misnamed in her present situation:

Her ensign dropped limp like a rag; the muzzles of the long six-inch guns stuck out all over the low hull; the greasy, slimy swell swung her up lazily and let her down, swaying her thin masts. In the empty immensity of earth, sky, and water, there she was, incomprehensible, firing into a continent. Pop, would go one of the six-inch guns; a small flame would dart and vanish, a little white smoke would disappear, a tiny projectile would give a feeble screech — and nothing happened. Nothing could happen. There was a touch of insanity in the proceeding, a sense of lugubrious drollery in the sight; and it was not dissipated by somebody on board assuring me earnestly there was a camp of natives — he called them enemies! — hidden out of sight somewhere. (P. 11)

The entire passage is brilliantly symbolic — one of the best things Conrad ever wrote. The sense of futility is of course appalling.

The name "enemies" is no more meaningful and effective than the performance of the man-of-war ("she") popping shells into the indifferent immensity of Africa. She is "incomprehensible" and futile in the same way that the idea of *war* and *enemies* is simply incommensurate with the reality confronting these names. The West, with its taste for decisiveness, endings, stories with kernels of meaning and definitions, is no match for the intractable immensity confronting it. The whole scene suggests, among other things, the futility of language in the face of an experience which eludes such authority. Guetti's emphasis here would no doubt be on the "alinguistic" character of experience. But Marlow sees the problem also in terms of authority: where is the authority that will allow him to give to experience names that have some substance. He is Adam in the Garden watching the parade of nameless experience, but without the complete sense of authority that Adam feels delegated from God. Ultimately, Marlow looks forward to meeting Kurtz — that marvelous "voice" — as a possible source of authority, as a penetrating honesty that will at least know the proper names for things. Whatever Kurtz's own moral condition, Marlow has learned enough about him to expect that he will offer correct and substantial names — names that have some connection with reality. He expects from Kurtz that most primitive sense of names: that they will have something intrinsic to do with the thing named, even that they possess in some way its magic. In that view, to name a thing is to invoke it.

The space that Conrad and Marlow had seen upon the map of Africa was blank, and as Marlow proceeds upriver he soon discovers that none of the names since associated with Africa bear any relation to reality. As I have suggested, everything associated with the natives is an unreadable symbol to him. He cannot name the importance of the piece of white worsted, of the cannibals' peculiar "restraint," or of the sound of the drums. Any name is at the very least ironic: that these rapacious colonials should be called "civilized" and the natives "savage," that with their long staves the company men should look like "pilgrims," and so on. The land itself seems to turn the products of Western civilization into natural things, a boiler "wallowing" in the grass, a truck "lying . . . on its back with its wheels in the air" (p. 12). Identifications, in short, slip and slide and will not hold.

Occasionally Marlow meets someone who can make "correct entries" (as presumably can the Lawyer, the Accountant, and the Director), but only within his carefully limited range of concern. Nevertheless, "when one has got to make correct entries, one comes to hate those savages – hate them to the death" (p. 15). Marlow, however, is concerned with a much subtler accounting and is all too ready to tell us how "inscrutable" it is. Where is the man who can make a correct entry with regard to the "implacable force brooding over an inscrutable intention"?

Until he meets Kurtz, however, he is continually offered riddles as names, almost as though he were in some kind of fairy tale where the magic name must be discovered before – before what?

"Tell me, pray," said I, "who is this Mr. Kurtz?"
"The chief of the Inner Station," he answered in a short tone, looking away. "Much obliged," I said, laughing. "And you are the brickmaker of the Central Station. Every one knows that." (P. 21)

Even the diction and syntax resemble the catechism so familiar in the fairy tale's quest for a magic name. And the uselessness of the names offered is carefully underlined: this is the brickmaker who makes no bricks, presumably because there is no straw, presumably because no one really wants the bricks. Yet reading "chief of the Inner Station" metaphorically, we may anticipate (as Marlow seems to) that things will somehow be final and absolute there. One hopes names will be used differently there. The peculiar oil sketch Kurtz has left behind, a blindfolded woman holding a torch, suggests that the allegory of Justice (blindfolded and holding scales) has now been given a different function: not to judge but to illuminate, and not to be aware herself of the results of her illumination. So Kurtz will do something for Marlow that he has been unable to do for himself. Presumably impartial Justice may feel the weight of her scales and know when she has balanced correctly; but if her function is to illuminate and not to judge, her being blindfolded takes on a new significance. Though he *will* judge, Kurtz's main function in the story is not to judge or be judged but to illuminate. Perhaps Kurtz's emblematic intention in the sketch was to suggest that he came to these savages not to judge but to light the way for them. As a comment on what Marlow is to find in Kurtz, however, the painting assumes other more resonant implications. Kurtz will teach Marlow something about the source of authority for real names, the kind of names a child expects and the world seldom provides.

Certainly the nature surrounding Marlow is "mute, while the man jabbered about himself" (p. 22). His mind returns many times to nature's inability to talk: "Could we handle that dumb thing . . . I felt how big, how confoundedly big, was that thing that couldn't talk, and perhaps was deaf as well" (p. 22). But Kurtz is primarily a voice and a talker: one of the principal oppositions in the story is between nature, which can neither talk nor hear, and Kurtz, who is really the archetypal talker, as the Russian (who is perhaps the archetypal listener) and Marlow avow. If the inarticulate universe surrounding them could talk it might offer some true names, some awful names. Perhaps Kurtz will.

Marlow defines one aspect of his own predicament involving words and language when, in the same breath, he insists both that he cannot bear to lie and yet is persuaded that it is "impossible to convey the life-sensation of any given epoch of one's existence — that which makes its truth, its meaning — its subtle and penetrating essence. It is impossible. We live, as we dream — alone. . . ." (p. 23). This visceral respect for truth coupled with the awareness of the impossibility of communicating it is characteristic of Marlow wherever he appears in Conrad, and partly accounts for his continued interest in names as the steamer continues upriver.

He notes with ironic interest the name of the "Eldorado Exploring Expedition" and with far greater interest the fact that Kurtz's name "had not been pronounced once. He was 'that man'" (p. 27). Cut off "from the comprehension of our surroundings," he suggests that as a civilized man he is too far removed from his primitive origins to penetrate the meaning, say, of the drums. But part of the "primitive" from which most of them *except* Marlow are

too far removed is its preverbal quality. Marlow may indeed fancy
himself "the first of men taking possession of an accursed inheritance, to be subdued at the cost of a profound anguish and of excessive toil" (pp. 30–31). The implication is, however, that the world
he inherits is fallen not in any orthodox way through Adam's and
Eve's sin, but in its meaninglessness, in the enormous toil and pre-
sumption required of man to give it meaning. The signs and sounds
coming from this primitive world are to these civilized men without meaning, as the world may have been to the first man regardless of his obedience or disobedience. Perhaps his original sin is to
want meaning. The need to create significance from this plethora
is "toil" of the most difficult and seminal kind. This is "truth
stripped of its cloak of time" in the *echt* Conradian sense. And to
its challenge Marlow affirms that

he must meet that truth with his own true stuff — with his own in-
born strength. Principles? Principles won't do. Acquisitions,
clothes, pretty rags — rags that would fly off at the first good shake.
No; you want a deliberate belief. An appeal to me in this fiendish
row — is there? Very well; I hear; I admit, but I have a voice too,
and for good or evil mine is the speech that cannot be silenced.
(P. 31)

This is surely one of the most important speeches in *Heart of
Darkness*. The temptation is less to unleash ego or, as the Freudian
would have it, to realize pure id satisfaction, than to abandon the
toil of giving meaning to this inheritance, names to this preverbal
mystery. Any meaning which has been given to you ("Principles")
won't do precisely because you have not had to bear the pain and
responsibility of creating it. Principles are usually acquisitions,
which like other things we acquire rather than generate, like
clothes, are easily shaken off. The power of "speech" which will
sustain a man is the power to create or affirm for one's self a "deliberate" (a chosen) belief. Interestingly enough, this power is verbal,
"the speech that cannot be silenced." It is prior to morality ("for
good or evil") and represents the choice to give meaning and to
bear the responsibility springing from this willingness. Such speech
can alone give true names to things, not necessarily the magic

names of childhood or of fairy tales — the names which go to the imagined essence of things — but at least names for which the speaker bears a personal and final responsibility.

This speech is the only proper response to unspeaking nature and to the essentially preverbal character of all experience. And it is Kurtz's achievement. Although the above passage occurs a long way from the end of the novel, its location is a nice bit of Conradian strategy. It cannot at that point possess its full significance for the reader, but it swells back upon him with enormous effect after he has finished the story. Kurtz opening his mouth at the end of the novel as though to swallow the whole world (one thinks of Goya's Saturn) may be an emblem of unleashed ego, but in the light of this earlier passage and indeed of the whole story's emphasis on speech, we may well think that in a sense Kurtz has swallowed the world verbally as well as egoistically. And he has spit it out again in a flow of words that establishes his principal identification for Marlow as a "voice." But not until his "The horror! The horror!" does he, to Marlow's satisfaction, achieve the speech described so much earlier. His last act of naming comes from no Principles that have been given to the man; if anyone has shaken off all acquired values it is Kurtz.

Marlow follows this early appeal to "the speech that cannot be silenced" with a review of his contrastingly pragmatic attitude while proceeding upriver. But clearly it is *Marlow's* speech ("I have a voice too . . . *mine* is the speech that cannot be silenced"), and Marlow's speech *after* Kurtz has affected him that is, in this brief anticipatory passage, important. As he tells this early part of the story his mind rushes ahead to a realization he cannot yet substantiate dramatically.

While the steamer plods upriver, of course, Marlow says he has no time or taste for such ultimate speculations. He distracts himself with repairs to the steam engine, the difficulty of navigating — anything that does not acknowledge the threat implicit in his recent experience with language, names, speech. He turns temporarily to the "surface truth" of his job and contemplates the savage who tends the boiler. Here is a man who has been told a myth about the boiler, accepts it, and asks no more questions: "What he knew was this — that should the water in that transparent thing disappear, the evil spirit inside the boiler would get angry through the greatness of his thirst, and take a terrible vengeance" (p. 32). But for Marlow there is no source of authority to function as he himself does for the savage. "Civilization" has deprived him forever of the savage's power of belief. The boiler is a puzzle and a cipher to the savage, but some apparently absolute authority exists to explain these ciphers for him, in terms he can understand and accept. Marlow calls him a "poor devil" because instead of watching the boiler he ought to have been "clapping his hands and stamping his feet on the bank." But relative to the mysteries he faces, he is in a far more comfortable position than Marlow, who on the following page notes that *An Enquiry into some Points of Seamanship* is full of pencilled notes in cipher: "I couldn't believe my eyes! They were in cipher! Yes, it looked like cipher. Fancy a man lugging with him a book of that description into this nowhere and studying it — and making notes — in cipher at that! It was an extravagant mystery" (p. 33).

The mystery is partially resolved when Marlow later discovers that the cipher is actually plain Russian. But of course the unreadable notes are designed by Conrad to emphasize the larger cipher which has, at this point, nearly paralyzed articulation and becomes paramount as Marlow approaches Kurtz. The Russian's hut has a flagpole with "unrecognizable tatters" flying from it; the boiler-watcher's hair is "shaved into queer patterns." And the discovery of the seaman's engineering manual only serves to remind Marlow how thoroughly different its reality is from the unreadable cipher that teases him: "The simple old sailor, with his talk of chains and purchases, made me forget the jungle and the pilgrims [the first of which cannot be "read" and the other, cruelly misnamed] in a *delicious sensation* of having come upon something unmistakably real" (p. 33; my emphasis).

Just before reaching Kurtz, Marlow is able to formulate the problem of articulation with at least some tentative clarity:

I fretted and fumed and took to arguing with myself whether or

no I would talk openly with Kurtz; but before I could come to
any conclusion it occurred to me that *my speech or my silence*,
indeed any action of mine, would be mere futility. What did it
matter what any one knew or ignored? What did it matter who
was the manager? One gets sometimes such a flash of insight. The
essentials of this affair *lay deep under the surface, beyond my
reach*, and beyond my power of meddling. (P. 33; my emphasis)

"Beyond my reach" is a key phrase. When Kurtz's natives first
cry out, unseen, one of the pilgrims stammers, "Good God! What
is the meaning – ?" (p. 34). This is very shortly followed by Marlow's speculation that the crew of cannibals had no "clear idea of
time, as we at the end of countless ages have. They still belonged to
the beginnings of time – had no inherited experience to teach them,
as it were . . ." (p. 35) Yet the implication clearly is that the savage timelessness is better suited to accommodating the mystery
than is a Western sense of history, of calendar and clock time. Marlow is not only returning to primeval time but moving behind time.
They enter a "blind whiteness of fog," and should they "let go our
hold of the bottom, we would be absolutely in the air – in space.
We wouldn't be able to tell where we were going to – whether up
or down stream, or across – till we fetched against one bank or the
other – and then we wouldn't know at first which it was" (p. 37).
Marlow's navigational problem is suggestive of the impossibility of
defining the cannibal's "restraint," a question that occupies him for
two pages before this description of the fog. Marlow is beginning
to sense that he must – analogically speaking – let go his hold of
the bottom, that he is entering a realm where all the old sense of
direction is futile. Nothing in his background can tell him the
meaning of these ciphers, certainly not of the savage restraint that,
in the circumstances, defies reason. Such restraint seems to him the
*ur*-morality; it appears to stand at the origin of value.

As the actual navigator and captain of the steamer, Marlow keeps
his anchor on the bottom. In most other respects, it seems to me, he
has now been prepared to let go his hold of the bottom and to seek
in the proper frame of mind the Kurtz who lies beyond time, as an
"enchanted princess sleeping in a fabulous castle" lies beyond time.

The old means of articulation have now been irreparably discredited, the usual navigational marks made useless: even now should he reach a bank he would not know which it was. The conversation of the pilgrims echoes through the scene like some subtle kind of Greek chorus: " 'Left.' 'No, no; how can you? Right, right, of course' " (p. 37).

When Kurtz's natives attack, Conrad treats us to a brilliantly visual scene predicated upon the misidentification of a spear. As I said earlier, even the first shower of arrows is called "sticks, little sticks." The inability to name things meaningfully persists:

The side of his head [the "fool-nigger"] hit the wheel twice, and the end of what appeared a long cane clattered round and knocked over a little camp-stool. It looked as though after wrenching that thing from somebody ashore he had lost his balance in the effort. . . . He looked at me anxiously, gripping the spear like something precious, with an air of being afraid I would try to take it away from him. (P. 40)

Conrad's impressionism is crucial here, transforming pain and death into possessiveness and even pride. The familiar motif is, however, again dominant: not even this fundamental fact of wounding and death can for the moment be properly identified.

Marlow's earlier and decisive "mine is the speech that cannot be silenced" is now solidly connected with his passion to hear Kurtz *talk*. This word undergoes a crescendo after the attack, largely because at that moment Marlow has reason to wonder just what it is he will miss should he never reach Kurtz. He makes the rather surprising discovery that it is hearing him, talking with him that he had "been looking forward to."

I made the strange discovery that I had never imagined him as doing, you know, but as discoursing. I didn't say to myself, "Now I will never see him," or "Now I will never shake him by the hand," but, "Now I will never hear him." The man presented himself as a voice. . . . The point was in his being a gifted creature, and that of all his gifts the one that stood out pre-eminently, that carried with it a sense of real presence, was his ability to talk, his words — the gift of expression, the bewildering, the illuminating, the most exalted and the most contemptible, the pulsating stream of light, or the deceitful flow from the heart of an impenetrable darkness. (P. 41)

This remarkably insistent emphasis is rather puzzling, especially since it comes before either we or Marlow have met the Russian and heard his testimony to Kurtz's power as a talker. But if we remember the emphasis throughout on names and articulation, it becomes at once clear that Marlow has reason to expect Kurtz may be beyond the need to corrupt names. The basis for this hope is not clear to Marlow, except that all the "pilgrims" (those prime corrupters of names) have suggested how fundamentally unlike themselves Kurtz is. He has, after all, the experience of the Inner Station.

Marlow is so overcome by the memory of the first attack and the real possibility that he might never have reached Kurtz, that he breaks the chronology of his narrative and leaps ahead to assure his listeners he had finally "heard more than enough."

And I was right, too. A voice. He was very little more than a voice. And I heard — him — it — this voice — other voices — all of them were so little more than voices — and the memory of that time itself lingers around me, impalpable, like a dying vibration of one immense jabber, silly, atrocious, sordid, savage, or simply mean, without any kind of sense. Voices, voices — even the girl herself — now — (P. 42)

At first Kurtz too seems almost to join the "jabber" that has characterized attempts at articulation thus far in the story. " 'My Intended, my ivory, my station, my river, my —' everything belonged to him" (p. 43). The supreme egotism of this sort of speech differs from the jabber, however, in its directness and honesty. Kurtz can be eloquent, as the tract for the International Society for the Suppression of Savage Customs indicates, but there his "unbounded power of eloquence — of words — of burning noble words" (p. 44) is still generically different from the articulation Marlow had earlier anticipated in his "mine is the speech that cannot be silenced." In short, Kurtz has yet to show Marlow the kind of naming that will constitute a "victory." Before the normal chronology resumes, Marlow wonders whether the life of the helmsman was worth the journey to Kurtz. The thought is important in understanding Marlow's state of mind: he emphasizes that the helmsman had after all "steered." "He steered for me —" (p. 45). Can we, in other words, easily conclude that Kurtz's contribution to our sense of ultimates outweighs the faithful performance of the need simply to steer in this world — not to wonder what the boiler is really all about but simply to get dutifully around the next bend. Such operational fidelity is not to be despised.

The anxiety to identify things continues when Marlow finally reaches Kurtz. The "round carved balls" on what Marlow assumes to be fence posts come into focus later as human heads on ceremonial stakes. Definitions continue to collapse. The heads are those of "rebels": "Rebels! What would be the next definition I was to hear? There had been enemies, criminals, workers — and these were rebels" (p. 52). Kurtz — through the explanation of the young Russian that Kurtz had to cope with these rebels — is remarkably close to being implicated in the dishonest use of language introduced by the Company and the pilgrims much earlier in the story. Marlow, however, still looks to Kurtz for the possibility of authentic names and language. Oddly enough, it is only when Marlow discovers that Kurtz had been acting God among these natives, had been an unchallenged namer and definition-giver, that he despairs of discovering in Kurtz something definitively different from the articulation of the pilgrims.

But on the contrary Kurtz's experience as a would-be God has evidently prepared him for the speech that assumes the whole burden of the preverbal chaos it confronts. In a manner suggested at the beginning of this chapter, Kurtz has by his effect on the natives been stripped of all acquired principles. Or at least Marlow assumes that this has been the case. After all, Kurtz's "The horror! The horror!" has no fixed meaning; the important thing for this impressionistic story is what Marlow's experience and perspective have led him to think it means. To sum up that perspective, Marlow when he meets Kurtz is above all men prepared to assert that in the beginning was *not* the word; and after we hear of Kurtz's acting God (doing what he pleased, the opposition automatically defined as rebels), he quickly assumes that whatever evil Kurtz has done, this common knowledge of radical freedom is a bond between them. Unlike the native who watches the spirit in the boiler, and unlike the pilgrims who chart contentedly the borders of their own self-interest, there is no satisfying myth for Marlow and Kurtz, no authority that articulates the measuring of experience. Thus, although most of Kurtz's "magnificent eloquence" is empty, a mere cover for his fundamental lack of "restraint," his final naming of what he has done is speech of a different order. What qualifies him for this final utterance is identical with his degradation: ". . . I had to deal with a being to whom I could not appeal in the name of anything high or low. I had, even like the niggers, to invoke him — himself — his own exalted and incredible degradation" (p. 59). Nor, correspondingly, will Kurtz invoke any higher authority for the judgment of his actions — and this, Marlow knows very well.

Thus "The horror!" is judgment of a sort we have not seen before in the story and seldom hear in life. It is based upon no allegedly transcendent sanctions, upon no authority other than the individual's new sense of freedom and thus of responsibility. (Certainly it is not based on any regained Christian perspective.) His articulation is analogous to Axel Heyst's naming of Lena in *Victory* — she has been called Alma and Magdalen in the orchestra — and is surrounded here as there with implications of the first naming in Eden. "There must be a lot of the original Adam in me, after all," says Heyst. And Conrad's implication is not only that Heyst is capable of *felix culpa*, of finally "falling" into life, but more specifically of assuming responsibility for such fundamental comments as this by Lena: "Do you know, it seems to me somehow, that if you were to stop thinking of me I shouldn't be in the world at all."

The same may be said for "The horror!": it wouldn't be in the world at all without the man who will assume responsibility for saying it is. Some other horror might — a traditional Christian one on the model of Dante or Calvin or St. John of the Cross. But Kurtz's articulation of his own judgment depends on this incredible sense of freedom demonstrated to the man himself by his experience among the worshiping natives. It is the declaration of a man who knows that while for him there is no myth, he is necessarily the myth-maker. It is probably not accidental that while Marlow alleges Kurtz has thereby had a "victory," that same word is reserved for the title of Heyst's and Lena's story. It was, after all, not a word that Conrad used loosely, though it is a strange victory of death and responsibility that Heyst earns.

When, in one of the final scenes, Kurtz's savage mistress shouts something incomprehensible from the shore, Marlow as we may well expect says, "Do you understand this?" Kurtz's reply suggests more than either his comprehension of the native language or of their anxiety at his leaving: "Do I not?" he says (p. 60). There are no more masks or mysteries for Kurtz. His, finally, is the articulation that while seeming to be solipsistic has an importance to Conrad that makes any such label irrelevant. Later, in Brussels once more, Marlow learns that Kurtz had been "essentially a great musician," that is, a student of the pure art, all form and no content in the sense that other arts possess it.

"He had faith — don't you see? — he had the faith. He could get himself to believe anything — anything. He would have been a splendid leader of an extreme party." "What party?" I asked. "Any party," answered the other. (P. 65)

Obviously, then, Kurtz, has always had this peculiar combination of emptiness and enthusiasm. Yet it is vital to remember at this point in the story that Kurtz has finally *used* his own emptiness, momentarily discovered an articulation that redeems Marlow's anguish about speech in general. An awareness of the quality of nothingness — and I think Marlow believes Kurtz has gained such awareness — has always been prelude to spiritual growth, whether we see it in Sartre's key metaphors for human consciousness in *Being and Nothingness* or in Buddhism or Christian mysticism. Kurtz, in sum, has been led to this sense of responsibility and freedom not only by his effect on the natives but from an increasing awareness of his own emptiness.

Although Marlow has by no means been instantly prepared by

Kurtz's example for his own new speech, he utters the first words on the path to his own achievement. He lies to Kurtz's Intended. The motif of names and naming is lent its final potency in this moment: " 'The last word he pronounced was — your name.' " The lie is interesting because it is a touchingly crude imitation of Kurtz's articulation. Marlow intimates that he has moved on from that moment with the Intended to a fuller appreciation of Kurtz's significance. But this lie, it must be remembered, was his first, almost unintentional attempt to create myths in the new manner, in the way Kurtz had begun to teach him. What he does is benevolent and a trifle mistrustful of women, but more important it is free and responsible and articulate in a way that is apparently new for him. He has lied — bitten into something rotten — and discovered no doubt that there was a lot of the old Adam in creating names that are in some narrow operational sense lies. The particular content of this lie is not nearly so important as Marlow's attitude toward telling it; it is, after all, the one activity he instinctively abhors. His decision to lie at the crucial moment is thus a tribute to the new sense of responsibility Kurtz's victory has taught him, a sense that does not encourage us to pursue magic names that are somehow already intrinistic but to give names in a new spirit. As *Nostromo* points out, the true name is the one we are willing to be responsible for.

Conrad suggests, then, that Kurtz's acting God has in large part been what any authentic man ought to do — that far from being an exotic experience, it is precisely the central experience for late-Victorian man. Which is not to say that we all ought to find our native mistresses and heathen rites as fast as possible. The god role was unquestionably one of Conrad's crucial experiences as a novelist: how to imagine values without recourse to any intimation that the universe made sense. It is roughly the experience of Pinter's characters in *The Dumb Waiter*, as they are confronted with demands — all taken from the dumbwaiter itself — for one exotic menu after another. If there is an "intelligence" upstairs, a carefully organized restaurant making these demands — at least we can never know whether there is or not. The only proper response is to recognize that we are free to behave as though there were, providing we then recognize that these menus — each a comic masterpiece — in a sense also come from us. The universe is really dumb underneath its seeming eloquence, really motiveless behind its precise demands for eight different Chinese dishes. And like Pinter's characters, if we choose to respect these orders we shall probably have, for the supplication, no more than broken bits of candy in our pockets — a long way from the *haute cuisine* demanded.

Conrad is by no means, however, prepared to alter his root conceptions in a way that would allow the full exploration of this freedom. And it is by no means easy to see just what the effect of Kurtz's vision might have been had Conrad pursued it with the intensity of Melville, say, in *The Confidence Man*. What did happen in part, was that Conrad intensified his sense that analysis according to a priori categories of mind was self-defeating, no matter how brilliantly imagined it was. From *Lord Jim* through his subsequent political novels, he has the mind in effect creating itself in a myriad of ways that defy the categories even of Conrad's Schopenhauerian model. No model other than "self-image" could accommodate the radical freedom that Conrad had seen in Kurtz. This much is entirely clear: although Conrad's creation of Kurtz was sufficiently guarded so that the full implications of this freedom were never allowed to surface, *Heart of Darkness* had made it impossible to return wholeheartedly to any models that were uncongenial to such freedom. And this is true even in such seemingly pure examples of the Schopenhauerian model as "Falk."

Though to point out Conrad's growing similarity with Sartre's arguments on "Existential Psychoanalysis" in *Being and Nothingness* would require an extensive technical exposition, a few general comments may serve to indicate how both men were forced to change their root conceptions of mind under pressure of this radical freedom.[2] Sartre's development, of course, goes philosophically much further than Conrad's, but they agree that the temptation to play God is fundamental to man and suggests how consciousness ought to be seen. The following comment by Sartre will suggest, I

think, why this temptation, though Conrad was unwilling to face
many of its implications, is central to any examination of the sort I
am making. By "in-itself" in the passage quoted below Sartre
means, as his translator, Hazel Barnes, says: "Non-conscious being.
It is the being of the phenomenon and overflows the knowledge
which we have of it. It is a plentitude, and strictly speaking we can
say of it only that it is." Being-for-itself is, on the contrary, "the
nihilation of Being-in-itself; consciousness conceived of as a lack of
Being, a desire for Being, a relation to Being. By bringing Nothingness into the world the For-itself can stand out from Being and
judge other beings by knowing what it is not." [3] Sartre conceives
of consciousness as that which secretes nothingness into the plentitude of Being, thus creating differentiation or, as he coins the
word, "nihilating" in-itself by secreting a shell of non-being about
it. Obviously Sartre is having a hard time talking about these fundamental matters; but it is too easy to smile at either Sartre or Conrad
when they have, often for good reason, nearly exhausted the re-
sources of language. There is nothing funny about the ideas involved, and though I should be hard pressed to argue the point, it
appears that at rare moments Conrad is incredibly close to seeing
consciousness as this fountain or gland of nothingness. It need hardly be pointed out how far this image is from any other of his conceptions. (In *Nausea* Sartre tries a great many metaphors to express
his conception of the mind, and, surprisingly enough, is most successful with the sound of a jazz phonograph record.) In any event,
Sartre, like Conrad in *Heart of Darkness*, defines man by his desire
to be God, but God defined in a special way. He has said that for-
itself desires the condition of in-itself, but

It is *as consciousness* that it wishes to have the impermeability and
infinite density of the in-itself. It is as the nihilation of the in-itself
and a perpetual evasion of contingency . . . that it wishes to be its
own foundation. . . . The fundamental value which presides over
the project is exactly the in-itself-for-itself; that is, the ideal of consciousness which would be the foundation of its own being-in-itself
by the pure consciousness which it would have of itself. It is this

ideal which can be called God. Thus the best way to conceive of the fundamental project of human reality is to say that man is the being whose project is to be God.[4]

In less technical language: the consciousness wants to exist like in-itself, but to be aware that it so exists and that it has enabled itself to so exist. This condition is what used to be called saving your cake and eating it too; it represents the impossible best of two contradictory worlds or modes. Yet is this not Lord Jim? And are not both *Lord Jim* and *Heart of Darkness* stories about "the man who would be king" in Sartre's sense of *God?*

Clearly the sense in which self-image is important in *Lord Jim* has been affected by the existential insights of *Heart of Darkness*. Thematically Lord Jim and Kurtz have a great deal in common, though it is interesting that the two are not usually compared in depth by critics of Conrad. Aside from the obvious fact that both men set up among natives as a Lord (Lord Jim nearly if not quite divine), Jim seeks his divinity in a manner easily comprehended in Sartre's terms. He wants the irrevocability and infinite density of the natural world, of a natural object, and in fact a good deal of the novel's symbolism suggests just this passion. He will not understand that his self is a free choice which must be continually chosen and projected onto a nature which is indifferent to that "project," as Sartre would call it. As I have said before, Jim always believes that he has been ordained to be a particular kind of hero, much in the way that Stephen Crane's Henry Fleming believes men are born either cowards or heroes and that nature has a distinct attitude toward his every action. One of the keys to understanding Lord Jim is the sense in which he desires to be in-itself, but, as Sartre argues, in the mode of consciousness, to be conscious that he can be nothing but a particular kind of hero. We surely do not need the existential model of the mind to see that the very fact of being conscious of one's irrevocability strongly suggests the contingency one is trying so hard to avoid. In fact, what I have just said sounds like a reasonable summary of *King Lear*. If the moon Jim is so fond of were conscious of its moon-ness, it would not be the moon. In the peculiar sense that Sartre establishes, then, Lord Jim wishes to have the "impermeability and infinite density of the in-itself," but *as consciousness*; Jim's ideal is "the ideal of a consciousness which would be the foundation of its own being-in-itself *by the pure consciousness which it would have* of itself." Such a Sartrean analysis explains, it seems to me, one of the most paradoxical aspects of *Lord Jim.* Jim unquestionably believes he was born a hero and seems able to rationalize any of his behavior that does not fit this self-image; yet it has never seemed quite true to say that he undertakes Patusan merely to prove to others that he *is* his kind of hero. Some would say that he needs to prove it to himself, but that does not seem at all an accurate description of a man whose every moment of thought depends upon assuming essence before existence. But if we think in Sartre's terms, it is clear that Jim undertakes Patusan in order more nearly to become God — not in the mundane sense of being worshiped by the natives but as a man who seeks to enhance his consciousness of his own being-in-itself, who is, in fact, seeking through that consciousness to found his own existence as some sort of natural force. It is only at the end of the novel, when Jim guarantees Brown's exit with his own life and then gives that life to Doramin, that Jim, suffering the inherent contradiction in his project to be at once cause and caused, takes the most direct and uncomplicated path to becoming unconscious matter. This is a "man who would be king" worthy to set beside Kurtz.

In the special sense that Lord Jim pursues his godhead, his story becomes more nearly a definitive myth for the late nineteenth century than Kurtz's. In neither *Heart of Darkness* nor the Kipling story is the definition of God so thoroughly saturated with implications springing from fresh conceptions of human consciousness. *Heart of Darkness*, however, reinforces our understanding of Lord Jim in the terms suggested by Sartre, and in its use of the "man who would be king" motif leads the reflective reader to the subtler definition of God in *Lord Jim.* We may be sure that for Conrad both *Heart of Darkness* and *Lord Jim* were part of the same upheaval in his root conceptions of mind.

There is one more thing necessary before we leave *Heart of Darkness*. In order to do justice to the true texture of that story and of *Lord Jim*, I have had to find an analogous model of the mind in Sartre. Unfortunately, doing so leaves the impression that Conrad must be understood primarily as a man ahead of his time. Since I want to use Sartre again near the end of my comments on *Nostromo*, it becomes important once again to indicate how thoroughly Conrad was immersed in a Western tradition, and that if analogous psychologies are sought they may be found nearly as well in the past as in the present. Instead of Sartre, for example, I might almost as well have used Shakespeare, particularly *King Lear* and *Hamlet*, plays Conrad apparently knew well from the complete Shakespeare that accompanied him on his voyages. To speak of Conrad as an incredible anticipation of our most modern philosophy is to misplace emphasis. I have used Sartre because he provides so brilliant an emphasis — in just the right spirit — on the crucial motif of the man-god. Very briefly, however, it can be shown that precisely this "existential" motif, if it does not go at least as far back as Job and *King Lear*, was conspicuous in the Victorian context. If Sartre is a great help, he does not hold the patent on "nothingness."

We need go no further than Kipling to define, perhaps even better than we already have, the nothingness that permeates *Heart of Darkness*. If Conrad ultimately moves in some sense ahead of his contemporaries, he does so with his feet planted solidly on the past and in his own times. To talk about him as a *fin-de-siècle* novelist generates the need to think back to St. Paul; to place him beside Sartre requires us to think once again of his own late-Victorian times.

In the last decades of the nineteenth century there was a widespread taste for stories about colonial whites asked or tempted to play God for native populations or whose morality was radically altered by contact with natives. It is odd that *Heart of Darkness* is so often isolated from these related stories, though the reason is clear enough: it is so much better than all but Kipling's "The Man Who Would Be King." [5] Aside from Kipling, Louis Becke, Robert

Louis Stevenson, and Rider Haggard had all made their contribution, though never with precisely the same motif. Stevenson's "The Beach of Falesá," for example, belongs in the category though it focuses rather narrowly at times on Stevenson's scientific interest in native taboo.[6] Similarly, Haggard's *She* and the sequel, *Wisdom's Daughter*, though it is not published until the twenties, raise many of the same issues and ironies. The conscience of a colonial power, anxious about the morality of its behavior in "uncivilized" parts of the world, was sometimes at the root of such narratives. Even Stevenson, however, with what he thought were realistic South Seas stories, pursued the moral question into metaphysical regions. The old gothic modes were often revived, with their popular appeal, and the degenerating white man become a cliché that was never abandoned by Hollywood. The revival of the gothic had also, however, enhanced the metaphysical flavor of even some of the worst of these stories; for reasons that we need not go into here, the gothic had often had similar effects.

Whatever else it may have been, the genre was also a response to the spiritual crisis that had made Schopenhauer's search for a morality apart from any supernaturalism predictable and thoroughly Victorian. The question was not new: how to found sanctions in the absence of supernatural (read "divine") authority. It was the Matthew Arnold problem. Anyone reading *Heart of Darkness* in 1899 may well have placed it at least tentatively in that genre, and this fact becomes an important context for Kurtz's qualities and for Marlow's response. For Conrad, of course, the archetype of such tales lay in the career of Rajah Brooke in Sarawak. I vaguely remember reading the memoirs of a man who was both his relative and administrator and who worries about the Dyaks making sacrifice to Brooke, calling him god. Brooke's relative quickly recovers his tranquillity, however, by remembering that after all the Rajah was more than able to assume such responsibility: they were fortunate to have a godlike man to make god.

The absolutely fresh perception provided by Kurtz's final self-judgment can best be understood by — paradoxically — realizing that *Heart of Darkness*, despite its preeminence, need not be read in isolation from other literature of the type. There is in Kipling's story "The Man Who Would Be King" a similar insight into late-Victorian man's sense of estrangement from all hope of transcendent moral sanctions. Kipling too felt what Irving Howe has called Conrad's appreciation of *nada* (the reference is, of course, to Hemingway's use of that conception in "A Clean, Well-Lighted Place"). The date of the Kipling story coincides, conveniently enough, with Conrad's Bangkok crisis of 1888, when, as the narrator of *The Shadow Line* puts it, he had felt the "menace of emptiness."

There is ample evidence to suggest that Conrad had read the story. Lawrence Graver suggests stylistic similarities between "The Man Who Would Be King" and "An Outpost of Progress," a colonial tale which clearly anticipates *Heart of Darkness*.[7] Conrad finished *Heart of Darkness* in February 1899. On Christmas Day, 1898, he wrote to his cousin in Poland, Mme. Angelé Zagórska, to say that "among the people in literature who deserve attention the first is Rudyard Kipling (his last book *The Day's Work*, novel)."[8] And in August 1897 to Cunninghame Graham:

> You understood perfectly what I tried to say about Mr. Kipling — but I did not succeed in saying exactly what I wanted to say. I wanted to say, in effect, that in the chaos of printed matter Kipling's *ébauches* [sketches or, better, short stories] appear by contrast finished and impeccable. I judge the man in his time, — and space. It is a small space and as to his time I leave it to your tender mercy. I wouldn't in his defense spoil the small amount of steel that goes to the making of a needle.[9]

Are the short stories "needles" which, though small, are nonetheless made of steel? Four days earlier, again to Cunninghame Graham:

> Mr. Kipling has the wisdom of the passing generations, — and holds it in perfect sincerity. Some of his work is of impeccable form and because of that *little* thing, he will sojourn in Hell only a very short while. He squints with the rest of his excellent sort. It is a beautiful squint: it is an useful squint. And — after all, — perhaps he sees round the corner? And suppose Truth is just round the corner, like the elusive and useless loafer it is?[10]

Conrad's attitude toward Kipling, at least at this time of his life, is quite nicely balanced and very respectful.

Kipling does indeed "see round the corner" in "The Man Who Would Be King." His heroes, Daniel Dravot and Peachey Carnehan, have moved from the ragged bottom of the colonial heap to the role of gods in a remote Afghan tribe by deciding to emulate Rajah Brooke's career in Sarawak: "We have decided that there is only one place now in the world that two strong men can Sar-a-*whack*. . . . They have two-and-thirty heathen idols there, and we'll be the thirty-third and fourth." "Rajah Brooke will be a suckling to us" (pp. 53, 81). They succeed in imposing their ludicrous though by no means immoral imitation of Brookean law and order on the tribes and finally imagine that like Brooke's Sarawak their kingdom may also be delivered to England's influence. But Dravot feels, despite his godhead, that he needs a wife for the long winter.

The girl chosen by the tribe fears that marriage to a god means death; when presented to Dravot, she bites his neck in fear, drawing blood and demonstrating Dravot's mortality to dissident priests who shout " 'Neither God nor Devil, but a man!' " (p. 89). Dravot is murdered, cut loose on one of the rope suspension bridges with which he had improved the mountainous country, and Peachey is "crucified":

He hung there [between two pine trees] and screamed, and they took him down next day, and said it was a miracle that he wasn't dead.
    . . . They was cruel enough to feed him up in the temple, because they said he was more of a God than old Daniel [Dravot] that was a man. [Peachey is talking about himself in the third person; p. 95.]

At the end of the story a mad Peachey, returned to civilization, is found bareheaded in the midday sun, singing

> The Son of Man goes forth to war,
>     A golden crown to gain;
> His blood-red banner streams afar —
>     Who follows in his train? (P. 97)

Throughout the story both men have occasionally spoken to the
natives in biblical language, as God to Adam and Eve ("Go and dig
the land, and be fruitful and multiply" [p. 70]) or as Christ ("Occupy till I come" [p. 72]). Certainly the most obvious point is —
as Brooks and Warren in their analysis of the story suggest — that
if one wants to play god he'd better *be* god. Having spoken like
Christ in a situation which can only make his words a parody,
Peachey must suffer crucifixion; having claimed the prerogatives
of Christlike divinity (even, in a grotesque sense, by playing a false
Christ to Dravot's false God), he must spin out the role to its end
and take all the consequences of his assumed godhead. Though
Brooks and Warren feel that ironically Dravot's not inconsiderable
solicitude for his people, his manly death, and Peachey's love for
Dravot finally achieve something of divinity, this is clearly not
Kipling's most compelling implication. Man, Kipling feels, cannot
accept only part of godhead; he cannot assume Christ's authority
without being prepared for the crucifixion as well. The Son of
Man goes forth a golden crown to gain — who follows? The simple
evangelical thrust of the hymn — which is its immediate significance
— is redirected into the most metaphysical questions when applied
to the events of the story: who dares to seek rather than only follow the golden crown which is Christ's alone to wear, to seek divine prerogatives *and* divine burdens, to emulate Christ's self-defining act of mediation between God's justice and man's sin? Which
man thinks his humanity will bear the weight of godhead as Christ's
divinity bore the weight of flesh? Dravot is unmasked as a god
simply because he wants a woman, because he is human; but the
beauty of the story lies in its uncertain attitude toward the man-
god. The disturbing implication in some late-Victorian thought is
that man must act as a god, not only or even mainly in the colonial
sense, but in the metaphysical sense as well: he must will his own
sanctions, erect a morality not necessarily on some kind of human-
ism but always from his awareness that there are no divine sanctions. Only on its most accessible level does the story suggest "The
White Man's Burden," with its implication that the white man may

at best expect "the blame of those ye better," and, as the poem also
implies, their hate.

Faulted though Peachey and Dravot are in their sometimes comic
version of imperialism, both are murdered for their trouble. And
the crucifixion is due, in this story, not so much to the native's per-
verse refusal to accept what is good for him but to the very act of
the white man's assuming godlike prerogatives. There is something
unholy in the position late-Victorian man occasionally felt himself
required to assume. His sense of blasphemy was profound, though
he had begun to recognize that in an absurd universe, value, if it
was to emerge at all, must come from a sense of his own uniqueness.
One critic, whose appreciation of Kipling's very difficult story
"Mrs. Bathurst" is most convincing, says of the fortuitousness of
life which that story suggests:

> This theme runs through all of Kipling's work and accounts, in
> part, for his pragmatism and for his refusal, so annoying at times,
> to take the "long view." The world, Kipling would say, is, as far
> as any man can tell, a chaotic place, ruled by blind chance. Sooner
> or later everyone comes to trial and must struggle to extract some
> order from chaos, to impose on the universe some law, useful at
> least to himself. At the crucial moment, Hooper [a character in
> "Mrs. Bathurst"] says, a man "goes crazy — or just saves himself";
> that is, either he echoes the disorder of the universe with the dis-
> order of his own mind, or else, through his own efforts, he some-
> how manages to organize at least one corner of the chaos so that
> he can go on living.[11]

It must have been as difficult for Kipling as it is for us to know
just where self-reliance ends and a sense of blasphemous godhead
begins, but there is certainly some such balance of blasphemousness
and nobility suggested in Peachey by his crucifixion. As with some
of his contemporaries, the thought of creating for one's self what
had earlier been at least initiated by divine authority awakened
childlike but by no means childish fears in Kipling.

Both Conrad and Kipling understand in their respective stories —
Conrad perhaps for the first time clearly — the burden that makes
both Peachey and Kurtz godlike, yet kills them for acting like
gods. Of course Kurtz has been evil by any ordinary standards,

and the two ex-troopers vaguely benevolent; but both stories faith-
fully imagine the paradox: late-Victorian man's distinction is both
to be god and, in a sense, to die for it. He is the reverse of Christ,
taking godhead upon his flesh. Kurtz's self-judgment is if anything
more godlike in its total acceptance of responsibility for asserting
value than any of his earlier corrupt dominion over the natives.
Both writers describe the tragic late-Victorian role of the man-
god, the sense of absolute responsibility not unlike that which Kierkegaard had called "the fear and the trembling."

Thus, much of the emptiness in Kurtz after his experience with
the natives corresponds to his sense that there is nowhere he can
look outside himself or within himself for innate or ordained sanctions. What he needs he must make through a sheer act of will, and
finally does in his exclamation, "The horror! The horror!" It is a
judgment that comes from the core of his awareness that there is
nothing man is meant to be. His experience as a god has led him to
this realization; and it has not been a rare, exotic experience so
much as the fundamental condition of man. His is the nothingness
from which all sense of being comes, from which, as Sartre says in
*Being and Nothingness*, all differentiation arises. The most basic
task of consciousness is to know what it is not, and it is not, as
Roquentin in Sartre's *Nausea* learns, the plenum of unconscious
being, the in-itself which continually threatens to engulf consciousness and excites the peculiar nausea which gives Sartre's novel
its title.

What I am offering here is not, however, necessarily an existential
reading of *Heart of Darkness*. I am simply restoring to the tale its
sometimes forgotten emphasis on Kurtz's acting God among the
natives and the metaphysical questions that activity raises in him
and in Marlow. He expects to be naturally guided in his standards
among the natives but is overwhelmed to discover no such guid-
ance at all. This is the "hollowness" that Marlow apprehends: the
complete absence in Kurtz of any innate or transcendental sanctions, and the inability to fill that emptiness. But such emptiness can
also be fruitful and the beginning of new conceptions of value, new

bases of value. Kipling's symbolic use of the crucifixion suggests such ambivalence. Certainly in Conrad's universe the man who acts God may well be crucified by the attendant burdens (as Abraham nearly is in Kierkegaard's version of the Abraham and Isaac story). It is our tragedy to need to act the god (in establishing value and standing responsible for it) without *being* one, without enjoying his other attributes. Metaphysically speaking, the late-Victorian sensibility had to Sar-a-*whack* it not in Afghanistan but on other frontiers, in Kipling's, Conrad's, Arnold's, and even Pascal's cosmos. If we understand that for the word "accident" Conrad really means "absurdity," he had summed it all up: "Our captivity within the incomprehensible logic of accident is the only fact of the universe." This comment, it may be noted, was written in a reader's report on a novel by Louis Becke, one of the exotic romancers who did not understand, as Conrad and Kipling did, what the new metaphysical terms of the "romance" often were.[12]

If we strive to give Conrad his full resonance, and ignore the more obvious antecedents of Job and Lear in favor of something Conrad may have known even better, it is not difficult to take this motif beyond the late-Victorian context to some of the best of Pascal's *Pensées*. What I have perhaps misleadingly called "acting God," Pascal on the contrary would have called his "wager." Pascal and Conrad both emphasize the "disproportion" between man and God, or whatever God would be if he existed. In the beautiful Pensée 72 he emphasizes the middle condition of man in a manner that reminds one uncannily of Conrad's men who would be king, men who violate their middle station between infinity and "nothingness." The term "nothingness" undergoes a crescendo in Pensée 72, as Pascal sketches universes beyond us and within us:

For who will not be astounded at the fact that our body, which a little while ago was imperceptible in the universe, itself imperceptible in the bosom of the whole, is now a colossus, a world, or rather a whole, in respect of the nothingness which we cannot reach. He who regards himself in this light will be afraid of himself, and observing himself sustained in the body given him by nature between those two abysses of the Infinite and Nothing, will tremble at the sight of these marvels. . . .[13]

As for Conrad, Pascal's man is on a tightrope between the infinitely large and the infinitely small, kin to neither, estranged from nature and alone in it:

Man is but a reed, the most feeble thing in nature; but he is a thinking reed. The entire universe need not arm itself to crush him. A vapour, a drop of water suffices to kill him. But, if the universe were to crush him, man would still be more noble than that which killed him, because he knows that he dies and the advantage which the universe has over him; the universe knows nothing of this.

All our dignity consists, then, in thought. By it we must elevate ourselves, and not by space and time, which we cannot fill [or devour, *pace* Kurtz]. Let us endeavour, then, to think well; this is the principle of morality. (Pensée 347)

By "thinking," Pascal does not here mean exclusively reasoning, since in this passage as elsewhere he is extremely critical of the powers of reason (in a manner reminiscent of Conrad). The process he describes as "thinking" involves the emotional, intuitive grasp of man's ontology as much as it does the rational analysis of that incredibly tenuous middle position. And the dignity which comes of this painful consciousness I take to resemble Marlow's after watching the spectacle of Lord Jim and Kurtz. For Marlow comes to apprehend the precise transgression involved in trying, as Kurtz does initially and Jim does eternally, to be God in Pascal's sense, to fill space and time, to embrace the extremities with which (as Pensée 72 emphasizes) man really has so little to do. We must pursue the Conradian ideal which will confer all our dignity: we must, as Pascal says, "take our compass; we are something and we are not everything. The nature of our existence hides from us the knowledge of first beginnings which are born of the Nothing. . . . Our intellect holds the same position in the world of thought as our body occupies in the expanse of nature." We prepare ourselves — in Conrad often by exercises in witnessing the extremes — for a humility which, to my way of thinking, becomes paradoxically godlike, since it prepares us for a wager. But this is my perspective and not Pascal's.

We are "incapable of knowing either what He is or if He is. This

being so, who will dare to undertake the decision of the question?
Not we, who have no affinity to Him" (Pensée 233). What, then,
may we achieve? Pascal and Conrad are here very close. We learn
the conditions under which we must create value in this universe:
⌜"Nothing stays for us. This is our natural condition, and yet most
contrary to our inclination; we burn with desire to find solid
ground and an ultimate sure foundation whereon to build a tower
reaching to the Infinite. But our whole groundwork cracks, and
ₗthe earth opens to abysses" (Pensée 72).
⌞

Man, as Sartre would say, seeks uselessly to be God. His dignity,
as Pascal and Conrad would both say, lies in creating value in the
light of the adjective "uselessly." We prepare ourselves if not precisely for Pascal's wager about the existence of God, at least for an
analogous wager about the value of human existence. After all, we
have seen Kurtz until his last moment erect a tower of Babel
(wherein language itself becomes nearly useless) "reaching to the
Infinite." And we have most certainly seen the earth open beneath
him.

Pascal concludes Pensée 233 by offering us an intuition about the
existential assumption of responsibility. The "wise" man says he
blames those who make the wager, because we cannot know: "No,
but I blame them for having made, not this choice [say, to believe
in God] but a choice; for again both he who chooses heads and he
who chooses tails are equally at fault, they are both in the wrong.
The true course is not to wager at all." Pascal answers as would
Conrad, though the two men choose to affirm value differently:
"Yes; but you must wager. It is not optional. You are embarked.
Which will you choose then?"

In short, a full appreciation of the man who would be king takes
us not only into the Victorian "death of God," but behind it at
least as far back as Pascal, to an appreciation of man's unique middle
condition first sounded in the Book of Job. It is really only in the
light of this middle condition that, say, Kurtz's career into extremity assumes its full meaning. Kurtz is not a Job figure, but he is used
to sound many of the same resonances. I shall not attempt to do
any more with the Victorian context here, except to note that ev-

erything a critic such as J. Hillis Miller has done with the disappearance of God in Victorian times aids immeasurably in restoring to *Heart of Darkness* its Janus-faced identity.[14] Criticism of such a story must be similarly Janus-faced if we are to appreciate the continuing traditions of ontology and mind in which Conrad worked.

No one expects Conrad to write in *Nostromo* a fable for precisely this new sense of consciousness and mind. But that something along these lines happened there can be little doubt. To be hollow inside was not only Kurtz's predicament. That metaphor and all the images surrounding it in *Heart of Darkness* come very close to suggesting the kind of nothingness that Sartre and Pascal discuss. Such nothingness, then, far from suggesting only that Kurtz could discover no values within himself after the veneer of civilization had been stripped off, further implies that hollowness is really in the nature of consciousness itself. Compare these images of hollowness, and the peculiar sort of freedom they suggest, with any psychoanalytic, Freudian analysis of Conrad's work during this fruitful period and the stark contrast of metaphors for mind must be apparent. As Sartre systematically dismisses Freudian assumptions about bundles of instincts or layers of instincts and controls, so it might be useful for the critic to do so when approaching even a story such as *Heart of Darkness*, where they seem to work so well. Despite their possible applicability to the relation of author and art, they do not seem to be at all congruent with the model that Conrad himself is creating in the work. Sartre contends that in existential psychoanalysis we must discover (by a method not unlike that of Freudian psychoanalysis) the original "project" of the individual, a free choice in his manner of being that, while it is not unconscious (Sartre admits of no unconscious), is prelogical and will not easily be understood by the individual. I cannot here rehearse the arguments by which he attacks the whole idea of an unconscious mind and replaces it by noting the difference between being conscious of something and understanding it, except perhaps to note that I am unconvinced and greatly impressed. Nor is it really possible, without hearing much more from Sartre about the nature of these

"original projects" of being, to understand when we have reached
the irreducible free choice of someone whose life we are studying.
Sartre's extraordinary discussion of the metaphysical implications
in the feeling "slimey" suggests the entirely prelogical and symbolic nature of this choice.[15] All I want to take from the rather mysterious end of his discussion, however, is the sense in which Conrad
too related his characters to some fundamental choice involving
self-image as the irreducible way of being. As with Sartre, this
choice is not unconscious so much as simply prelogical and not understood by the character until events force him to backtrack and
acknowledge its primacy, a primacy even over those erotic feelings
a Freudian might have taken as basic and irreducible. And what is
so striking in Conrad is his sense of this primal choice as free, though
of course not many of his characters are allowed to see so far into
this radical freedom and responsibility as Kurtz. Finally, with a
haunting persistency, many of Conrad's characters who do not
outwardly resemble Lord Jim nonetheless remind us that they may
be compared with his project, fundamental for Conrad as for Sartre:

Every human reality is a passion in that it projects losing itself so as
to found being and by the same stroke to constitute the In-itself
which escapes contingency by being its own foundation, the *Ens
causa sui*, which religions call God. Thus the passion of man is the
reverse of that of Christ, for man loses himself as man in order that
God may be born. But the idea of God is contradictory and we
lose ourselves in vain. Man is a useless passion.[16]

In Charles Gould and Nostromo, Conrad has come closer to
showing the birth of the fundamental "project" than he has in
either Jim or Kurtz. We can watch both men forming their most
basic modes of being in relation to in-itself, to the silver of the San
Tomé mine. In a grotesque sense much human life in *Nostromo*
courts the mode of existence of in-itself, of silver and of the earth
itself. Whether or not that observation is entirely true, however,
it is clear that this novel is written with an acute awareness of the
way consciousness defines itself by fundamental projects into
nonconsciousness, by continually evoking the irreducible sense of

difference between material and the peculiar "nothingness" of consciousness, and, often, by attempting to lose itself in order that God
may be born. It is possible to see in Gould at least as good an example of this process as Lord Jim. His quest for "stability" grows
increasingly ominous. What, after all — and in a metaphysical
rather than political sense — is the final "material interest"? What
can it be like to live in the interest of "material"? It may be useful
to see *Nostromo* as a deeply metaphysical novel rather than as primarily a political one.

# 6

# The Psychology
of Self-Image:
*Nostromo*

*Nostromo* is a study of identity and self-image
as a source of value, and as such the novel has deliberately been
made pseudopolitical. Political maneuvers and ideals, so apparently
the source of value for many men, are here seen as masks consciously and unconsciously used to disguise and reveal simultaneously the true source of value; and this is true for everyone in the
novel (with the possible exception of Don José Avellanos), from
Pedrito Montero with his poetic vision of Second Empire decadence to Charles Gould and his rule of law.

While it seems harmless to regard *Nostromo* as a political novel,
doing so may obscure the manner in which various conceptions of
self are brought into elegant parallels and contrasts. A political
awareness ought not confuse us about Conrad's use of the political
drama in Costaguana as a kind of wood stain necessary to bring out
the grain of intricately compared self-conceptions. Political belief
and action may be an aspect of the "formal cause" of *Nostromo*,
but it is wrong to consider it part of what Aristotle would have
called the final cause of that novel. Politics, like love, has always
been one of the witches' brews in which the self feels it can grow
to recognizable form. Especially the young mind has often sought

to define itself by some confusion of love and politics, as did Conrad himself with "Rita" in Marseilles. What I shall try to make clear in the course of this argument is that politics in *Nostromo* is distinctly an aesthetic means to an end, and that despite its surface the novel has little to contribute to Conrad's nearly compulsive interest in human solidarity except in a negative way. For at least this novel I am inclined to take the side of Irving Howe against that of Mrs. Hay.[1]

Charles Gould is essentially apolitical. We are told he broods about the silver mine as though it were a powerful personality that had killed his father only because it had not been properly disciplined. So long as Don Carlos must pay blackmail to chaotic local authority, the mine is likely to find an unexpected and destructive way of expressing its power. To discipline the mine is, for Charles, a means of relating himself to the father he had known mostly through long letters describing his defeat by the mine and by a government which had punished him with it. Don Carlos can transcend the pathos of his father's death and perhaps achieve a victory that has been honored throughout centuries as a way of achieving identity: one continues the role of the father but kills the dragon he could not master, not through indignation or for revenge but as a self-defining gesture. I do not mean to sound either psychoanalytical or to pursue archetypes, but the early pages of *Nostromo* insist on this relationship between father, son, and mine.

Thus Charles initially does not want the silver or a stable government in themselves, for any intrinsic reasons. Without political stability he cannot succeed where his father has failed; and without the stream of silver there is of course no power and no overt measure of success. Conrad suggests that the mine becomes a demanding mistress: Emilia Gould will bear no children, and Charles is insistently described as riding off to spend the night at the mine. For reshaping his father's dilemma, Charles has what Conrad regards as the Northern, even English talent for idealizing "material interest," for making material success mean more than measurable quantities of silver and power and for justifying the pursuit of that success by some "idea." The American capitalist Holroyd will, he says, abandon Gould should the mine get into fairly deep trouble and cease to be a good investment; he will see Gould through the kind of difficulties that can reasonably be expected to have a silver lining, but his immediate motives are severely practical. He has, however, that same Northern talent for idealizing material interests and so actually believes that his ultimate purpose is to introduce a form of Protestantism into Catholic Costaguana and to extend the moral rights of North American empire. One of the comic ironies of the novel springs from the fact that the old priest Father Roman, having been shown how to blow up the mine should anything happen to Gould and Don Pépé, thereby helps save Costaguana for the militant Protestantism of Holroyd (pp. 566–67).

Conrad is far from despising the idealized materialism of Gould. At first, Emilia is able to take her sense of purpose almost entirely from her husband's: "And at once her delight in him, lingering with half-open wings like those birds that cannot rise easily from a flat level, found a pinnacle from which to soar up into the skies" (p. 65). The project of the mine becomes indistinguishable from their new love: "It was as if they had been morally bound to make good their vigorous view of life against the unnatural error of weariness and despair [meaning, of course, Charles's father]" (p. 82). The skeptic, Decoud, likes to imagine that he is precisely opposite to Charles Gould, but even Decoud acknowledges that Gould's "sentimentalism" ("The sentimentalism of the people that will never do anything for the sake of their passionate desire, unless it comes to them clothed in the fair robes of an idea") constitutes illusions which "somehow or other help them to get a firm hold of substance" (p. 265). Ironically, the men most successful with the material things of this world (Holroyd and Gould) are never called "materialistic" by Conrad: that adjective is reserved for Nostromo, whose identity is contrasted with Gould's: "It was not the cold, ferocious, and idealistic self-conceit of a man of some northern race; it was materialistic and imaginative. It was an unpractical and warm sentiment, a picturesque development of his character, the growth of an unsophisticated sense of his individuality" (p. 461).

This is not to say that Nostromo depends upon material wealth; on the contrary he gives or gambles away most of his money and silver buttons until, imagining himself exploited, he turns with a vengeance to the treasure of silver bars. The point is that the idealistic Gould disdains the merely material as even the reputation-mad Nostromo never would, yet perhaps because of this disdain is able literally to move mountains while Nostromo gets himself killed trying to move a relatively few silver bars. As *Lord Jim* suggests, Conrad is amazed at the power of the idea over the material world and perhaps over the organic pulse of the material that might be called nature.

Gould changes the face of nature, transforms the paradise of snakes so often alluded to in the novel (and the subject of a sketch by Emilia Gould) into the scarred gorge of the San Tomé mine. Perhaps it is not stretching an idea too far to remember that the color of the mine, the color of hope, is also the green of nature and especially of the paradisical gorge before it is transformed by Charles's instruments of hope. The phrase "paradise of snakes" of course invites symbolic readings. Although it is suggestive of the Fall, it seems to me we are invited primarily to speculate about the inevitability of what Charles has done to that state of nature in the gorge and to that paradise of snakes Sulaco had been before the great victory: nature innocent of power and sophistication beyond the direct danger of passionate self-interest. When Emilia Gould looks at the sketch of the virgin gorge late in the novel, she may simply wish it had never been disturbed. Yet as I read *Nostromo* it is easy to believe not in the Fortunate Fall, but in a necessary one. The great victory will lead, as Dr. Monygham suggests, to new conflicts inherent in the "democratic" spirit so welcome to Nostromo and his Italian compatriots, and in the intensified, idealized materialism of the foreign interests. What Gould has done to Sulaco, however, is no more nor less evolutionary than what Europe has done to Kurtz; yet just as Kurtz can become more vicious than his savages, so presumably can future conflicts in Sulaco surpass the anarchy which opens the novel and even the battles which establish the independent state. Charles insists, however, there is no turning back:

> And Mrs. Gould gazing at the last [her watercolor sketch of the San Tomé gorge] in its black wooden frame, sighed out:
> "Ah, if we had left it alone, Charles!"
> "No," Charles Gould said, moodily; "it was impossible to leave it alone."
> "Perhaps it was impossible," Mrs. Gould admitted slowly. Her lips quivered a little, but she smiled with an air of dainty bravado. "We have disturbed a good many snakes in that paradise, Charley, haven't we?"
> "Yes; I remember," said Charles Gould, "It was Don Pépé who called the gorge the paradise of snakes. No doubt we have disturbed a great many. But remember, my dear, that it is not now as it was when you made that sketch." He waved his hand toward the small water-color hanging alone upon the great bare wall. "It is no longer a paradise of snakes. We have brought mankind into it, and we cannot turn our backs upon them to go and begin a new life elsewhere." (Pp. 231–32)

This conversation occurs late at night, just before Decoud is to give Mrs. Gould the rumor that a battle has been fought near Sta. Marta and the Riberists defeated. As she leaves her husband and walks down the hall toward Decoud and the news that will finally commit Charles and all his energies to the independence of Sulaco, she is described in a brilliantly visualized paragraph as though moving through "patches of sun that checker the gloom of open glades in the woods"; she would like to be a creature of that paradise, wandering still in the innocence she and Charles once shared. Yet paradise was full of snakes to begin with, and man was born to fall: this is perhaps Conrad's emendation of the Christian story.

Charles's and presumably Conrad's main point lies, however, in the paradox of the phrase itself, "paradise of snakes." There is no paradise once the consciousness of man is introduced. The gorge may well have been a paradise *for* snakes, but with the introduction of man it becomes a Garden of Eden with not one serpent but many working for the fall of man. The idea of there being many snakes underlines Conrad's new metaphor for the creation of self and the description of consciousness. Each man will discover his own serpent, will see his fall in a different light and with different metaphors for its understanding. The idea of "passion" scarcely applies at all to Charles's and Nostromo's falls; neither of these losses of innocence has any meaning at all outside the unique self-image or project each man has chosen for himself. The only common denominator lies in something like Sartre's description of the way all men lave their freedom about the unconscious world — about, in the case of both these men, the silver. Sartre argues that "doing" is really a form of having or appropriation, and that the self in having things really tries to make them part of itself according to the archetypal pattern of self trying to found itself, trying to become God. Something of the sort is clear in Gould's later behavior and self-conception. Of Nostromo we learn that he wants to "clasp [the silver], embrace, absorb, subjugate in unquestioned possession . . ." (p. 590). Something like Sartre's model will provide a convenient generalization about many of the self-images in *Nostromo*, largely because Conrad perceived some of the same qualities in human consciousness. The keynote of this novel, however, is nonetheless a kind of relativity. In *An Outcast*, "Karain," "The Lagoon," and so forth, there was one serpent. Now there are many; indeed, one man's fall is another's salvation.

Although Conrad had always spoken of the problems involved in creating self, nowhere before *Nostromo*, not even in *Lord Jim*, does he employ so direct a vocabulary for the discussion. The novel is full of phrases such as "self-discovery," "sense of individuality," "conscious and subconscious intentions," "betrayed individuality," "thinking, acting individuality," "lost personality," "doubt of his own individuality" and so on and on. Of course Marlow could not have used the vocabulary appropriate to an omniscient author. Nevertheless, the existence of such a vocabulary suggests Conrad's preoccupation with pursuing value behind politics and beyond even the subtlest conception of man as a political animal. Mrs. Hay's excellent chapter on *Nostromo* rests finally on the claim that Conrad wants to denounce a political theory which is

devoid of genuine moral principle but insists that whatever is good
for material interests is good for the nation. No doubt Conrad
hated the implication that a capitalistic wave of the future had
made it unnecessary for a nation and its citizens painfully to discover moral relationships between the individual and society. Material interests, as we can all agree, bring with them peculiarly cold
forms of inhumanity, in which the individual can no longer locate
his authentic self among the proffered economic identities. What
begins with the desirable outfitting of Gould's miners in protec-
tively green and hopeful uniforms ends in the leviathan imperson-
ality of economic process. One has the feeling that Gould's growing silence and stolidity are the inevitable result of his dedication
to the mine, and that his single principle is an unconscious attempt
to put man in some kind of grotesque sympathy with the earth itself.

Despite Conrad's distaste for the arrogance of this "progressive"
capitalism — suggested to him most directly by the rationalizations
of American imperialism in Cuba and the Philippines — he subordi-
nates the political issue to a more resonant and ultimately more important objection to Gould. These material interests — especially
the mine — have a metaphysical as well as political importance.
(We cannot pursue here their origins in religious doctrine, in issues
discussed by Tawney and Max Weber as inherent in the rise of
capitalism.) Such interests represent, in effect, the seduction of human nature by the nonhuman in-itself (to use Sartre's word); and
this seduction usually involves treating the "material" as though it
lived a superior, clean life of its own, above — in the case of the
mine, literally above — the tangle of human moral error. Thus
Gould gives a personality to the mine and thinks of his father as a
man who did not "understand" it.

We cannot then say that the silver, symbolizing these material
interests and their progressive capitalism, kills Nostromo; and, in
fact, the entire sense of the contrast Conrad meant to suggest between Charles Gould and Nostromo must be reexamined as a problem in forms of identity. Gould has lost himself by idealizing an
economic function, as many men are able to in an age when eco-

nomic romance perhaps appears superior to that between a man and a woman or a man and his country. It is to Conrad's credit as a sympathetic artist that he can summon at least a cool understanding of the mine's appeal. But what Conrad sees in Gould's attitude toward the silver is not what he sees in Nostromo's after his return from the Isabels. As for the doubloon in *Moby Dick*, we must here describe a paradigm of meaning for the silver ("I look, you look, they look") rather than argue that simple Nostromo joins Monygham, Mrs. Gould, and Conrad in appreciating the destructiveness of material interests. There can be no doubt that the silver is meant as a symbolic axis; but we need not assume that its meaning will be largely or ultimately political to a sensitive reader watching the characters revolve about its influence.

To Nostromo the shipment of silver at first seems to offer a capstone for his vanity. Rescuing the ingots will secure a reputation already approaching legend. This expectation is of course undercut ironically by the "builder of railways" who suggests that since no one could have run off with such a load of silver, "Gould, Decoud, and myself judged that it didn't matter in the least who went." "He took a slightly different view," says Monygham in partial sympathy with Nostromo's own grand estimate of the affair (p. 356). It does not at the outset matter to Nostromo where the silver comes from or what it symbolizes to his employers, so long as they obviously value it.

The silver and the idea of the mine induce in Gould a loss of moral sensitivity; in Nostromo, on the contrary, the treasure causes the very birth of moral awareness in a man who has always found his identity in vain reputation. Gould depends on the absolute will of the inanimate, on the irrational demands of the earth; Nostromo listens only to the voice of others, of his people and of the ruling Europeans. I suggest that Conrad meant to show two opposite directions both leading to a form of inhumanity, two apparently opposite means of achieving a sense of self which end nearly in the destruction of individual identity.

When Nostromo swims ashore and falls asleep in the fort, he has completed the first step in his loss of identity. In a famous passage he arises from his "lair in the long grass," as "natural and free from evil in the moment of waking as a magnificent and unconscious wild beast"; but then "in the suddenly steadied glance fixed upon nothing from under a forced frown, appeared the man" (p. 458). In his passion to enhance a reputation, Nostromo, "our man," has gotten into a situation where he cannot even show himself in Sulaco. Secrecy is imperative, and secrecy is one of the demands that will erode Nostromo's sense of identity. This man who has fed upon the regard of even the lowest Indian must go sneaking about the waterfront avoiding the contacts so necessary to his psychic well-being. Before meeting Dr. Monygham he believes that the arrival of Sotillo had decided the fate of Sulaco, and that no one except Decoud "cared whether he fell into the hands of the Monterists or not. . . . And that merely would be an anxiety for his [Decoud's] own sake" (p. 463). Nostromo's position would not be so difficult for a man taking his identity from something other than vain reputation; but Nostromo, suddenly deprived of adulation, childishly feels victimized, betrayed into a scheme which seems after all to have been an insignificant part of the complex crisis. He refuses to leave Sulaco without something to show for his career there, something material which cannot, as his popular role does, suddenly disappear like mist over the harbor. Conrad tells us at this moment that Nostromo has "no intellectual existence or moral strain to carry on his individuality, unscathed, over the abyss left by the collapse of his vanity" (p. 466). Except for his anger at the fine gentlemen who have exploited him (a sentiment he borrows to fit the occasion from old Viola), Nostromo shares none of Conrad's disgust at the subtle corruption spread by material interests. Nor is the reader encouraged to see Nostromo's plight as the result of material interests working their merciless logic upon human frailty.

If we are to suggest that Nostromo's destruction is, along with everything else in the novel, in the service of Conrad's attack on the mystique of progressive capitalism, then surely his possession of the silver must be our principal evidence. His first reaction to the debacle is that he has simply been "betrayed" out of his old

identity, and must now, in all his unintelligent simplicity, create a
new basis for an identity: "The word [*betrayed*] had fixed itself
tenaciously in his unintelligence. His imagination had seized upon
the clear and simple notion of betrayal to account for the dazed
feeling of enlightenment as to being done for, of having inadvertently gone out of his existence on an issue in which his personality
had not been taken into account" (pp. 469–70). Later he is extraor-
dinarily ready to feel guilty for Decoud's death. But we may be
sure that had he been able to retain faith in his old identity neither
event would have affected him morally. The loss of that self has
created a moral sensibility or allowed a weak, innate one to grow
sizably. His mind — "the popular mind is incapable of scepticism"
(p. 470) — must believe in something; and, after all, he is surrounded with the insistent argument that the universe is run according to "power, punishment, pardon," quite apart from whether
or not one accepted the priests' claims of earthly power. Thus the
silver which has clouded and finally obliterated a true moral sense
in Charles Gould has ironically developed one in Nostromo. The
silver may kill "our man" who has become his own man, but it cannot easily be said to have corrupted him. He is no longer reliable
and — according to Captain Mitchell's sort of definition — incor-
ruptible; but he is morally awake as he never has been before. Who
other than Nostromo himself is to say this is a loss? If we are to
condemn material interests for contributing to such changes in
Nostromo, we shall lose our case. What kills Nostromo is not the
taint of silver, symbolizing progressive capitalism; the silver might
have had the same effect on him had it been melted down from the
trinkets of the ladies of Sulaco by Don José Avellanos personally.
Nor is he destroyed through moralizing the amoral, a sin which
would indeed connect his death with the corruption of Charles
Gould and of progressive capitalism in general. He feels, rather,
that there must be compensation for the betrayal which has forced
him "out of his existence." The escape with the silver has irrevoca-
bly shown him how easily his identity could be dissolved, a basic
truth which the fame of his subsequent ride to Cayta cannot erase.
He demonically wants from the silver a rudimentary sense of re-

compense; had he lost his identity in another way, his method of
seeking restitution might easily have been different.

What connects the story of Nostromo with that of Charles
Gould is thus not the objection to progressive capitalism but the
drama of identity — cohering, dissolving, finding new form, always producing a sense of value or its equally powerful absence,
destroying and creating. As a rule the attempts of various characters to take identity from abstractions, especially from one kind or
another of political idealism, fail. Neither Viola nor Don José
Avellanos fails in the attempt (though Avellanos is sorely tested
when the sheets of his history of Costaguana are used for gun wad-
ding), and Captain Mitchell seems able to identify himself with
"historic events." But on the whole one wonders whether dedication to even the most enlightened political morality and idealism
would not dehumanize its champion; if we are to take Dr. Monygham as in significant part the voice of Conrad, then, as he says,
there is "something inherent in the necessities of successful action
which carried with it the moral degradation of the idea" (p. 582).
Though Conrad is amazingly farsighted, even prophetic in his criticism of the pseudo ethic of material interests, he is even wiser in
the above observation. A man must take his identity not only from
ideas but from the painful commitment to other human individuals
so conspicuously absent from Nostromo's final state of mind and
— as he becomes absorbed in the mine — from Charles Gould's.
Concerned always with his reputation, with the verdict of the
many, Nostromo is remarkably distant from even those closest to
him, from old Viola and, as Conrad makes brilliantly clear in her
death scenes, from Teresa. In one of the many structural ironies
which create the unity of this sprawling novel, Nostromo is deeply
moved by another human soul — for all its weakness and naivety —
only just before he dies. Concerned that recompense be made for
his lost identity, "the only thing lost in that desperate affair" (p.
485), he is shot by Viola before Giselle can affect him permanently. As Gould grows further from all intimate human contact, so
Nostromo dies essentially alone, both men destroyed by modes of
identity that make no room for the dependence on another single

human being which sustains Monygham, Teresa, and Mrs. Gould, to name only conspicuous examples. Faith in another fallible human may ultimately be no more secure a source of identity than a faith in ideas that will be corrupted by their very enactment or in a reputation established by the impersonal crowd; but at least such intimate dependence defines one's humanity as Gould's and Nostromo's never can be.

There is in this novel an intricate playing on the name Nostromo, and it is probably for this reason rather than for any centrality in the plot that "our man" gives his name to the whole performance. As long as he depends on being their man (his European employers' and the crowd's) he cannot really be his own. After sinking the lighter and abandoning Decoud on the Isabels, Nostromo says that the "captain" is no more. All along, Teresa has objected to the name given him by the fine gentleman, *Nostromo*, as no *name* at all — that is, no indication of independent individuality. But when he realizes that his own name — Giovanni Battista Fidanza — must supplant the other names and titles, Nostromo reserves none of his energy for the love which might genuinely confirm a new identity. His visits to Viola and the girls become — until the moment he is captivated by Giselle — only an excuse to accumulate a silver recompense for the loss of his most ominous and perhaps most accurate name, Nostromo.

Nonetheless the man who cannot even entertain seriously the abstract ideal, political or otherwise, is destroyed as surely as Nostromo and Gould. So much has been written about Decoud's skepticism that it is unnecessary to rehearse its failure in detail. Obviously, however, Conrad meant us to compare it not only with Nostromo and Gould but with Emilia Gould, whose life also pivots on love for another human being. What, then, are the differences between these two, or between Monygham and Decoud? Monygham, tortured like some Sartrean hero until he finds himself capable of anything, exists only in the light of Emilia Gould's regard. He has, however, a peculiar ability to idealize the distinguishing feature of his life: "For Dr. Monygham has made for himself an ideal conception of his disgrace" (p. 418). He has, as Conrad says, exaggerated a correct feeling, failing to explain at least partially his fantastic confessions under torture by "physiological facts or reasonable arguments." Partly guilty, he is also partly innocent, but shapes his life to the contour of that guilt. He denies the perfectibility of man even while worshiping the nearly perfect Emilia Gould, and offers himself in sacrifice not to the new state of Sulaco or to Emilia's love for her husband (and hence to Charles's success), but to the idealized guilt that in his own eyes makes him the man for such dirty and deadly work as the deception of Sotillo.

Mrs. Gould, sustained by love for her husband, is also for a time capable of idealizing the mine and even material interests. When that idealism fades with the slow corruption of her husband, she is after all surrounded by people in whom she can readily believe: Antonia, Monygham, even for a time Decoud himself. Furthermore, neither Monygham nor Emilia is primarily an intellectual creature, though Monygham has a quasi-intellectual farsightedness that enables him to see the long-run oppressiveness of the San Tomé mine. Monygham is also both intellectually and emotionally aware of the threat that Decoud, because of his unsupported intellect and his inability to idealize more than his fragile love for Antonia, cannot tolerate. The identities Conrad imagines here demand a sense of *individual* existence; but as Monygham has reason to know, the element common to all physical dangers is "the crushing, paralyzing sense of human littleness, which is what really defeats a man struggling with natural forces alone, far from the eyes of his fellows. He was eminently fit to appreciate the mental image he made for himself of the capataz, after hours of tension and anxiety precipitated suddenly into an abyss of waters and darkness, without earth or sky, and confronting it not only with an undismayed mind but with sensible success" (pp. 484–85). Of course the danger facing Decoud when he is isolated with the treasure is not physical. Yet Decoud and Nostromo would seem to react in opposite ways to such physical and psychological isolation. Monygham in the above passage sees that there are times when the sense of identity is so fragile that one feels himself absorbed as just another part of the physical universe. And it is this threat, this terrifying sublimation, which awaits the man who cannot idealize his actions and is denied the presence of a human love that might have continued to define him. Decoud is very nearly the kind of skeptic whom Stein had suggested tries to climb out of the destructive element of dreams and ideals and to deny that they are a necessary part of our humanity. Decoud drowns and dies, as Stein said he would, because he tries to be the natural man, avoiding that "unnatural" fervor of idealism except as a formal exercise.

Once again it is easy to see how a great many of Conrad's characters are placed by their relation to nature, by the degree to which they accept, deny, distort, or are simply unaware of the seemingly unnatural position Victorian science had created for human consciousness. Decoud's isolation on the island reminds us how that situation was used in the eighteenth century as a means of expressing not only theories of nature but maps of the human mind as well. Robinson Crusoe bends nature zestfully to his middle-class economic will; and we can imagine an American transcendentalist isolated as Decoud was and mystically penetrating even the dispiriting nature of the placid gulf. Far from discovering in nature a profound symbolic revelation of the God-given stuff of economic and spiritual success, Decoud (like Marlow in *Heart of Darkness*, unable to read his environment) "beheld his universe as a succession of incomprehensible images." He does not even feel, as Ishmael in *Moby Dick* does, that there *is* a meaning though man will never penetrate the symbolic masks to its presence. The nature which absorbs Decoud is an impersonal process, the ghostly and amoral analogue, on the metaphysical level, of material interests.

Decoud cannot finally resist the temptation to merge with unconscious nature; he cannot even distinguish himself from it. Yet — appearances to the contrary — is not the same or a very similar attraction characteristic of the ultimate projects of both Nostromo and Charles, and is not the silver symbolic of this? Though, as I have said, Nostromo initially defies absorption by the placid gulf (in a scene that is meant on a very accessible level as a contrast to Decoud's later suicide in those same waters), both men are finally carried to their deaths literally and figuratively weighted with silver. In desiring to "clasp, embrace, absorb" the silver, Nostromo has also lost the sense of boundaries between the human and unconscious matter. Indeed Conrad focuses here as in *Lord Jim* on man's various attempts to be self-caused and self-founded, to become in-itself (to "absorb" the silver or be absorbed by it). Such a project, the archetypal project for Sartre, is, however, futile and destructive. We can well understand the different motives in all three men (Charles, Nostromo, and Decoud) that bring them to the same grotesque imitation of matter. It is especially clear why "our man," having grounded his identity in the opinion of others, should now turn to what seems to him most permanent and unlike that ephemeral acclaim. He will later continue his life in the public eye, but only because he can simultaneously hoard the true foundation of his being.

What happens to Decoud is the most conspicuous example of the pattern I am suggesting. When he weights his pockets with silver before shooting himself and plunging into the placid gulf, an important symbolic connection is made between men who otherwise seem unlike one another. After all, Decoud unlike Nostromo has cared nothing about public opinion, though the two share an inability to idealize their desires. Charles, on the contrary, is expert at idealizing his passions and epitomizes the spiritualized material interests for which Decoud can summon no real enthusiasm. Nonetheless, when Decoud reaches his extremity, it is the silver that comes to symbolize the metaphysics of his disappearance into the plenitude of an indifferent nature:

After three days of waiting for the sight of some human face, Decoud caught himself entertaining a doubt of his own individuality. It had merged into the world of cloud and water, of natural forces and forms of nature. In our activity alone do we find the sustaining illusion of an independent existence as against the whole scheme of things of which we form a helpless part. (P. 556)

The bars of San Tomé silver are chosen to speed and perfect his entry into this world: "Don Martin Decoud, weighted by the bars of San Tomé silver, disappeared without a trace, swallowed up in the immense indifference of things" (p. 560). The intimation is that the silver satisfies a related project on the part of Charles and Nostromo. The language surrounding Charles's hopes for the mine echoes, as I have said, with the idea of permanence, incorruptibility, stability, purity, and, in short, with the infinite density of in-itself. Although his talent for the idealization of material interests would seem to lift the silver out of its existence as in-itself by the sheer energy of human significance, the movement of his character away from all forms of human contingency (even from his wife's love, which is barely contingent at all) uncovers the true nature of his project. Claire Rosenfield senses his similarity to Lord Jim:

As Thomas Moser suggests, Conrad found the subject of love uncongenial; but in Charles Gould he reveals the successful characterization of a man unable to love for reasons which were congenial to Conrad. He is attempting to be faithful to an image of himself; he is a romantic like Lord Jim. Like Lord Jim he allows his egoism to isolate him completely from other human beings. The man who attempts to sentimentalize his actions is simply another portrait of a type which Conrad successfully created again and again — the self-deluded idealist.[2]

But we ought to be suspicious of any claim that such a figure was simply congenial to Conrad. Gould's increasing isolation is intuitively seen by the man himself — and by many others — as godlike. Gould sees Holroyd as a kind of god (as Miss Rosenfield observes), and he himself is Holroyd's chosen one in Sulaco. The evidence that Charles projects a godlike role for himself and the mine is too numerous to mention here. It is his mode of establishing this godhead that really reminds one of Lord Jim. Like Jim, he very subtly desires to be like the unconscious natural world, specifically like the silver, but also to be entirely conscious of — and in that sense also to have founded — his own immutability. The familiar paradox and futility of Lord Jim is repeated. Needless to say, Conrad is far from simply "congenial" to the idea that man may be lost so that God can be born. Conrad knows that in the sense of founding values man must be godlike, but not at the expense of losing his humanity. The abandoned Jewel and Emilia Gould are the most conspicuous signs of this betrayal, although there are much broader trails of such indications left behind both men. I suspect that although Conrad appreciated the importance of any such project to become God, he would have insisted on several perspectives. First, that although it is difficult to say how aware either Gould or Jim is of the true nature of his project, both have consciously chosen it and yet are unwilling to take the responsibility for having done so. Their projects continually dodge the one quality that Conrad would have insisted on as godly: responsibility. It is precisely at this point that Kurtz becomes important in Conrad's contemplation of the man-god, for though Kurtz's path to divinity has been more direct and in pattern somewhat unlike Jim's and Charles's, he alone has had the courage to assume responsibility for his divine prerogatives. Compare his "The horror!" with Jim's hand placed carefully over his mouth at the moment of death.

Charles, Nostromo, and Decoud have all failed in the fundamental necessity of consciousness to distinguish itself from the dumb world. That sounds like a strange way of describing what is wrong with them, but it seems to me the most basic way. Although Decoud and Nostromo are not striking examples of the man-god in either the Lord Jim or Kurtz pattern, both are seduced by initself and both strive to be continually aware of the immutability they can never really establish.

The San Tomé silver, then, whatever political implications it may have, serves primarily as a symbol of the most primitive and yet perhaps most difficult task confronting consciousness: to know what it is not, to appreciate its own unique mode of being. The implication of *Nostromo* for Conrad's psychological models is enormous but not essentially different from *Lord Jim*. *Nostromo*, however, suggests that Conrad had become more nearly aware that Kurtz's hollowness was not so much the failure of consciousness as its permanent condition of radical freedom, continual becoming, and total contingency. In *Nostromo* he was never further from resembling Freudian or depth-psychology models, nor from the rubrics of will and passion or ego and sympathy. Decoud on the Isabels is much like Roquentin in the park, both men threatened by the plenitude of being to the point where neither feels capable of that fundamental, self-defining act of consciousness: negation, the secretion of nothingness which is the nature of consciousness. Though Roquentin sees and feels the threat everywhere (in the very roots of the tree he watches), Conrad has made it much more difficult to see the ultimate threat in the silver. There are, after all, subtle temptations for Conrad to use more conventional language. We are told, for instance, what terms to use for understanding Decoud's suicide:

He had recognized no other virtue than intelligence, and had erected passions into duties. Both his intelligence and his passion were swallowed up easily in this great unbroken solitude of wait-ing without faith. Sleeplessness had robbed his will of all energy, for he had not slept seven hours in seven days. (P. 557)

The review of categories is hastily made: intelligence, passions, duties, faith, will; and the very breakneck pace of the list indicates how little it interests Conrad except in its suggestion of the way Decoud, in contrast to Steinian idealists, creates his imitation of ideals. But see what has happened to will: from the ostensibly prin-cipal subject of enquiry it had been in the early work we now find it checked off almost as an afterthought and weakened by so mun-dane (though admittedly devastating) a thing as lack of sleep. The truth is that the conception of will has little bearing on any of the characters in this novel. For Gould and Nostromo, passion and will — insofar as we can use these categories at all — are one, sub-sumed by the more viable conception of identity and self-image. The very language of the novel shows how the drama of identity has replaced the vocabulary of classical psychology. If there is any place in *Nostromo* where the struggle between will and passion might have been adduced, surely it is the moment when Nostromo decides to possess the treasure. Yet, as I think most readers will agree, no such frame is suggested for that decision. We can imagine how in an earlier novel, nonetheless, there might have been a rhet-

oric of classical psychology seriously designed to universalize the
particular in a distressing and occasionally dishonest way.

*Nostromo* still demonstrates, to be sure, Conrad's tendency to
doubt the power of intellect. Nor is the idea of conscience entirely
absent. But on the whole the old conceptions (intellect, conscience,
passion, duty, will, sympathy, ego) are all reshaped by approaching a character through his own sense of identity, as of course they
were in a small way in even his first novel. Since the classical categories appear to hinder Conrad's appreciation of human behavior
that simply escapes or eludes them, it becomes vital that he consider the birth of value without the dubious aid of these models.
Granted, he had produced great art with their powerful economies
of thought and emotion, but he could not have written either *Lord
Jim* or *Heart of Darkness* while strongly under their influence.
When any one of them preoccupied Conrad — as, say, Schopenhauerian will did in "Falk" — the true subject of his story was
often submerged and lost in the more easily managed expectations
of the model. Thus the threat from absurdity that seems to have
been the real importance of his experience in Bangkok never
emerges in "Falk," as it most certainly does in *Heart of Darkness*,
where the conception of unbridled ego very soon proves inadequate to adduce Kurtz's significance.

For reasons that are not entirely clear, Conrad's increasing interest in self-image as the arbiter of value parallels the development in
Europe and the United States of what has been called the psychology of personality. British behaviorism and the study of "mind
in general" gave way in the work of Freud and of the Gestalt psy-
chologists in the first two or three decades of the century to a concern with unique personality (even if only eventually to return to
mind in general with a vengeance). In the thirties the United States
added the work of Gordon Allport, Henry Murray, and Kurt
Lewin — among  others — to advances in Freudian and German
Gestalt psychology until, as one contemporary psychologist summarizes the matter, "Concern with the self and self-image is one
of the most striking features of recent theoretical developments."
"The self, which perished as a psychological entity some time be-

fore the turn of the century, has been rediscovered as a vital and necessary conceptual referrant. I predict that it will not soon be lost again." [8] Of course in art the self did not "perish as a psychological entity some time before the turn of the century"; on the contrary, so-called Impressionism and the Romantic influence of Schopenhauerian solipsism had given it a vogue. But there is undeniably a strong taste in much of Conrad's work for displaying mind in general, a taste which has, by the way, enabled an occasional student to underline all Conrad's comments on conscience, intellect, will, passion, and so on, and offer the sum as Conrad's "psychology." Though it is an absurd critical method, the fact that it can be done at all shows Conrad's often rather slavish enthusiasm for a Victorian pastime so much at odds with his avowed impressionism and with the surpassing power of his imagination.

While it is undeniable that my analysis of *Lord Jim*, *Heart of Darkness*, and *Nostromo* also depends to some extent on a sense of mind in general, it must be clear that none of the Conradian insights that may be compared with Sartre are given labels in the novels, nor are they manipulated as categories and faculties. The only fundamental categories necessary in this model are consciousness and what it is not. The individual choice of project is as various and unique as the fundamental fact that everything is either conscious or not will allow. The fresh existential insights of these three novels are perfectly and unavoidably dependent on what I have called Conrad's metaphor or model of self-image. The cliché is, after all, no cliché at all.

# 7

# The Whole Man:
# "The Secret Sharer"

In testing the conclusions I have reached about *Lord Jim, Heart of Darkness,* and *Nostromo,* "The Secret Sharer" and the novel for which it was interrupted, *Under Western Eyes,* became quite important. "The Secret Sharer" is one of a very few stories where Conrad rests content with presenting intimations of unconscious mind, as though such dark, egoistic forces marked the limit of his penetration into the nature of mind. My feeling, however, is that in "The Secret Sharer" he exploits this almost Freudian model at the expense of the all-too-painful sense of nothingness he had manfully confronted in the triad of novels we have just discussed. Perhaps without his knowing it, he drew from that existential awareness a strength and honesty missing (to my taste) from "The Secret Sharer," but present again with all its force in *Under Western Eyes.* I do not mean to suggest that when he is existential he is good but when *less* than existential less than good. On the contrary, "The Secret Sharer" is in many ways a marvelous story. It is, however, a conservative, almost reactionary one.

By 1902 and the publication of *Nostromo* no other English novelist with the exception of Henry James had had so unsettling an effect on the classical psychological models and metaphors of the nineteenth century. Neither James nor Conrad purports to cut immediately to anything that might be called the key assumption upon which nineteenth-century "mind in general" rested, largely because that classical psychology could not be so easily summarized as, say, William Blake felt the eighteenth century could by Urizen's usurpation of the whole mind. But like Blake, both James and Conrad helped inspire a return to ideas of subjective wholeness from the rubric of naturalism and the categories of mind in general, whether classical or Schopenhauerian. Tending in a similar direction, W. B. Yeats had discovered a not unpredictable affinity for the holism of Blake and had begun in his poetry as well as in *A Vision* to use a complex unity of being as an ultimate value. It is extremely difficult to say how deep are the similarities between Conrad's and Yeats's ideals, but in their common concern for the possibilities within the self of antiself, for the integrity of egoism against selfless values, and for a harmony of self in which neither part of the "duality of man's nature" is bruised to pleasure the other half ("How can we tell the dancer from the dance . . .") both men are representative of deep currents at the turn of the century. In his essay on Henry James written in 1905, Conrad appears to feel that such harmony of self is unlikely if not impossible and that renunciation is the drama generated by man's dual nature.

. . . from the duality of man's nature and the competition of individuals, the life history of the earth must in the last instance be a history of a really very relentless warfare. Neither his fellows, nor his gods, nor his passions will leave a man alone. . . . All adventure, all love, every success is resumed in the supreme energy of an art of renunciation. . . . Like a natural force which is obscured as much as illuminated by the multiplicity of phenomena, the power of renunciation is obscured by the mass of weaknesses, vacillations, secondary motives and false steps and compromises which make up the sum of our activity. But no man or woman worthy of the name can pretend to anything more, to anything greater. . . . Wherever he stands, at the beginning or the end of things, a man has to sacrifice his gods to his passions or his passions to his gods. That is the problem, great enough, in all truth, if approached in the spirit of sincerity and knowledge.[1]

Although Conrad goes out of his way to make this a universal pronouncement, he is clearly thinking of James's characters in their most characteristic and morally defining acts, of Isabel Archer, for example, returning to Osmond at the end of that novel. If, however, the idealizing aspect of man's nature and what often seemed to Conrad the dark egoism of his animal inheritance must always be either victim or victor, we shall never approach wholeness and scarcely be able to explain so crucial a story as "The Secret Sharer." Renunciation may be the fate of man, but the term suggests the will and passion that Conrad had long since abandoned in his novels and short stories if not, apparently, in his formal essays. Of the characters in Conrad's work who try to integrate the dual nature of man, not to control passion but to encompass it and occasionally to deny the morality of speaking as though it were somehow not part of the self, "The Secret Sharer" is obviously crucial.

We need only ask how Nietzsche or Freud would have reacted to Conrad's rather official assertion that a man must sacrifice either his passion to his gods or his gods to his passion, in order to realize how anxious the late nineteenth century was to find a way of solving that classic dilemma. Freud's manner of changing the problem was to suggest that it was entirely possible a man's gods grew from his passions — which, if we do not take the term "passions" too narrowly, is really not a bad description of political idealism in both *Nostromo* and *The Secret Agent*. The question for Frazer, Freud, Jung, Nietzsche, D. H. Lawrence, and even Joyce — all contemporaries of Conrad — was how man could turn from artificial and damaging schemes of renunciation as a means of creating value to new forms of acceptance. The Nietzschean *Übermensch*, the hero who embraced his darkest impulses, was of course impossible for Conrad as for all of the other names I mentioned; but these others were all nonetheless anxious to confront modern man with the continuity of what seemed to them his primitive origins and drives, not so that those impulses might be despised and rejected but so that a new appreciation of their ineluctable presence and value in all civilized life might create a new authenticity.

According to Albert Guerard's definition of Conrad's undeniable attempts to imagine some sort of night journey, the hero becomes partly aware of his unconscious life. But this claim — despite Guerard's open-mindedness — exaggerates Conrad's use of the distinction between conscious and unconscious mind in "The Secret Sharer" at least. As Conrad's biographer, Jocelyn Baines, has said:

> However, Guerard goes on to assert that Leggatt is not merely an "other self," he is a "lower self," "the embodiment of a more instinctive, more primitive, less rational self." I believe that this misses the whole point. Leggatt is not a symbol of the unconscious but a man on precisely the same level as the young captain; their selves are interchangeable (the epithet "secret" might imply the opposite but its context and the whole tone of the story show that the word was intended in its literal sense: Leggatt was "secret" because he had to be kept secret or hidden).[2]

One of the persistent flaws in Baines's biography of Conrad is his desire to play the role of sane Englishman against the all-too-clever "alchemical" American New Critics. Though undoubtedly we deserve more than one rap on the knuckles, Baines in his desire to wield the stick often grows awkward. Guerard does not usually suggest that the character of Leggatt is in all its significance simply equal to a lower self; but in Leggatt's action aboard the *Sephora* he certainly has been instinctive and primitive, as, increasingly, is the captain once Leggatt has come aboard. Guerard would probably agree that Leggatt is otherwise pretty much on "the same level as the young captain"; which is, as Baines says, the whole point — otherwise the sharing could not begin and the captain's realization that he must also share Leggatt's proven capacity for primitively instinctive acts would have no emotional logic to it.

Nonetheless, Baines's conservatism has at least as much of the truth as Guerard's depth psychology. The whole man, I believe, was never intended by Conrad to be only one who had recognized and accommodated the primitive unconscious, but also anyone who had violated his own self-image and had begun to realize that he was at once more and less than the image, not in fact one with it. Often when one of these characters is forced to recognize his own unsettling and potentially disintegrating acts, the action is described as will-less either by the character himself (whose judgment may then be treated ironically by Conrad, as is Willems's) or by the author, who has by no means decided just how the idea of will is involved in such actions as Leggatt's or Lord Jim's. This quality of will-lessness, however, ought not always to be taken to mean that a primitive, irrational portion of the mind has shown its claws. Usually the sense of will-lessness suggests that the character himself cannot contain the act within his self-image, and hence considers it beyond the gravitational forces (often called "will") of that self-image. It is so strange to him that he cannot imagine having chosen it, though if there is any substance to the idea of free will he must at least consider the possibility of having done so. There is a vast difference between these two senses of wholeness. The first is distinctly Freudian and Jungian; the second bears signs of being genuinely existential, despite the fact that Conrad in much of his writing shared with Freud and Schopenhauer, as I have said, the idea that man bore always with him a primitive *essence*.

I feel much more comfortable reading Conrad if I can determine what, because of a character's unique self-image or project, he will consider dark and untoward, unacceptable to this image. Most readers who are, with Guerard, anxious to savor the night journey in "The Secret Sharer" fail, however, to understand the implications of "Falk." Though a poor story, it is nonetheless the first of at least three in which the author returns to the crisis in Singapore and Bangkok and attempts to assess its importance in — undoubtedly — his own life, but also in the imaginatively controlling metaphors of his art.

Conrad makes no attempt to disguise the Bangkok setting of "The Secret Sharer." While no one is likely — having read both "Falk" and "The Secret Sharer" — to assume that the later story takes up where the other stops, we are indeed told that the tugboat has just left the captain and his new command at the head of the Gulf of Siam. The Paknam pagoda, as in "Falk," still dominates the horizon; and the young captain suffers from the same anxiety about his adequacy that lies just below the surface in "Falk." On the whole, Conrad seems to be returning to the same terrifying and yet promising experience in Bangkok for a second imaginative time around. But even this second time, the narrator's reasons for feeling so inadequate are veiled, and even granting that it is his first command we may wonder at the rapidity with which he comes to feel nearly "insane."

Of course the history of Conrad's fears for his own ego since leaving the *Vidar* are behind the imagining of this captain's anxiety as surely as they are behind the narrator in "Falk." In neither story, however, is Conrad willing to provide that background, to give the captain a past as surely as it finally purports to give him a future. At least this sharer of Leggatt's crime tries none of the amused distancing, the grotesque humor, so objectionable in "Falk." We have all sometimes noticed that in narrating disturbing events, people may originally couch the story in false and unsuccessful humor, possibly as some sort of a control. On retelling, that comedy usually disappears, leaving only the grotesque and drawing us closer to the narrator's genuine state of mind. There is nothing amusing about Conrad's sense that his emergence from late youth had depended upon a delicate and not altogether clear sharing of something with another human being. What that something was, and how the sharing proceeded, may have required three or more stories and many years of imaginative reflection to decide, if indeed it has yet been decided.

Certainly the first structuring of this experience in "Falk" suggests that the one person more confused than the reader is Conrad himself. The story is full of portentous clues, shaky generalizations, and very ambiguous relations between narrator and author. Nevertheless, it appears quite vividly that Conrad's fear in Singapore and Bangkok was of losing identity. He had fled Poland and Marseilles and found a measure of romance and security in the role of English merchant seaman—something, at least, that offered the solidity and simplicity Uncle Bobrowski had long touted in his letters to the wayward young suicide. The routine in tropical waters aboard the *Vidar*, however, gave Conrad an enervating dose of the craft he had perhaps chosen for reasons like those of the young captain in "The Secret Sharer": "And suddenly I rejoiced in the great security of the sea as compared with the unrest of the land, in my choice of that untempted life presenting no disquieting problems, invested with an elementary moral beauty by the absolute straightforwardness of its appeal and by the singleness of its purpose" (p. 96).

But duty aboard the *Vidar*, routine life at sea unglamorized by early youth, was unsatisfying enough for him to bolt the ship. What better intimation that this identity was not wearing well, that he might not be able or willing to devote a life to that "elementary moral duty." So long as the sea appeared an escape from unrest, temptation, and, above all, moral complexity, it was not likely to satisfy a man of Conrad's moral discernment. In "The Secret Sharer" Leggatt demonstrates to the captain just how complex and unstraightforward life at sea could become; the story erodes any "elementary moral beauty" and in doing so ironically makes it eminently possible for the captain to continue in the profession.

Conrad could never have remained in any craft that might genuinely be described as a refuge from life. Command — the task facing both this captain and Conrad aboard the *Otago* — is full of obscure choices and dubious results; what is necessary to give the captain his full identity and to pay his debt to Leggatt endangers the whole ship (which is taken dangerously near Ko-ring). Leggatt's raw impulse to rig the sail and thereby save the *Sephora* is also, the young captain says, behind his strangling the mutinous sailor: the group is saved by a force which takes individual life, damages Leggatt's own life, and is approved by neither Captain Archbold nor the crew. It is necessary for our captain both to share Leggatt's knowledge and to rid himself of that criminal-not-criminal. And so on, ambiguity heaped upon uncertainty and paradox until it becomes clear not only that we have an allegedly whole man in the captain, but one now aware how inadequate his motives for seeking this profession have been. One further implication of this new professional and moral awareness: the captain shares Leggatt's

crime as much because both have been in or are in positions of professional responsibility as because he feels within himself an equally
dark potential for what is instinctive and violent.

In one sense both "Falk" and "The Secret Sharer" are wishful
thinking by a writer thoroughly afraid he might have become indifferent, seduced by the terrifying view of the East revealed especially, it seems to me, in the yawning, shuddering Eurasian police
chief of the "Falk" manuscript and by the Paknam pagoda with
its implications of Buddhist withdrawal. The following passage
was never published, perhaps because it was too nearly autobio-
graphical. It shows our captain threatened and courted by a sense
of meaninglessness, the "menace of emptiness" so prominent in
*The Shadow Line.* The captain's small cash reserve has been stolen,
and he and Captain Hermann have pursued the thief; they come
to a native police hut and are interviewed by the native chief of
police.

Their chief a tall dissipated looking Eurasian in a tunic with pew-
ter buttons fastened all awry and tucked up anyhow as though he
were in the habit of going to bed in it received my deposition in
tired disillusioned silence. As soon as he attempted to speak he was
overcome by a fit of immense yawning with profound shudders
and contortions, like the symptoms of some convulsive disease.
They would catch the Chinaman, he managed to utter, if I liked.
— What do you mean? Why shouldn't "I like" I asked ruefully.
   In that moment I may say I sounded the lowest depths of desolation in my whole life. I have been in danger and difficulties since
up to my neck but never so near understanding what a man means
when he professes himself ready to curse the day he was born in.
That Eurasian's yawning horrified my very soul. I shall never forget that police hut, the hot night tasting of dust and paraffin, the
extraordinary stuffiness of that plain with the Buddhist temple
upon the invisible horizon. I could hear alternately the croaking
of frogs from a mudhole nearby and the bursting shrieks from a
Chinese theater that marked with white flares of light the obscure
vastness of the town on both sides of the river. Whiffs as of rotting
corpses and smoldering joss sticks passed faint and overcoming in
tepid gusts. The crescent of the moon seemed to be the only cool
and wholesome thing left in the general fatigue and decay of the
universe.[3]

The appearance of the chief touched a neurotic fear in, I assume, Conrad himself. "They would catch the Chinaman, he managed to utter, if I liked. — What do you mean? Why shouldn't 'I like' I asked ruefully." Why indeed shouldn't he like? Perhaps because he had become nearly accustomed to the relatively easy cruises in tropical waters, with native crews and heat so bad even the officers remained in "sleeping suits" all day; he fears the menace of emptiness, perhaps even as Conrad feared a repetition of the attempted suicide which had concluded his absurdly unenthusiastic involvement with the Carlist cause in Marseilles and along the Spanish coast.

Not surprisingly, both "Falk" and "The Secret Sharer" are about men who discover within themselves great natural impulse, energy and determination, not painfully emerging from volition but flowing from primitive, essential wellsprings. It is therapeutic, for a man who had begun to feel empty, to be suddenly presented with the possibility that man does contain this natural energy — all the better "dark," if by that we may assume it is inherent in our animal nature.

What Conrad offers in his vision of Falk and Leggatt is not his belief in the night journey or his spontaneous discovery of that archetype, but three identities, Conrad himself and his two complex projections into the narrators of both stories, who because of a largely unspecified anxiety about their own selfhood *need* at least the possibility of naturally sustained ego. For a man in the state of mind Conrad seems to have experienced in Singapore and Bangkok, Falk might have seemed a comfort. Albeit the narrator and through him Conrad have difficulty sharing anything with Falk, here is someone who faces no threat of meaninglessness, whose will to live never allows even the thought of suicide; and in Leggatt, though his impulse is as we might expect more complex than the crude Schopenhauerian will of Falk, there is equally a natural and morally ambiguous instinct the sharing of which is not so disturbing as comforting to this amalgam of author and character.

It is likely that at times — certainly in Bangkok and in remembering that episode – Conrad may have welcomed the idea of primitive instincts. These were far better than the threat of emptiness Decoud carries with him, better than the symbolically stifling plain of Bangkok suggesting the "general fatigue and decay of the universe." Conrad seems willing to accept the undesirable aspects of these primitive impulses largely because, as one critic has said of "The Secret Sharer,"

A man must act, must be in part impulsive, instinctive – and this side of him is in a sense amoral. It may produce good (the giving of the hat) or evil; but the basic point is that it is essential for life and action. . . . A kind of moral spectrum is set up, in which Conrad recognizes the moral importance of vast differences of degree: at one end of the spectrum is the criminal instinct, which imperceptibly merges through the instinct for right action and the giving of certain orders to the other extreme of pity. The management of this spectrum – where there is no logical way of drawing a dividing line – is the art of life. Conrad is saying that there is no difference in moral kind between the making of a certain sign [giving the hat to Leggatt] and the killing of a man; the attribute of impulsive action contains within it the seeds of savagery. To deny it is at best foolish, to be unaware of it (the Captain at the beginning of the story, or the early Leggatt) is to imperil all.[4]

But what has not been said and needs to be, is that for these captains there is something far worse than primitive impulse. The night journey blurs differences between Kurtz's discovery and that made by Leggatt and the captains in both "The Secret Sharer" and "Falk." The metaphysical context in which Kurtz, Marlow believes, victoriously judges his darkest ego points beyond that ego, toward the implication that there is an even more fundamental threat of the sort that Decoud and Gould and Nostromo and Lord Jim encounter, a threat grounded in the difficulty of consciousness knowing what it is not. The impulse revealed in Leggatt, however, suggests that such primitive spontaneity – usually of self-love – is the irreducible spring of human nature, and this is a faith which ignores the corrosive action of self-consciousness in the new universe upon such relatively comforting primitivism. As Conrad knew all too well, man has the unique ability to divest himself of all sense of ordination, animal no less than spiritual, irrational no less than rational.

The sympathy of the captain for Leggatt is seemingly based on the kind of self-knowledge that had purified the sympathy of Marlow for Lord Jim and Kurtz. But in "The Secret Sharer" as in "Falk" that knowledge of man's irrational nature never goes beyond a kind of self-congratulation at discovering that man is not absurd, that he is always at least possessed of instincts that can give meaning even to the life that has flirted with meaninglessness. *Heart of Darkness* and *Nostromo* are not so optimistic.

We have in these two stories the return of Conrad to old problems of sympathy and ego, but this time with the hope of creating a vision of psychic wholeness — not Jim's ego blindness, but a genuine alternative to the renunciation suggested in the article on Henry James. Marlow's development in *Heart of Darkness* is not conducive to the whole man. How is he to accept the total contingency of value that makes self-love seem desirable by comparison? Conrad saw in writing *Heart of Darkness* and perhaps in his own Congo experience more than the black ego of man's animal nature, or of his participation in Schopenhauerian will. What Kurtz and Marlow confront, what he faced himself, was the knowledge that not even animal self-love could be counted upon — that man, unlike the rest of nature, was sometimes suicidal because of his nearly unbearable estrangement from nature, that his self-consciousness made him unique. The vision of ego in "Falk" and "The Secret Sharer" emphasizes, on the contrary, that man's animal nature can be sustaining, actually a refuge from the far more disturbing existential vision that clouds the background of both stories.

Something goes wrong, however, even in the attempts to share this seemingly unlimited but actually censored night journey. I have already suggested some of the aesthetic failures in that aspect of the "Falk" narrator. In "The Secret Sharer," the sharing seems far more successful, not only to the captain and Conrad, but to the reader who feels that the story is after all a very satisfying work of art. It is, however, apparent, as Carl Benson suggests, that *The Shadow Line* was written as a counterpart to "The Secret Sharer"

in order to reevaluate the wholeness and new competency demonstrated by the captain at the end of the story.[5] As a result of the
nearly Christian sharing, the captain nonetheless becomes a rather
proud, isolated figure more concerned with his self-possession than
with the humanity it is his responsibility to command. And it is not
always true that such self-possession will automatically be good
for the crew: he does bring the ship dangerously close to the rocks
of Ko-ring, an act the crew takes as a sign of his competence
(though they have had no reason to expect it of him up to this
point), but a risk actually far beyond his knowledge of either the
waters or the ship.

The captain of *The Shadow Line* is, on the contrary, sustained
by a crew that continues, though sick to a man, to run a ship he
can offer almost nothing. He is afraid to come on deck and face
the problem of windless weather, a sick crew, and the nagging conviction that in failing to check carefully the quinine he has let his
men down unpardonably. In acknowledging his dependence on
the crew and especially on Ransome — who expends himself un-
selfishly despite a heart ailment — this captain, though he does not
achieve the self-confidence of his earlier counterpart, realizes "that
no man, not even one upon whom dynastic rule has been con-
ferred, is truly *self*-sustaining, that the lot of the one is ineluctably
involved with that of the many." [6] If self-possession is a necessary
prelude to one's achieving any kind of human community or love,
it is only a prelude. In short, the effect of Leggatt on the captain
is, on later consideration, undercut by Conrad just as surely as that
still earlier captain's sympathy for Falk is — aesthetically speaking
— stillborn.

So many of Conrad's contemporaries were struggling to achieve
an ideal of synthesis that we should not be surprised to see him ex-
pend a great deal of imaginative energy on these confrontations
with primitive levels of human nature, even when he had begun to
suspect that the self-sustaining man was a fiction and the ultimate
confrontation, with the "menace of emptiness," crippling. Although there is something aristocratic and solitary about the hero
who seems to undergo the night journey — even the censored ver-

sion in "The Secret Sharer" — *The Shadow Line* looks very much
like a public gesture and in itself does little to persuade us emotionally that there has been anything inadequate in the earlier captain's response to Leggatt. *The Shadow Line* is, after all, dedicated to Conrad's son Borys and those serving with him in the
British army during World War I. In many ways, the story is a
patriotic gesture, an affirmation in wartime of the individual's dependence on the community, from a man who had gained an un-
deserved reputation as the natural historian of solitaries.

There is a path from self-possession to human solidarity, but it
necessitates a confrontation not to be found in "The Secret Sharer"
or *The Shadow Line*. It is to Conrad's lasting credit that in novels
such as *Under Western Eyes* and *Victory* — late works which bear
unmistakable signs of his physical and psychic weariness — he once
again sees the enigma of self-possession and human solidarity
whole. Of course no one disputes that self-possession of one kind
or another is a necessary condition for any form of human solidarity; but it is a dangerous, precarious achievement that may trap
the individual. It is by no means likely, as some students of Conrad
have suggested, that the fundamental sympathy of the captain for
Leggatt becomes both self-possession and the microcosm of all human solidarity, the acceptance of common human guilt and inadequacy. Says Walter Wright of the captain's acceptance of Leggatt: "With [Lord] Jim's delicacy of conscience, he cannot condemn to punishment a man who is his *alter ego* without feeling
that he has been a traitor to his own soul and has forever separated
himself from any standard of decency which makes society ten-
able."[7] If this were a fair description of either the captain's final
disposition toward his crew or of Leggatt's significance against the
background of other more disturbing threats to individual and social order, the captain's symbolic gesture of giving the hat would
indeed be the juncture at which self-possession becomes human
solidarity. But Conrad himself did not apparently feel it was, and
*The Shadow Line* attests to this. In a sense, sharing Leggatt's crime
is far too easy: witness the surplus of critics who have, to my way

of thinking, made a kind of festival out of doing so. We all learned at the age of ten that Leggatt was a hero.

Conard's compulsive exercises in sympathetic sharing continue, however, into *Under Western Eyes*, where the sharing is not easy, and where the connection between self-possession and human solidarity becomes the hero's central passion. And this issue is just what needed to be faced in all its complexity before it could be coupled, in *Victory*, with at least echoes of the radical metaphors I have discussed earlier. Conrad was never again to work so experimentally and so freshly with conceptions of consciousness as he had in the three key novels, but in *Victory* — which is by no means a great novel or even a very good one — he explores the impact some of those earlier experiments might have had on the ideal of human community. Of course that impact fully realized could have been tremendous — possibly analogous to that of the Marabar Caves in *A Passage to India*, where the ultimate threat of the caves (those images of in-itself, older than spirit, perfect spheres reflecting immemorial blackness and plenitude) are potentially a spur to Godbolean spirit. The full impact was never to be realized; but on the basis of his achievement in *Under Western Eyes*, we can see clues in *Victory* as to what it might have been.

# 8

# The Psychology
# of Self-Image:
# Under Western Eyes

In the sense of the word "political" used by Mrs. Hay in her study of Conrad, a sense which opens out from her definition of *méchanceté* in Conrad's famous "*l'homme est un animal méchant*," it can hardly be denied that *Under Western Eyes* is a political novel — or, for that matter, that *Lord Jim* fits the same category.[1] We need not, however, expand the definition of either *méchanceté* or "political" so generously: the best political novels, novels that very often use rather limited definitions of "political," end by transcending politics in a region where root emotions create all our enthusiasms and allegiances — political, erotic, religious, or otherwise. Not that such novels ultimately lose the political flavor; they may, however, use it for symbolic purposes without diminishing its more immediate significance and effect. In this regard *Under Western Eyes* joins the distinguished company of *A Passage to India*: Russia and India are what they are, but they intimate symbolic dimensions that have little directly to do with the political reality of either country. No less than the Marabar Caves, India is itself symbolic. No less than India in Forster's novel, Conrad's Russia will forever elude attempts to make it the subject of *Under Western Eyes*.

Jean-Aubry suggests that it was the visit in October 1909 of Carlos M. Marris, a captain who now sailed Malayan waters and had enjoyed Conrad's early work immensely, that caused him to interrupt work on *Under Western Eyes* in favor of some early memories and to produce, in two weeks of relatively easy writing, "The Secret Sharer." [2] Regardless of whether or not this speculation is true, the fact that "The Secret Sharer" came as a rather painless interlude in the composition of *Under Western Eyes* suggests that we may equally in that novel have a case of sharing, but a sharing from which the short story may have seemed a refuge. It is at least possible that "The Secret Sharer" and its amendment in *The Shadow Line* provide as valid a context for *Under Western Eyes* as Conrad's lifelong involvement with the enigma of Russia. I should like to play down the political implications of the novel in favor of an intriguing guess: that Conrad had in this novel become so bound up in the problems of wholeness, self-sufficiency, and commitment that "The Secret Sharer" was created in an access of oversimplification and escapism. The novel does not appear to be nearly so resonant as the short story and has, perhaps for this reason, seemed to many readers a less original and significant vision of sharing; but in its own more intricately symbolic manner, *Under Western Eyes* considers the consequences of that sharing with far more honesty and penetration than the glamorous example of Leggatt can stimulate. "The Secret Sharer" is in many ways more richly imagined, but its widely advertised recognition cannot compete with the macabre tenacity and somber wealth of the novel.

There are many phrases in *Under Western Eyes* that invite the reader to guess when Conrad's mind may have returned briefly to some of the Bangkok feelings or when he may have had first intimations that the well-known story of the *Cutty Sark* and second mate John Anderson could enrich the motif of sympathetic identification. Leo Gurko points out the line which says of Razumov, "He was as lonely in the world as a man swimming in the deep sea" (p. 10); [3] and I am fond of Razumov's reaction to the portly feminist, Peter Ivanovich, after they have left Madame de S——'s salon and have talked in the hall for some time: "He felt, bizarre as it may seem, as though another self, an independent sharer of his mind, had been able to view his whole person very distinctly indeed" (p. 230). But these are at best suppositions about an affinity that needs no such fragile evidence. Razumov, like our captain, discovers a totally unexpected visitor who raises the twin questions of identity and community. The texture of both these opening scenes is remarkably similar: both visitors have committed a crime and have appeared before our heroes almost fortuitously — Leggatt because he must rest for a moment and has seen the ladder, Haldin because the watchman at the lumberyard had been unable to bear his haunted "ugly eyes." Of course, there are more substantial reasons for Haldin's choice of Razumov, but that "confidence" is built on little more tangible evidence than is Leggatt's quickly felt confidence in the captain. Both encounters are meant to suggest the inevitability of this demand on human nature: the sense in which most of us will be called on to "share" for markedly less valid reasons than we should have liked or expected. Peculiarly, the fact that neither of these visitors has what might ordinarily be called a good claim on our heroes becomes a compelling part of their claim.

Their crimes, too, are not really so different, although Leggatt's impulse has been made almost attractive. Razumov detests chaotic upheaval perpetrated in the name of democracy, but he is devoted to a centrally guided evolution toward a more just society, and he certainly agrees that Mr. de P. was a beast. Thus Haldin's crime is sufficiently marginal for Razumov to feel the need to think, " 'For it is a crime,' he was saying to himself. 'A murder is a murder. Though of course some sort of liberal institutions . . .' " (p. 26). Rather than wonder about the correctness of calling Haldin's act a crime, however, Razumov spends most of his time insisting that the real crime is Haldin's attempt to involve him in that act. Neither Razumov nor the captain in "The Secret Sharer" can believe that a murder, simply and without qualification, is a murder; any such oversimplification kills the moral life of both stories. In both confrontations, then, there is a marginally criminal act to be shared despite great dangers to the captain and to Razumov. Interestingly, although the captain shares the crime and Razumov refuses to, both decisions tend to evoke the same human issues.

The problem of sympathy in both stories involves each hero's conceptions of his own identity. The captain shares Leggatt's marginally criminal act and thereby seems able to recreate and fulfill a self-image — not, of course, the simplistic one he brought on board. In *Under Western Eyes* Conrad spends what is even for him an unusual amount of time suggesting Razumov's difficulties with identity. He is the illegitimate son of Prince K——, and that fact shapes the very mode of his thought and of his first anxiety after leaving Haldin in his room. Haldin says he has chosen Razumov partly because Razumov has no family that might be involved and hurt: "The peculiar circumstances of Razumov's parentage, or rather of his lack of parentage, should be taken into the account of his thoughts. And he remembered them too. He had been lately reminded of them in a peculiarly atrocious way by this fatal Haldin. 'Because I haven't that, must everything else be taken away from me?' he thought" (p. 26).

Even though he turns eventually to Prince K——, he at first feels there is nowhere to go, no home to run to: "Other men had somewhere a corner of the earth — some little house in the provinces where they had a right to take their troubles" (p. 32). Razumov continually reminds himself and others that his name — which translated suggests "man of reason" — is no name, that there are figuratively and literally no Razumovs, no men of reason in Russia, and certainly no relatives for him. He draws a tragic conclusion from these facts: identity must come not from the bare acknowledgment given him by Prince K——, but from his mother, Russia herself, and from nowhere else. His first real awareness of this goal has ominous overtones. Having said that there is for him nowhere to run, he asks:

To whom could he go with this tale — in all this great, great land?

Razumov stamped his foot — and under the soft carpet of snow felt the hard ground of Russia, inanimate, cold, inert, like a sullen and tragic mother hiding her face under a winding-sheet — his native soil! his very own — without a fireside, without a heart! (Pp. 32–33)

This mother will be cold and tragic, offering an illusory quest for an identity that cannot be achieved — as *Nostromo* suggested it could not — solely between a man and an abstraction.

Much later, having told Peter Ivanovich that he has "no name," Razumov retraces his early argument with equal anxiety:

"The very patronymic you are so civil as to use when addressing me I have no legal right to — but what of that? I don't wish to claim it. I have no father. So much the better. But I will tell you what: my mother's grandfather was a peasant — a serf. See how much I am one of *you*. I don't want any one to claim me. But Russia *can't* disown me. She cannot!"

Razumov struck his breast with his fist. "I am it!" (Pp. 208–9)

Razumov is partly tailoring his remarks to what he imagines is the great feminist's egalitarian bias (in this assumption about Peter he is wrong), but he is nonetheless still seeking his mother with tragic intensity. Like Peter (p. 211) and even Natalia Haldin (pp. 104–6) — each in a different way — he believes in what may be called a transcendent Russia. This mystique of Mother Russia annoys him in others, especially when it implies a faith in the noble peasant and in the collective will of the people; but he is himself devoted — as Mrs. Hay points out — to a variety of the Holy Russia myth, of the belief that Russia alone among nations has a messianic destiny. Razumov believes that the authority and power of the single great ruler must be preserved for the day when it will be necessary to that messianic role, to the mystical unity which, as Natalia Haldin suggests, will transcend the democracy achieved by the artificial conflict of equally artificial political parties. Even today the monolithic Russian Communist party is forever comparing itself favorably with the allegedly phony conflict of Western parties, thus echoing the idea of mystical unity that permeates most Russians, revolutionaries *and* autocrats, portrayed in this novel. So strong is this sense of Russia as his parent, that we are told of Razumov: "Whatever good he expected from life would be given to or withheld from his hopes by that connexion alone. This immense parentage suffered from the throes of internal dissensions, and he shrank mentally from the fray as a good-natured man may shrink from taking definite sides in a violent family quarrel" (p. 11).

In giving these Russians distinctly national characteristics, Conrad does not mean to suggest that they have no more than secondary problems of identity. On the contrary, their national psychology — which the Western teacher of languages is forever trying to summarize — provides only the peculiar materials with which they are destined to work, the ethnic assumptions upon which the painfully achieved individual identity must be erected. Now Razumov is indeed partly victimized by a "violent family quarrel" which tears apart the source of his identity. All the other Russians in the novel more or less rely on the mystique of Holy Russia for their identity, but none so directly as Razumov and none as a would-be man of reason tragically seeking support for that ambition in a country and within an inherited psychology defined by mystical irrationality. Much like Conrad, Razumov apparently wants a constitutional hereditary monarchy in which the rule of law and the will of the leading figures are indistinguishably just. What he gets, however, is the trap between an autocracy and a revolution that are equally arbitrary and violent. He is to be ground between these millstones because, psychological and biological orphan that he is, there is as he conceives of the dilemma nowhere else to turn. The reader can agree with Conrad and the "Western eyes" that Razumov's hopes for a rational, central will to shape Russia are contrary to the mystical irrationality of that land and to the deepest reality of Razumov's own character.

Razumov's quest for a genuine name is illuminated by a similar problem in Madame de S——'s *dame de compagnie*, Tekla. When Razumov meets her and, after a frank conversation, asks her name, she replies that no one is told her name: "No one cares. No one talks to me, no one writes to me. My parents don't even know if I'm alive. I have no use for a name, and I have almost forgotten it myself" (p. 235). Then, alluding once more to the suffering of her poor lover Andrei years earlier, she says:

"That is the lot of all us Russians, nameless Russians. There is nothing else for us, and no hope anywhere, unless . . ."

"Unless what?"

"Unless all these people with names are done away with," she finished, blinking and pursing up her lips. (P. 236)

One is reminded of Madame de S——'s insistence that there is only one family in Russia that must be extirpated. Such is the problem of identity when reduced and simplified, as Razumov never can reduce and simplify it, to revolutionary ardor: some names eliminated, other blanks assume their rightful identities. Hearing the thoughts of the arbitrarily named Tekla ("You may call me Tekla, then") and of Madame de S—— only serves to remind us how subtly different Razumov's related problem is.

Razumov's sense that his identity can only come from Russia herself makes him peculiarly vulnerable to Haldin's visit. The Russia Razumov must depend on is not the magnificently rational will he would like, but a quixotic autocracy that will fit him into its side or the other and admit nothing in between. Indeed the behavior demanded of Razumov by the state is much more like the relations between actual sons and parents than is the ideal fantasy Razumov imagines. Can Mother Russia be both rational and loving? Isn't love by its very nature irrational, categorical, and inflexible? Razumov's metaphor for his relations with the state is confused, for he wants parental warmth along with the rational objectivity necessary to a man of reason. It is only by understanding the contradictions in this metaphor, it seems to me, that we may equally grasp the sense in which betraying Haldin was, as Razumov finally says, betraying himself.

What Haldin wants Razumov to sympathize with (at least so far as to help his escape) is mystical, revolutionary ardor. Razumov too has his own version of the Holy Russia mystique, but Haldin's visit precipitates in Razumov certain idealistic, conservative principles that — albeit they are partly inspired by fear of official punishment and rejection — are peculiarly his and not genuinely the spirit of either side in this war of attrition. It would have required an automaton with no problems of identity to have recognized the diabolical dilemma thus presented by Haldin's visit, and to have sought the neutrality of refusing both aid and betrayal.

Indeed the situation—considering the myopic zeal of both auto-cratic state and revolutionaries—does not admit of neutrality: in-action will be interpreted as action, and neutrality will seem hostile to both sides. Razumov considers this practical fact, and there is consequently a good deal of rationalization in the assertion that he is after all opposed to everything Haldin represents and basi-cally in agreement with the state.

But we must not conclude, as Leo Gurko does, that Razumov betrays Haldin out of "pure self-love," or, as Mrs. Hay does, that "Razumov never felt simple remorse for having sent a fellow mor-tal to death, for this kind of contrition was always overshadowed by an insistence in his mind on the criminality of Haldin's ac-tions." [4] The two views are extreme in opposite directions: the one gives the betrayal no coloring of moral integrity, the other, too much. There is so much selfish rationalization in Razumov's sud-denly intensified conservatism that we can hardly accept it at face value, and elsewhere in her scholarly chapter on this novel Mrs. Hay seems not to want us to do anything of the sort. On the other hand, Razumov's rationalization is surely built on the moral con-viction that throwing bombs into crowds of innocent people for the sake of killing one beast is wrong, and that anarchy is never a justifiable means to an end. The reasons for Razumov's growing sense of guilt are elusive at best; the man himself resorts to a vo-cabulary of supernatural influences in order to explain what is happening to him toward the end of the novel.

We need not speak of "devils," however, to understand that he has betrayed himself by accepting, partly for selfish reasons to be sure, an autocratic role that is no more satisfactory morally than the revolutionary violence he deplores. Morally isolated (as he is often described) he intrinsically lies between the categorically re-pressive autocracy, symbolized by the eyes of General T——, and Haldin's bomb throwing; in aiding Haldin he would have betrayed himself fully as much as he has by reporting to the police that far more disturbing version of Leggatt. Razumov finally recognizes that the ideal evolutionary course is impossible in Russia and per-haps also in the psychology he as a Russian has inherited. The tragedy of autocratic repression breeding revolutionary violence (which inspires even worse repression) is perhaps only accounted for by the mystically irrational faith in Holy Russia that remarkably enough inspires both sides.

It is not, however, entirely clear to Razumov just what he has helped murder in Haldin until he experiences the purity of Natalia's heart and of her faith in the messianic destiny of Russia. The mystique that has moved Haldin to murder innocent people has equally had its part — along with self-love — in making Razumov a deadly police spy, whose business it is to parade an identity he does not have. It is only after seeing what he can sink to, despite the nobility of his mystical faith in Russia, that Razumov can understand the equal — but no more than equal — corruption of Haldin. We are led to believe that Natalia can remain pure because upon her return to Russia she seeks not political action but the relief of the suffering. The implication surely is that anybody in turn-of-the-century Russia who tries to take political action in accordance with his noble ideals will — as Dr. Monygham in *Nostromo* reminds us about political action in general — stain those pure abstractions. Both sides, operating with a Holy Russia mystique that in many essentials they share, inevitably become brutal.

Haldin, then, has a significance to be shared which becomes clear only after Razumov has experienced a kind of Haldin purified in his sister. These are the "twins" necessary to the themes of *Under Western Eyes*. Further, although he rejects Haldin, Razumov finally sees that he too has spawned evil from a tragically noble assumption about Russia's destiny. Razumov even admits that of the two paths, his and Haldin's, the revolutionaries have the better claim to "right": "After all, it is they and not I who have the right on their side! — theirs is the strength of invisible powers" (p. 361). This is a puzzling statement, but whatever else it may be it is not, in context, at all ironic. A revolutionary such as Haldin (and despite what many critics have said, even Madame de S—— and Peter are better than their obvious self-contradictions would imply) had at least not severed himself from the power of his original mystical insight. But Razumov, choosing finally to be "independent" (p.

362) of either side, has cut himself off from the passionate sanctions which allow feelings of right and wrong. What Razumov is now doing he cannot call right any more than he can use his irrational faith in the future of Russia as a justification for his new independence. Ultimately he finds the limbo not of those who refuse to take sides but of those who have imaginatively taken too many. Simple justification by invisible powers, the sort of faith and right that distinguishes the two young Haldins, is not now available to him. His increasing powers of sympathy — especially an understanding through Natalia of her brother — have freed him not for the guilty torment of one who has betrayed another human being, but for the ultimate moral isolation of a man overcome by the tragic view of this Russian dilemma.

To see the disastrous consequences of nearly all the action a man might attempt in this tragic impasse (be he revolutionary, autocrat, or a Razumov trying rationally to believe in the irrationally "perfect plant") is to flirt with a paralysis inherent in the tragic view. From the spiritual exhaustion of that vantage point, the faith, action, and moral absolutism of such people as Sophia and Mikulin, revolutionaries and autocrats, is the very breath of life. Razumov warns Natalia in his final message that having called the revolutionaries right, in the sense I have tried to establish, he has not, however, been converted. Is he then ignobly indifferent to the claims of either side? "Have I then the soul of a slave? No! I am independent — and therefore perdition is my lot" (p. 362). The tragic view is the price of that independence, and its symbol in this novel is the isolation of deafness. As we have of late been told in innumerable spy stories, the tragedy of human affairs is nowhere so apparent as to the double agent, the man who in exploiting human loyalties loses his soul.

What may have begun as something of an indictment of Russia, develops in *Under Western Eyes* into an extraordinary further view of sympathy. Because he is an extremely complex hero, Razumov is not basically approved or disapproved for his original betrayal of Haldin or for his confession to Natalia and to the assembled revolutionaries. He is, rather, a paradigm of all the ironies inherent in the kinds of sympathetic sharing so prominent in Conrad's work from the beginning. We can occasionally say that what he has done is better or worse than what he might have done, but such judgments on the part of Conrad and the reader do not discover the true moral importance of a character like Razumov. Conrad has poured into him all the frustrations, all the sense of dilemma confronting a man who must settle the claims of his independence against the claims of human community. Some readers may feel that all Razumov's problems stem from the unique social and political problems of Russia: but Russia, by the end of the novel, had itself become symbolic of the inevitably unsatisfying and possibly tragic nature of the call to human community, of the unwanted visitor waiting in one's room or in the sea next to one's ship. For many men, certainly for Conrad, there is an inevitable conflict between one's own ideal self-image and the social reality in which that image must be made to take shape and substance. Razumov, we may say, never has a chance to achieve the rational identity and the evolutionism he set up as an ideal for himself and for Russia. He says at one point that he *is* Russia; but he and the reader become quite aware that, although he shares Russia's fatal mysticism, Razumov despises it as much as he embodies it. So acute is his lack of identity that he must identify with Mother Russia even though he abhors the essence of that national psychology.

But is this dilemma (the need to identify with a community that characteristically frustrates one's ideal self-image) really unique to Russia? It seems obvious that Conrad has again rendered the dilemma that touches so many of his sympathetic characters: to move toward some form or sense of human solidarity is unsatisfactory; not to do so is worse. To admit, for example, that Lord Jim is "one of us" is terribly disturbing; to suggest on the contrary that his problem is unique is no better than a subtle form of savagery. Razumov too is one of us, just as Russia is suggestive of a human dilemma that is far from limited to the special agony of that giant.

The demonstration in *The Shadow Line* of a man's dependence upon human community for his own sense of self-possession is facile compared with *Under Western Eyes*. Such dependence is for

Razumov a richly tragic necessity, not only because he is the natural son of Prince K—— and emotionally alone in the world (Conrad has, after all, given him that position for symbolic purposes), but because Razumov feels the pull of human solidarity as surely as those in whom he initially mocks the sentiment, in Haldin and Natalia for the most part. As I have said, his faith in the destiny of Russia is no less than Natalia's, though he would not sentimentalize the alleged blood-wisdom of the peasant. We have seen Conrad try to make other of his heroes feel some form of human community as an imperative, but seldom have the details of the character's background been arranged to suggest the paradox seen with such clarity in *Under Western Eyes*: that Razumov must identify with a nation whose mystical essence precisely denies his aspiration to be a reasonable man.

It is not only Razumov Conrad is talking about, not only the Russian who has no parents and no authentic name. If Conrad's work — especially *Nostromo* — has established anything, it must be that many of us really have no name, that most of us are in one way or another somebody else's man, and that self-possession, while it is the only source of value in an absurd universe or at least in a cosmos where man has only an absurd role, depends almost mystically on a sense of human solidarity. Almost regardless of how any single reader interprets the details of this relationship between self-discovery and human solidarity in *Under Western Eyes*, we can agree that what may seem to be the special circumstances of Razumov's birth and Russia's national soul are really symbolic of our common experience.

The principal ironic symbol of this strange relationship between self-discovery and community is Rousseau's island and statue in Geneva, where Razumov goes to write his first secret letter to Mikulin in Russia and to compose his diary (p. 316). The allusion to Rousseau here is not, as one critic has suggested, important because of that philosopher's emphasis on emotion and sentiment (in contrast to Razumov's would-be rationality) but because he is the author, as Conrad specified, of the *Social Contract*. That no such rational, contractual ties between a man and human community are true to our experience is a large part of Conrad's point in this novel. He may have been familiar in detail with Rousseau's recommendations to the government of Poland for a constitutional monarchy; but we may be sure that his understanding of the *Social Contract* was vividly colored by Rousseau's reputation as the father of the French Revolution and of political freedom in general, and that he saw Rousseau as the son of Geneva, that dull, complacently rational denial of all that was passionate and mystical in Conrad's own, his father's, and Razumov's social experience.

Of course, Rousseau's own use of the ancient idea of social contract is not so patently rational as Conrad might have supposed. Like so much of the essay *Social Contract*, it is dependent on the nearly mystical idea of the general will and is used to express not an historical fact but a moral judgment about what the source of political authority *ought* to be. Further, the idea of the contract in that essay is distinctly something that Rousseau has inherited from many earlier writers, a container for ideas that ultimately transcend the legalistic fiction of contractual association. To Conrad, however, the relation of a man to the state and to the various other forms of human community was, unlike Rousseau's vision and Conrad's own in *The Shadow Line*, tragic, paradoxical, and no less mystical than the Holy Russia enthusiasm he finds in autocrat and revolutionary. It must be remembered that Conrad's own father was a zealous believer in the messianic destiny of Poland and that Conrad himself believed in the charisma of national identity. The value he saw in individual ego has its counterpart in the national identity tested by a thousand years of history; one always suspects that he associated the selflessness of Buddhistic or Schopenhauerian withdrawal with the specious "brotherhood" of international socialism. Thus Conrad often felt and spoke of various nations as having a "purpose" to fulfill; and in doing so he does not make the error of Holroyd in *Nostromo*, confusing the secular and the sacred. Nations can, for Conrad, be sacred associations, largely because they bear (with, he felt, the conspicuous exception of the United States) the stamp of compelling traditions to an even greater extent than the crew of a ship at sea.

Viewed unsympathetically, Rousseau seemed to imagine the individual relinquishing his natural state of freedom for the greater security and largely material advantages of society. What Conrad, after his experience in the Congo and after being for years the subtle artist of the primitive mind, may have thought of such speculations about the natural state, I can leave to your comic imagination. The importance of Rousseau's statue and island in *Under Western Eyes* turns more precisely on what must have seemed to Conrad the suggestion that the metaphor of contract expressed adequately the relations of an individual and society. Razumov is born Russian; his desire for rationality is hence a veneer covering inadequately an inner mysticism. Russia is his mother, whether he likes it or not. Contrary to Rousseau's warning in the *Social Contract* that relations between an individual and the state are not familial, Conrad seems to feel that they are, in an almost Freudian sense of intensely patterned love and resentment. And as with a family, the individual is born in a society, is at once a part of it, learns what is expected of him and that, again as with a family, those expectations are largely irrational claims on his private sense of wholeness and purpose. He may even come to see that paradoxically his sense of private identity is more dependent on a community of men than he would like to admit — as a son, having spent years protecting an identity from his father, may suddenly discover that he is nonetheless his father's son.

Razumov attempts to refuse the often irrational claims that community, or even only an implicit sense of human solidarity, makes upon individuals. It is no accident that while he is on Rousseau's island Conrad says of him: "And it occurred to him that this was about the only sound [the current breaking against the point of the island] he could listen to innocently, and for his own pleasure, as it were. Yes, the sound of water, the voice of the wind — completely foreign to human passions. All the other sounds of this earth brought contamination to the solitude of a soul" (p. 291).

Razumov would like to make some sort of rational contract with society, with Russia. But he cannot have it both ways: if Russia is his mother, one does not make contracts with mothers or fathers

or, in general, one's own blood. Once involved with the bureau-
cratic apparatus because of his reporting Haldin, Razumov has no
choice but to cooperate with official desires; he can only rationalize that he favors such central authority in any event. But he cannot himself accept the irrational claim society makes on autocrat
and revolutionary alike in this novel until he has experienced an
equally irrational love for Natalia. After confessing to her and free-
ing himself from his imitations of allegiance to both sides, he can
accept his own tragic independence and acknowledge that, if there
is no satisfactory response to his nation, there are nevertheless re-
sponses which have a profound claim on his sympathy. He cannot
want to remain a government spy, he cannot want to become a
revolutionary, but he can admit the authenticity of the passionate,
irrational claims human community may have on a man even when
it offers him nothing but a tragic dilemma of anarchy and autocratic repression.

It has been said that *Under Western Eyes* fails because Conrad
could never sympathetically understand the revolutionary state of
mind. But it seems to me that not only in Sophia, Tekla, Natalia,
and Haldin, but often in Peter as well, Conrad is anything but pa-
tronizing; so too the autocratic Mikulin is shown to have achieved
humanity partly through his irrational loyalty to the very system
that tries and kills him. We can approach our humanity through
what might coldly be called error; and for that we ought to be
thankful since, if our membership in the human race were measured by the correctness of our beliefs and action, we should all
be lost. In this sense Razumov's betrayal of Haldin may be seen as
a fortunate fall. It is only when one's beliefs are essentially what
Saint Paul called "fences" designed to isolate us in self-love — as
Madame de S——'s clearly are for the most part — that Conrad disapproves on the most profound moral level.

Frederick Karl argues that Sophia's later sympathetic visits to
Razumov in Russia (where he is deaf, ill, and cared for by the ir-
repressible Tekla) are incredible and a flaw in the novel:

That Sophia Antonovna, an ardent revolutionary, and her comrades
would visit the counter-agent Razumov after he has admitted be-

traying Haldin and spying on them, is, in the sequence of the novel, impossible to believe. When she goes on to praise Razumov's character in glowing terms, she destroys the illusion of the revolutionaries as a serious group and reduces them to ridiculous actors in a make-believe drama. If Conrad has succeeded in making his revolutionaries seem ridiculous, then Razumov's feelings of guilt, along with his dramatic self-effacement in their presence, all becomes meaningless. If they are contemptible one may ask how can they be Haldin's heritage? [5]

Karl errs here because he has earlier in his discussion of the novel mistaken the nature of Razumov's victory: "Then he . . . recognizes that Haldin is sincere and that the police and the General are despicable — he senses that Haldin's sympathies should have been his." [6] Razumov, however, does not feel he has been wrong in betraying Haldin, although inevitably a certain amount of guilt attaches to the deed. Far from being converted to Haldin's sympathies, he himself denies any such conversion in his final letter to Natalia. Razumov has, rather, lost his pride in nearly the way that tragic heroes traditionally lose it, though he is unable to grow spiritually on the basis of that newfound sympathy. Sophia can visit Razumov as she does because her sympathetic powers — her role as an individual who refuses sterile hate and has earlier reminded Razumov of his failure to love — are just as important as any simple revolutionary identification.

In a letter to Mrs. Garnett dated October 20, 1911, the same day he had written angrily to her husband protesting that *Under Western Eyes* was certainly not full of "hatred" — Conrad admits that he knows "extremely little of Russians":

Practically nothing. In Poland we have nothing to do with them. One knows they are there. And that's disagreeable enough. In exile the contact is even slighter if possible if more unavoidable. I crossed the Russian frontier at the age of ten. Not having been to school then I never knew Russian. I could not tell a Little Russian from a Great Russian to save my life. In the book as you must have seen I am exclusively concerned with ideas. [7]

He had told Edward Garnett that he was in this novel interested only in "ideas, to the exclusion of everything else, with no *arrière*

*pensée* of any kind." All his comments in these two important letters suggest that he was warning his friends against making the
novel too much a special study of a unique nation. Sophia, for instance, cannot be properly understood as merely a Russian revolutionary, any more than Razumov's final decision can be seen to
confirm an awareness that "Haldin's sympathies should have been
his." Dwelling upon the Russian and the revolutionary identity of
Sophia will indeed make it hard to accept her visits to Razumov,
just as a preoccupation with choosing sides between the best of the
revolutionaries and the worst of the repressive autocrats (the general) will tempt the reader to see Razumov's two confessions as
guilt for betraying the "right" side. Actually both confessions expiate the far more disturbing sin of refusing sympathy for the compelling demands of human community and for seeking the rational
contract that Razumov uselessly dreams about. His original judgment of Haldin is changed only in a peculiar way: he still feels as
strongly as ever that Haldin had been disastrously wrong, but now
is able to sympathize with his error — an act of sympathetic power
that equals Marlow's best and is a triumph of its kind.

I do not mean that in *Under Western Eyes* Conrad has become
some kind of zealot advocating the honesty of violent emotions between country and individual. But he had abandoned many of his
somewhat easier visions of the relations between an individual and
the human community, and he had begun to lose the self-confident
irony that works so well the first time we see it sustained in *The
Secret Agent.* Jocelyn Baines's analysis of *Under Western Eyes*
treats many of Razumov's statements as though they were a con-
tinuation of the sardonic, continually evaluating author's voice introduced in that earlier political novel. Of course Razumov's list of
social maxims might have been Conrad's, and Razumov's judgment
of the revolutionaries (with the exception of Sophia) is very close
to the position we easily infer from much of Conrad's work. But
in *Under Western Eyes* Conrad eventually begins to separate himself from Razumov's assumptions; there is from the outset something quite wrong about the conservatism that becomes an excuse
for avoiding love, for scorning the passionate, if misguided, enthu-

siasm of one human being for the soul of another, as when Kostia steals his father's money (at great emotional expense) so that Razumov can throw it out the train window, thinking with unpardonable sarcasm, "For the people" (p. 315). In fact, a great deal of the moral certainty Conrad had felt in his politics disappears in *Under Western Eyes*, which is in that sense scarcely a political novel at all. The use to which Razumov puts his Conradian conservatism is repugnant — until Natalia, oddly confirming at least a fragment of Peter's easily despised feminism, awakens in Razumov a capacity for love and community far more important than the quality of his political beliefs.

The "Western eyes" which read and see Razumov's story may originally have been part of Conrad's desire to show a chasm between Western psychology and its resultant political systems and the unique Russian dilemma. But slowly it becomes apparent both that the West provides no lofty moral plateau from which Russia can be scorned for its errors and that Razumov's original unsympathetic sterility is a moral issue far from being explained by even the enormous differences between Russia and the West. The special conditions in Russia allowed Conrad to exaggerate and confront questions about the relation of self-discovery and human solidarity that he was sometimes tempted, especially later in *The Shadow Line*, to make less mysterious and tragic than they are. Russia itself, however, had in a sense liberated his imagination and become not a political subject but one of the potent symbols in his late work.

Razumov's problem of identity and its symptom, his constant difficulty with names and naming, suggests how close *Under Western Eyes* is to *Nostromo* in this regard. A study could be made of Conrad's preoccupation with names and naming, but it would in any event conclude that Marlow's "mine is the speech . . ." in *Heart of Darkness* is seminal. How is Razumov to justify his name, finally, except by the kind of responsibility Marlow affirms in Kurtz? Like Charles Gould and Lord Jim, Razumov would like to be irrevocable; his desire to be at one with the very earth of his Russia bears some of the ominous implications suggested by the silver in *Nostromo*. Although it is clear that these potent metaphors are not so active in *Under Western Eyes* as they had been in the great triad, still it is interesting that Conrad could not face passionately this issue of the relation between self-possession and community without at least feeling himself in their presence. The symbolic implications of so much in *Under Western Eyes* take us back almost unconsciously to Nostromo mulling over the implications of his acquired name, to Lord Jim in a pseudosympathic gesture to Gentleman Brown that is nearly the antithesis of Razumov's final state of mind, to Marlow's comment on Kurtz's name, and so on. The affinity is there in *Under Western Eyes* but not, I think, in "The Secret Sharer." And the reason is that "The Secret Sharer" deliberately shuts off these metaphors in favor of another that despite superficial resemblances is really not much like them — no more than Freud or Schopenhauer is like Kierkegaard or Sartre.

The problem of human association and community is, however, very much before Conrad at this time in his life, and it is probably inevitable that having finished *Under Western Eyes*, which does not bring directly to bear on the problem the existential insights of earlier years, he would eventually proceed to a novel some of whose characters are overtly suffering from the metaphysical view that led Conrad to visions of nothingness. True, the metaphysics of the two Heysts in *Victory* is a pale reflection of the intensely dramatized existential issues raised in Lord Jim, Marlow, Kurtz, Charles Gould, and Nostromo. But we have clearly, in *Victory*, returned with a vengeance to one question that has always been implicit in Conrad's existential view: can there be any impulse toward community in a man suffering from such metaphysical anguish? In a sense, *Victory* is an exhausted, shorthand approach to creating the man himself, the hero who is articulately aware of the Pascalian middle position and who, like Axël, seems able only to abandon mankind under the pressure of that awareness. *Under Western Eyes*, though it is a passionate and complex affirmation of the impulse toward community, does not imagine that impulse for all men. May we say, then, that *Under Western Eyes* had not even imagined that impulse for a man like Conrad?

# 9

# Renewed Existential Models: *Victory*

$W$e know that when Conrad presented the finished manuscript of *Under Western Eyes* to J. B. Pinker, the literary agent who had advanced him modest sums of money since handling "Typhoon" in 1901, the two men for some reason quarreled bitterly, and Conrad went home to a physical and nervous breakdown lasting well into the year 1910. Jessie Conrad said of this period, "There is the MS complete but uncorrected and his fierce refusal to let even I touch it. It lays on a table at the foot of his bed and he lives mixed up in the scenes and holds converse with the characters."[1] This hallucinatory anguish was for Conrad something of a watershed, on the other side of which lay *Chance* and success, money at long last and popular recognition. Unlike many of his earlier heroes' exercises in what Irving Howe has called "order and responsibility, restraint and decorum, fortitude and endurance," *Under Western Eyes* had been a Dionysian vision of man and society that passionately resolved logical contradictions in Razumov's tragically sympathetic intuition. Razumov's is a purification of sympathy that approaches tragic recognition, while in *Chance* and *Victory* sympathy very nearly remains in its lowest form, pity — that of Captain Anthony for Flora and, in *Victory*, of Axel Heyst for the entire world of action and aspiration.

The Dionysian symbol of Russia seemed to work on Conrad in ways that may have taxed his reason no less than Pinker's apparent blow to his identity. Irving Howe has said that

the claim sometimes made for Conrad, that these attitudes [of a stoical dedication to "order and responsibility, restraint and decorum, fortitude and endurance"] lead to a redeeming vision of solidarity, must be sharply discounted. Conrad reaches for such a vision and believes in its necessity, but it is almost never found, and in his political novels, those terrible surveys of desolation, it never is found. For Dostoevsky human life is always drenched with terror, yet men turn to each other for comfort and support; in Conrad the terror is also there, but each man must face it alone and the only solidarity is a solidarity of isolated victims.[2]

But in *Under Western Eyes* Conrad has given us a tragic affirmation of human community that comes not from what Howe sees as Conrad's need to control a devastating skepticism but from the vital depths of his sense of man's absurdity. In Conrad's work it is often true that the assertion of human solidarity is an official view which covers and controls the anarchic truth; but in this novel he had achieved a sense of that solidarity just as ineluctably passionate and free as Howe feels the forces of dissolution always are in Conrad's work. We can expect no such affirmation in *Victory* despite its title. Yet the two novels are closely related.

In Axel Heyst, Conrad once again plays upon the Schopenhauerian background he had so often used as a stimulus to his own original attitudes; he sets out to refute a variety of skepticism that is unmistakably Schopenhauerian. As I suggested briefly in my first chapter, Conrad's Axel is a conscious reflection of a play he must surely have heard of after its 1894 production in Paris: Villiers de L'Isle-Adam's *Axël*. Although we may disagree about how directly details of the novel suggest the play, there can be no doubt that Heyst's skepticism is "metaphysical" in the sense I have established earlier in discussing Schopenhauer — and that the escape from life in *Axël* is dictated by a precisely Schopenhauerian fear of the insatiable will. Since the will in its more idealistic "ideas," or "representations" as one translator calls them, can never be satisfied by "real" life or even by actual human relations, Axël and Sara achieve through suicide what has been called a victory over the two illusions, wealth and carnal love. Unlike Schopenhauer, however, Villiers welcomes suicide as a means of escaping will. The Rosicrucian magic both Axël and Sara profess is indeed the mysticism described in *fin-de-siècle* terms by Stanislas de Guaïta's 1885 preface to his poems, *Rosa Mystica*: "Mysticism? It is the love of our hearts for the dreams of our brains; it is what makes the vulgar hate us, what makes us into outlaws!" [3]

Heyst claims that his reasons for abandoning what we ordinarily think of as life are purely rational, based on the irrefutable logic of his father's demonstrations and his own experience with Morrison. As Conrad never tires of reminding us, however, "the use of reason is to justify the obscure desires that move our conduct, impulses, passions, prejudices and follies, and also our fears" (p. 83). Even a boy who, at age eighteen, is subjected to three years of the "pitiless cold blasts of his father's analysis" (p. 92) does not reach the decision to drift, to disengage from life, solely as an intellectual matter. We have a clue to the emotional quality of this decision in the line, "for the son of his father there was no other worthy alternative" (p. 92). Or, more precisely, after his father's death:

He became aware of his eyes being wet. It was not that the man was his father. For him it was purely a matter of hearsay which could not in itself cause this emotion. No! It was because he had looked at him so long that he missed him so much. The dead man had kept him on the bank by his side. And now Heyst felt acutely that he was alone on the bank of the stream. In his pride he determined not to enter it. (Pp. 175–76)

But more than pride is involved, for Heyst's father had warned him that even "flesh and blood" were not to be believed in and that a form of contempt for man, pity, was the only legitimate attitude. A son who is thus warned by his own father not to believe even in that paternal flesh and blood has been emotionally alienated at the outset (p. 174). Too proud or perhaps wounded to embrace a man

who had refused that allegiance, Heyst is humble enough never to
forget that, as his father had said, he too is as pitiful as the rest. But
it is the way in which his ego becomes involved in this apparent
humility that holds the key to transcending pity, changing it into
sympathy and finally love.

Heyst's relations with his father had, as Conrad insists, taught
him emotionally that if he is to retain a sense of worth and dignity,
the rest of mankind must be shown to be no better than he, worthy
of no more than pity. He must accept his father's philosophy in
order to explain or to understand imaginatively the coldness of
that parental relationship. He has, in short, an egoistic stake in remaining aloof; his thoughts late in the novel are permeated with
the sense that he is inadequate, that he cannot offer enough to war-
rant the love of Lena and Morrison. (Some critics, Guerard included, have speculated about sexual inadequacy, though I see neither a thematic need nor evidence for such impotence.) Thus pity
has been a defense against discovering an emotional inadequacy at
least partly created, Conrad would have us believe, by his father's
behavior. Believing that pity is the only appropriate attitude
toward the world, one can safely pity oneself without learning the
true reason for that emotional disposition, without learning how
ego is involved in what purports to be a rational philosophy.

Like so many of Conrad's heroes, Heyst must become aware of
that ego involvement if he is genuinely to sympathize with and
eventually love another human being. So far as Morrison has been
concerned, Heyst has been more than able to carry his end of a human relationship. He rescues Morrison, becomes a partner, and
supports against the grain of his own temperament the wildest visions of the Tropical Belt Coal Company. But he has withheld exactly what his father has denied him, a genuine emotional risk that
he may in any event be incapable of. There is a marvelous irony in
his conversation with Lena about Schomberg's accusations (p.
211). Heyst is indignant that Lena should even momentarily believe him capable of robbing and, in effect, of murdering Morrison.
She insists that it was not actually murder Schomberg had alleged,
and Heyst replies that when Schomberg suggested he had de-

spoiled Morrison and sent him, a ruined man, to die of a cold in England, he had described something worse than murder. "As to killing a man, which would be a comparatively decent thing to do, well — I have never done that." This sentence is loaded with irony. Heyst is not quite aware that earlier in the conversation Lena has put her finger on just what in his behavior has been worse than murder — not Schomberg's fantasy of Heyst sending Morrison back to England a ruined man, but the absurdity implied in Heyst's description of his connection with the man:

"I have never been so amused as by that episode in which I was suddenly called to act such an incredible part. For a moment I enjoyed it greatly. I got him out of his corner, you know."

"You saved a man for fun — is that what you mean? Just for fun?" (P. 199)

Lena is understandably shocked. She too, after all, may then suggest that she has been saved "for fun." His tone remains disturbingly light, the rhetorical sign of his urbane skepticism. But he continues to betray the real horror of what he has done by asking her, with regard to his relations with Morrison, "The people in this part of the world went by appearances, and called us friends, as far as I can remember. Appearances — what more, what better can you ask for? In fact you can't have better. You can't have anything else" (p. 204). What is the "appearance" of his running off with Lena? He seems insensitive to the extrapolation Lena continually and with every right makes from Heyst's first fall to this, his second.

Those who doubt there is any artistic achievement in *Victory* would do well to examine this long conversation as a sustained exercise in irony. To my taste it reaches a peak in those comments by Heyst that some few critics use as evidence for his impotence: "No, I've never killed a man or loved a woman — not even in my thoughts, not even in my dreams." And: "To slay, to love — the greatest enterprises of life upon a man! And I have no experience of either" (p. 212). Even if Conrad had not meant to suggest that intercourse occurs during the interval between the conclusion of part three, section four, and the beginning of section five, these two comments are too good to waste on pseudopsychoanalytic guesses. The connection between murder and love that Conrad intended is that both may be saving involvements, and not, as Heyst implies despite the apparent note of regret in his voice, the principal candidates for his pity. As a kind of categorical imperative, there can be no doubt that Heyst's amusement at Morrison's belief in him is far worse than murder sprung from deep emotional commitments, even considering that Heyst is by no means prepared to disappoint Morrison. Thus Heyst's inability to attempt killing his three evil visitors is no moral recommendation, and Lena's stealing the knife (not merely to disarm Ricardo) has more than the sexual implications suggested by Thomas Moser.[4]

Throughout the conversation there are at least three layers of meaning, deriving from Lena's anxiety about Heyst's amusement in the Morrison affair, Heyst's obtuse fear and anger that she will simply believe some fragment of Schomberg's fantasy, and the haunting implication that Heyst by no means understands Lena's fear of his saving a man for fun. Nowhere in the conversation does he appreciate either the true source of Lena's anxiety or of his own inadequacy. Toward the end of part three, section four, "experiencing a closer communion than they had ever achieved before," he nevertheless feels a "sense of incompleteness not altogether overcome — which, it seemed, nothing ever would overcome — the fatal imperfection of all the gifts of life, which makes of them a delusion and a snare" (p. 212). Of course imperfection is not in the gift but in Heyst's reception of it.

Lena imagines that she is unworthy of Heyst; insofar as she can grasp his motives for refusing the world of involvement and action, she is unable to decide whether his subtle remoteness is due to the apparent fact that she has done little to earn his love or to the puzzling quality of mind and feeling revealed to her in his narration of the Morrison affair. Heyst, of course, considers that he has shown more feeling for her than for anyone else in his entire life: as late as the end of part three, section four, immediately before the arrival of the evil trio, he says, "I don't even understand what I have done or left undone to distress you like this." His idea of what constitutes love is so imperfect that he mistakes for genuine progress the slightest alteration of pity into sympathy. Conrad does not pretend to explain love, but so long as Heyst blames the nature of the world for the imperfection of his relations with Lena, there can be no awareness of his own ego involvement, no purification of sympathy, and certainly very little love. Heyst submerges his sense of unworthiness until it is far less apparent than Lena's, although in final view of her sacrifice Heyst's guilt will drive him to suicide. Had he been asked why he looks on life and makes no sound, Heyst could not until the very end of the novel have blamed the emotional crippling accomplished substantially by his father. In those relations with his son that the novel describes vividly if briefly, the old philosopher has seen — as we say — nothing personal; he feels no sense of having rejected the boy as his son, and would like Axel to feel that every detail of that remoteness has been dictated by intellectual conviction, by an accurate vision of an absurd universe where there can be no fulfillment and no authority.

The elder Heyst's last book claimed for mankind the "right to absolute moral and intellectual liberty of which he no longer believed them worthy" (p. 91). That liberty, however, suggests not only a social and political freedom that may be achieved and preserved with some difficulty, but the frightening contingency of man in a universe that has no moral plan, the irrevocable freedom of a creature who is, as both Heyst and his father agree, an "accident." The old philosopher's vision is thus not really Schopenhauerian (though his disengagement is made superficially to resemble that of Villiers's Axël and his personality that of Schopenhauer), because unlike Schopenhauer he cites no authority for any value except disengagement. Schopenhauer's metaphysics, with its dependence on will as the irreducible ontology of man, made the sympathetic penetration of maya, of appearance, a prime moral authority. To sympathize was the beginning of the truth that individual free choice was often merely appearance, that all life suffers together in the great will that transcends individuation. (I shall, however, need to say more about Schopenhauer's general effect on the idea of free will in my last chapter, while considering that giant ruin of the will metaphor, *The Rescue*.) From his metaphysics Schopenhauer had no difficulty deriving an ethics in which he could consider ascetic holiness and the appreciation of art (escapes from will) some sort of moral imperative. But Conrad could not, for reasons I have already discussed at some length, and the elder Heyst could not. The elder Heyst and Conrad share an existential fear and awareness that cannot be attributed to Schopenhauer in any sense.

What disturbs Conrad in the philosophy of the elder Heyst, however, is that he uses his knowledge of the truth about man's position in nature to deny life. On the contrary, Conrad himself has in some of his work shown signs that his metaphysical vision is reason enough to encourage the human creation of value, perhaps in defiance of an absurd universe. Marlow is morally awakened by Kurtz; in fact, though the effect of his godhead is terribly dangerous and possibly too dark altogether, the implication is that understanding the onslaught may provide the only unshakable basis for human value. The initiation may be worse than fatal, but if survived the reward is an entirely new sense of the need for human community and solidarity. In contrast, even Schopenhauer's "sympathy" seemed a withdrawal from life because of an overwhelming sense that no effort could escape the futility of will (and it is something like this pessimism that Conrad works into the character of both Heysts). Lena, of course, has no view of man's position in the universe; but plain Mr. Jones does, and we shall need to examine Jones and Heyst as counterparts shortly.

Heyst, unlike Conrad, never is able to use his father's metaphysics to justify engagement in life rather than withdrawal from it. He cannot reach such an awareness by intellectual means alone, and perhaps Conrad himself could not entirely; it is the emotional impact of Lena's sacrifice that moves Heyst and not any logical refutation of his father's pessimism. What has impelled him to aid Morrison is a mystery that Conrad associates with a complex reworking of the Eden myth. So many critics have discussed this aspect of the novel that I must be cautious not to claim originality for all my comments here. But no one has considered the fact or condition under which any interpretation of the Eden symbolism must operate: that this Adam and Eve, this serpent, this peculiar Eden, are all in Conrad's universe rather than the Old Testament's (and you can choose from a great variety even there) or Milton's. This means, for one thing, that the sense of evil must be carefully redefined, as must the whole conception of a fall.

Among the first substantial and rather awkward clues that Conrad intends to develop the Eden myth are Heyst's reflections at the beginning of part three as to why he had helped Morrison:

"There must be a lot of the original Adam in me, after all."
He reflected too, with the sense of making a discovery, that this primeval ancestor is not easily suppressed. The oldest voice in the world is just the one that never ceases to speak. If anybody could have silenced its imperative echoes, it should have been Heyst's father, with his contemptuous, inflexible negation of all effort; but apparently he could not. There was in the son a lot of that first ancestor who, as soon as he could uplift his muddy frame from the celestial mould, started inspecting and naming the animals of that paradise which he was so soon to lose. (Pp. 173–74)

The Adamic quality contains not only a taste for action but for involvement with other human beings and for giving names to things. Surely it is not coincidental that Lena has no name until Heyst gives "Lena" to her. She has been called by Zangiacomo's group Alma and Magdalen, both names undoubtedly meaning less to the reader than their portentous use might imply. Frederick Karl suggests that Alma is "soul" and that Heyst prevents Lena-Magdalen from becoming a prostitute—all of which is likely. But it is more interesting, it seems to me, to note that he does, Adam-like, name her, and to ask what this naming means to Conrad against the background of the same motif in so much of his earlier work. Heyst says at one point, after reiterating "he who forms a tie is lost," that nonetheless she "gave him a greater sense of his own reality than he had ever known in all his life." And Conrad ends the section with this thought.

What Heyst has begun dimly to perceive, Conrad means to sug-

gest as another part of the Adamic heritage: part of our instinct for
involvement with others is simply the egoistic urge better to identify ourselves. Our sense of identity depends as much, if not more,
on our giving "names" to others as on their "naming" us. The unity
and identification of self depends a good deal on our ability to
stimulate that same effect in others. In creating important aspects
of Lena, Heyst creates himself. ("Do you know, it seems to me,
somehow, that if you were to stop thinking of me I shouldn't be in
the world at all," she says [p. 187].) Perhaps there is no other
way. This may be one of the most primitive means by which man
is led to community: through his own egoistic desire to achieve
identity. (A number of biologists have recently begun to speculate
that the defense of territory in many species is also explained by
the need to achieve individual identity, and is indispensable to the
formation of what is called the "biological nation.") Thus we do
not ordinarily depend upon the threat of an indifferent universe to
stimulate solidarity in its defiance, but upon the *usually* reliable
power of self-love and a desire to feel that thrilling sense of our
own individual wholeness.

Heyst, then, is not only using Conrad's metaphysics to deny life
(which is bad enough), and is not only unable to see that the same
metaphysics may induce commitments and action and genuinely
heroic attempts to create human value in defiance of that universe:
he further denies or fails to understand the fullness of his own motives in aiding Morrison and Lena — to see, as I have already suggested, that his ego is involved in this pity, and that such involvement may be an innately human requirement of self-love.

Samburan does not look much like Eden, but the entire set of allusions to the Judeo-Christian myth is in any event meant to be
analogical and basically to reverse the key conception of that story.
Heyst and Lena are both innocent of what they have to learn
through the visit of evil — Heyst especially, in the sense I have suggested. But, again, it must be remembered that evil in the form of
Jones, Ricardo, and Pedro takes any definition it may have from
the metaphysics Conrad and both Heysts share. There is for Conrad precious little in his view of man's position in the cosmos that

a sensitive man may use to create his own morality. Similarly, given the elder Heyst's sense of man as an "accident" (p. 196), Axel can only conclude that behavior suggesting an ordained purpose for man (an "essence" in philosophic jargon) is dishonest and immoral. To refrain from action and commitment is, for Axel, consonant with the cosmic indifference he has felt. We may well wonder, without becoming positively psychoanalytic, whether it is not his father's indifference rather than a cosmic one that he feels and that he seeks to imitate in his relations with this world.

Heyst's heritage from Adam, his nature simply as a human being, runs quite contrary to the code advocated by the elder Heyst in order to achieve harmony with man's absurd place in the universe. Axel comes to Morrison's and possibly Lena's aid partly for the "amusement" he describes to Lena, but also for egoistic reasons and with a compassion he does not understand; and it is just these rudimentary egoistic needs (the need to create himself by participation in the creation of others, a process suggested, as I have noted, by Adam naming the world and Heyst naming Lena) that he cannot escape whatever his intellect may advise. What Axel's reason thus advises is really quite dishonest in that it tries to avoid a kind of tragedy inherent in the difference between what man is and where he finds himself in the cosmos.

In view of these pervasive redefinitions of good and evil in *Victory*, how are we meant to understand Jones, Ricardo, and Pedro as evil? No one doubts that Ricardo is meant to suggest Satan, though even critics who cite all sorts of evidence for this often ignore the most obvious item:

Having been ejected, he [Jones] said, from his proper social sphere because he had refused to conform to certain usual conventions, he was a rebel now, and was coming and going up and down the earth. As I really did not want to listen to all this nonsense, I told him that I had heard that sort of story about somebody else before. His grin is really ghastly. He confessed that I was very far from the sort of man he expected to meet. Then he said:

"As to me I am no blacker than the gentleman you are thinking of, and I have neither more nor less determination." (Pp. 317–18)

Admittedly this is a peculiar passage, since it is impossible to tell whether after Axel's saying he has heard "that sort of story about somebody else before," Jones is henceforth talking about Satan or Heyst himself, who also fits the description Jones provides. At least he suits that description nicely if we understand that Jones is still full of Schomberg's lies about Heyst's behavior to Morrison. This confusion of Jones, Satan, and Heyst is, however, apparently deliberate, or at least so consonant with Conrad's redefinition of evil in the novel that his mind may spontaneously have written the ambiguity into the passage. Heyst and Jones are meant in many ways to be counterparts. And the visit of the evil trio to Samburan is compared with "those myths, current in Polynesia, of amazing strangers, who arrive at an island, gods or demons, bringing good or evil to the innocence of the inhabitants – gifts of unknown things, words never heard before" (p. 228). Their visit is not quite that ambiguous, for Heyst and Lena are in a sense innocent, and the evil that visits them is a fortunate initiation, albeit a fatal one: we are watching a fortunate fall.

In the foregoing quotation about the outcast rebel, both Heyst and Jones are implicated in evil, not, as Jones imagines, because of what Heyst has done to Morrison, but for reasons complex and at the heart of the novel. This novel, like so many of Conrad's, works with doubles: Lena and Morrison, Ricardo and Lena, Heyst and Jones. The vital similarities in any one of these sets are not at once apparent but insinuate themselves with growing force. Both Axel and Jones are gentlemen, outcast gentlemen if you will, though Jones at first thinks Axel an outcast only because he, Jones, believes Schomberg's lies. More important, both disdain genuine human commitment, partly out of their pessimism, their sense that there are no sanctions in the artificial fictions of society. Conrad tries to prepare us for the appearance of Jones and for the similarity of Heyst and Jones in the following quotation from the elder Heyst's book, *Storm and Dust*:

Men of tormented conscience, or of a criminal imagination, are aware of much that a peaceful, resigned cast do not even suspect.
. . .

We all have our instants of clairvoyance. They are not very helpful. The character of the scheme does not permit that or anything else to be helpful. Properly speaking its character, judged by the standards established by its victims, is infamous. It excuses every violence of protest and at the same time never fails to crush it, just as it crushes the blindest assent. The so-called wickedness must be, like the so-called virtue, its own reward — to be anything at all. . . . (P. 219)

This is nothing less than Conrad's metaphysics; the universe is indifferent, offers no sanctions, and if it is to be measured at all must be judged by the standards of its victims. But the passage also says that men of criminal imagination have a special capacity for seeing this, as Jones and possibly Ricardo apparently see it; and the elder Heyst further suggests that such criminal intelligence relies on the absurdity of all allegedly transcendent sanctions, realizing that both so-called wickedness and so-called virtue must be their "own reward — to be anything at all."

Now Conrad, the elder Heyst, Axel, and Jones all believe this, and its results in the lives of Axel and Jones are surprisingly similar if we consider their otherwise vast differences in temperament and character. Heyst avoids action while Jones seems to court it; but Jones's schemes are primarily designed to deny the efficacy of human effort, to frustrate another man's (Heyst's) supposedly ill-gotten security. Jones's vision is not even the Darwinian jungle Ricardo calls the world, although both he and Ricardo continually emphasize that they couldn't care less whether they kill or not, unless someone stands in their way. This indifference is intensified in Jones's occasional periods of neurotic boredom, and is only lifted in this special contest with Heyst, which, he says, gives him considerable fear and pleasure. Both men sense something of these resemblances without being able or willing to articulate them.

Conrad classifies the evil trio as "evil intelligence, instinctive savagery," and, in Pedro, "brute force." This ought to be enough allegory for anyone's taste, but the distinctions are nonetheless important in designating the source of what the world by consensus would call evil in these three. Jones's indifference to most of life does spring from a dim but intellectual awareness of its metaphysical futility; his indifference is not instinctive. Ricardo is described otherwise: "Cross-legged, his head drooping a little and perfectly still, he might have been meditating in a bonze-like attitude upon the sacred syllable 'Om.' It was a striking illustration of the untruth of appearances, for his contempt for the world was of a severely practical kind" (p. 267). Which, one might add, is a good deal unlike Jones's contempt. Pedro is simply raw force with no intelligence and no Ricardo-like savage contempt. He has a capacity for good or evil and is directionless without the aid of his two companions, those higher steps up the ladder of evolution. Ricardo's impression of the world as a jungle (in which Conrad makes him alternately a cat or a serpent) leaves him a strong taste for action and accomplishments, while Jones has begun to undercut all meaning, except a narcissistic egoism, through an intellectualized contempt for all achievement not unlike the elder Heyst's and Axel's. Even his homosexuality is narcissistically symbolic in the vein of Heyst's comment that he had never murdered and never loved a woman. Jones murders only when necessary, not because of any distaste for the act, but rather because he is indifferent to it and has none of Ricardo's bloodlust.

I should not like to dwell too long on these similarities, for they work aesthetically in the novel largely because they are covert, or at least remain covert until Lena, late in the novel, confronts Heyst with her sense that they are being punished for their illicit relationship:

"Punishment?" repeated Heyst. He could not understand what she meant. When she explained, he was still more surprised. "A sort of retribution from an angry heaven?" he said in wonder. "On us? What on earth for?"

He saw her pale face darken in the dusk. She had blushed. Her whispering flowed very fast. It was the way they lived together — that wasn't right, was it? It was a guilty life. For she had not been forced into it, driven, scared into it. No, no — she had come to him of her own free will, with her whole soul yearning unlawfully.

He was so profoundly touched that he could not speak for a moment. To conceal his trouble he assumed his best Heystian manner.

"What? Are our visitors then messengers of morality, avengers

of righteousness, agents of Providence? That's certainly an original view. How flattered they would be if they could hear you!"
. . . He regretted that he had no Heaven to which he could recommend this fair, palpitating handful of ashes and dust — warm, living, sentient, his own — and exposed helplessly to insult, outrage, degradation, and infinite misery of the body. (Pp. 354–55)

The passage intimates through irony that in a sense the evil trio has come as retribution not for Axel and Lena living together but for Axel's deeper sin, his disdain and pity for life, and his use of a metaphysics that Conrad also suffers under to escape the responsibility of defying man's absurd role in the cosmos. Heyst's acceptance of his father's metaphysics is all too clear as he nonetheless treats Lena's belief in a retributive God gently and with more than pity. He cannot finally, however, allow himself even the minimal Christian virtue he recommends to Lena: hope. The whole passage serves to remind us that Axel's errors spring from a particular use of his father's philosophy and that *Storm and Dust* had attributed to the criminal intelligence an equally clear view of that cosmic indifference. It is likely that some of the more subtle, latent similarities between Axel and Jones emerge only after the reader has mulled over this conversation. Of course there is no Providence in this novel except the aesthetic one and the latent rhetoric which requires that the trio be used as a kind of messenger of morality.

Finally unable to plumb the source of Heyst's pride, of that cold undercurrent chilling her even in the heat of his passionate rhetoric, Lena tries to become worthy of him through a great sacrifice. Conrad values this womanly talent, but Lena's death is a victory only in a very narrow sense. Although her capacity to trust in the feelings of another human being does make possible the climactic sacrifice, neither that sacrifice nor that capacity can alter Heyst's hard-core reticence; as he says to Davidson, a man must "learn" while young to put his trust in life. This ability must be acquired while the spirit is still malleable, and it must be learned as a skill not entirely natural to man, an implication that still shows Heyst a long way from appreciating just what it is he inherits from Adam, what it is that has led him to Morrison and Lena. Heyst is finally capable of suicidal guilt, but largely because despite Lena's sacrifice and example he still cannot simply love her. Lena, we may conclude, has in many ways been like Kurtz's Intended. She is protected from seeing the awful metaphysical vision that nearly incapacitates Heyst, and, given her own belief in Providence, is capable of a faith in Heyst that is admirable but not definitive. Within her own spiritual economy it is a victory; under the black canopy of those cold, indifferent stars that Marlow so detests in *Chance*, there are other victories to be won:

"It was one of those dewy, clear, starry nights, oppressing our spirit, crushing our pride, by the brilliant evidence of the awful loneliness, of the hopeless obscure insignificance of our globe lost in the splendid revelation of a glittering, soulless universe. I hate such skies. Daylight is friendly to a man toiling under a sun which warms his heart; and cloudy soft nights are more kindly to our littleness. I nearly ran back again to my lighted parlour . . ." (P. 50)

Even in her moment of greatest doubt and fear, Lena is still in that lighted parlour. *Victory* is not a sentimental affirmation of the power in some women to save us all; the question it poses but cannot answer is whether a faith in life can be created and sustained by the *initiate*, not by Lena or by Kurtz's Intended, but by Heyst (even if we grant that he still has little knowledge of his ego involvement), or the Marlow of *Heart of Darkness*, or Kurtz himself.

*Victory*, like *Under Western Eyes*, *The Shadow Line*, and possibly *Nostromo*, demonstrates that self-possession is contingent upon some form of human solidarity; and the novel perceives further that the requirements for such a larger sense of community are also necessary for what Heyst calls "faith in life" and for the love of a single human being. Although stated thus, in summary, these claims sound flat, they are really quite extraordinary. For at least the probing of these delicate relationships, it is fortunate that Conrad had often stopped looking so intently at the ties between a captain and his crew, a community which is after all very special and not easily — as *Lord Jim* shows — compared with other forms of human association.

Both Razumov and Heyst try to come to rational terms with society and discover on the contrary that they are inevitably caught by irrational tensions. There is no social contract just as there can be no rational decision to look on and make no sound. Conrad, perhaps more than any other writer, is anxious to dismiss the metaphors that have always proved convenient for understanding an individual's relations with "human solidarity." It is true that the metaphor of a child's relation to his parents goes a long way toward explaining some of Razumov's feelings about Russia, but even there Conrad is painfully aware he is only exploiting a model of sorts.

Significantly, the manner in which evil comes visiting both men — Haldin to Razumov's room, the trio to Samburan — suggests to both heroes the improbability of any rational attitude toward human solidarity. There is a calculated absurdity about both visits, about Haldin's exit from the lumberyard and his choice of a fellow student he barely knows, and about Schomberg's incredibly impelling lies. The world seems perversely to court those who temporize with it or deny it; avoided, it becomes not an imperative but a nemesis. In both novels love for a woman suggests to the hero a new understanding not only of himself but of his involvement with mankind; his sympathetic understanding of those who have developed one or another irrational tie with community is vastly increased. In short, the love for Natalia and Lena serves to destroy the hero's intellectual pride and to deny him a satisfactory identity outside the messy and often fatal demands of human solidarity. There is very little sense in either novel that love is being explored on its own terms, romantically, apart from these issues of community. In neither case is love isolating, as it tends to be in romantic literature, in Byron or Hemingway; the claims of amorous loyalty are not played off against the claims of society, as, again, they are in so many romantic writers and, interestingly enough, in Conrad's last important novel, *The Rescue*.

On the whole, *Victory* posed an ultimate difficulty for Conrad: could he imagine not Razumov but a man with something of Conrad's own temperament and metaphysics passionately affirming his dependence on feelings of human solidarity? Officially there's little doubt that in much of *Victory* he felt Heyst to be in fundamental error and, unlike himself, to be using a metaphysics from which they both suffered as a reason for denying life. But it seems to me much more accurate to see Heyst as a man doing exaggeratedly what a part of Conrad had always done; Conrad seems to recognize himself in the example of Heyst as much as he disapproves it. The sympathy finally suggested by Razumov is simply not available to Heyst, as it apparently was not to Conrad except possibly within the pressure of *Under Western Eyes* itself. A victory may be what Conrad would have liked for himself and his reticent hero in *Victory*, but it is not what has been achieved. If *Under Western Eyes* is the apotheosis of sympathetic sharing in Conrad, *Victory* comes close to being its ultimate failure for the Heyst-Conrad so often mistaken as its affirmation. It is nonetheless true that Heyst changes a good deal toward the novel's end, in a way that I shall speculate about in my final comments on Conrad's changing moral and psychological models. The aristocratic Swede has at last developed a sense of moral responsibility for his isolation equivalent to what the aristocratic Pole may have felt.

# 10

# The Exhaustion
of a Model: "The Planter
of Malata" and *The Rescue*

*Victory* is really the last time in Conrad's work
that the existential models have any potency — and even so *Victory*
does not channel that awareness in the way that *Lord Jim*, *Heart of
Darkness*, and *Nostromo* do. Simply as personalities, Razumov,
Gould, and Lord Jim are not very much like Heyst. My reasons
for concluding this study with *The Rescue*, then, need to be made
clear.

Thomas Moser is right in seeing that the evil in some of these late
heroes is not "inside" them in quite the way it had been in Conrad's
early work. But often in the late work (in *Under Western Eyes*,
*Victory*, and *The Rescue*) Conrad is not particularly interested in
the hero coming to terms with some of the frightening, lawless
aspects of his own ego, as he most certainly was in his portrayal of
the imaginative egoist. Parts one through three of "The Rescuer,"
a first version of *The Rescue*, had been finished by December 1898
and contain many details of characterization suggesting that Conrad's original conception of Lingard was quite close to the character he was to give Lord Jim within the year. Moser laments the disappearance in *The Rescue* of Lingard's "egoistic longings for power, his lack of self-knowledge, his moral isolation," the "increasing

isolation that results from his egoistic involvement in an unlawful
adventure," and "his powerful, if unacknowledged, longings for
self-destruction." [1] Which is to say, apparently, that Moser regrets
*The Rescue* was not written about another Lord Jim. Why should
it have been? The character of Lingard as it appeared in sections
one through three in 1898 did, in fact, find much more than predictable fulfillment in Kurtz and in Jim by 1900. When Conrad
returned to Lingard in 1918 he had undergone so much in his art
and life that a return even to variations on the imaginative egoist
would have been no less disappointing than the unsuccessful hybrid
*The Rescue* really is. Ego is not the same issue it had been for Conrad in 1898, largely because he had evoked a seminal vision in
Kurtz, *Lord Jim*, and *Nostromo*, and had felt that metaphysical,
existential awareness on and off for years. He resurrects it full-
blown (and not devoid of the emotional power it had created for
the reader in *Heart of Darkness*) in the metaphysics of the two
Heysts.

Although it must have been difficult for Conrad to return to a
story of romantic passion at any time, the portions of "The Rescuer" that had been written so much earlier were, in short, conceived in root metaphors that had been rejected in *Lord Jim*, *Heart
of Darkness*, and *Nostromo*. "The Rescuer" is a survival of the
passion-subverting-will formula so common in the first two novels
and *Tales of Unrest*. As he completed the novel in 1918, however,
he intuitively altered the original rubric to accommodate not only
some of the Heystian metaphysics that had been so important in
*Victory* but also some of the grotesque confusion of consciousness
and in-itself that had marked *Lord Jim* and *Nostromo*. Though
Conrad obviously suffers from great fatigue in completing *The
Rescue*, he nonetheless finally refuses simply to return to root
metaphors he had outgrown twenty years earlier. To study *The
Rescue*, then, is to observe the disastrous effects of a key metaphor
that has outlived its usefulness. Yet its appeal is still strong enough
so that the author cannot replace it with insights which, though
greatly disturbing, represent a good part of the achievement of
twenty years' creation. Returning to *The Rescue* was probably not

an act of courage on Conrad's part so much as it was an attempt to rest with relative comfort on old metaphors. As Conrad was quickly to learn, such rest did not suit him and did not become him.

There is nonetheless a key to understanding all these seeming inversions. Conrad's interest in 1918 pivots on the imaginative egoist as hero only insofar as he can be treated to reflect the preoccupations of a Heyst, a hero who seeks justification for any commitment with ambiguous results. But how is such world-weary skepticism to descend on a character like Lingard, a hero originally designed as the imaginative egoist (albeit, as Mrs. Hay says, an "Emersonian" egoist).[2] It seems to me that Edith Travers is made to carry some of the symbolic importance and the emotional impact given to Heyst's father and his metaphysics in *Victory* — that in a sense she becomes analogous to the absurd universe which debilitates Heyst. Lingard's passion for Edith affects him much as the elder Heyst's vision and charismatic presence affects Axel; and Edith's level and texture of society is made to suggest a similar meaninglessness in people who, while they do not look on and make no sound, are just as far from a real faith in life as Heyst. Their manner of disengagement is different, but the results are remarkably similar to Axel's.

Edith's significance is anticipated in Felicia Moorsom, a metaphysically important femme fatale in "The Planter of Malata." This story was written in 1913 while Conrad was still working on *Victory* and provides a link between the absurdity envisioned by Heyst's metaphysics and that possible to a particular kind of society. Of the two stories written while Conrad completed *Victory*, "Because of the Dollars" may actually contain the basic plot he intended to use in that novel; the other, "The Planter of Malata," may equally have been connected in his mind with *Victory* and spun off somewhat in the way that "The Secret Sharer" had been produced while he was still working on *Under Western Eyes*. Certainly "The Planter" leans toward allegory with a frequency and seriousness of allusion suggestive of what may have been the parent story.

"The Planter of Malata" concerns a man of action, Renouard,

who falls in love with a young, empty, yet egocentric society woman, Felicia Moorsom. Renouard has a reputation for being a ruthless adventurer, but nevertheless behaves more like an introspective romantic. Miss Moorsom, her father (a famous and popular philosopher), and his sister have come East seeking Miss Moorsom's fiancé, who has disappeared after a business scandal in England and has subsequently been proven innocent in the affair. She searches for the man only in order to repair her own vanity by making reparation for her earlier failure to believe in his innocence; she is in love with the sentimental image of herself doing this, and intends to mend his reputation through marriage to her eminently respectable name. Renouard has unknowingly hired this man (down-and-out, taking drugs, and using a different name) as his assistant on the remote island of Malata; there he has died just before the story opens. Having fallen in love with Felicia and having discovered that his dead assistant is the man she seeks, Renouard allows her to believe that her fiancé is still alive and ferries the entire party over to his island. He feels trapped by an earlier disdainful reluctance to tell a prying newspaper editor that his then-unidentified assistant had died, and now cannot bring himself to blurt out information that will not only stun Felicia but cause others to wonder why he had said nothing earlier. They may think he has concealed the death for some untoward reason; and, in fact, Renouard seizes any chance to keep Felicia near him a bit longer, even to advising her that his assistant is off on an island cruise of indeterminate length. Nevertheless, in a short time he confesses his love violently, tells her that the assistant is dead, and has his passion sharply rejected as though he had just made some awful faux pas at a fashionable West End party. After Felicia and her group leave, Renouard commits suicide, swimming "beyond the confines of life — with a steady stroke — his eyes fixed on a star!" (p. 85).

It seems to me that Paul Wiley has taken the story seriously in exactly the right way — as an awkward revelation, all the more revealing because of its faults.[3] He is perhaps too far committed to his thesis of the "knight" to see in the right spirit the mythological allusions intended by Conrad, but he does note the insistent references to Renouard's profile: "His face shaded softly by the broad brim of a planter's panama hat, with the straight line of the nose level with the forehead, the eyes lost in the depth of the setting, and the chin well forward, had such a profile as may be seen amongst the bronzes of classical museums, pure under a crested helmet — recalled vaguely a Minerva's head" (p. 38). And later: "He flung his hat far away, and his suddenly lowered eyelids brought out startlingly his resemblance to antique bronze, the profile of Pallas, still, austere, bowed a little in the shadow of the rock" (p. 75).

In addition to these two portraits the story is literally full of heads. Felicia's head, and especially her hair, startle Renouard the first time he sees her: "The light from an open window fell across her path, and suddenly all that mass of arranged hair appeared incandescent, chiselled and fluid, with the daring suggestion of a helmet of burnished copper and the flowing lines of molten metal" (pp. 9–10). She is in face and profile like a helmeted statue, and is in this respect visually similar to Renouard. Her statuesque head appears in one of two dreams he has during the story, where its fate constitutes a nice bit of dramatic irony: the head falls to dust, anticipating the destruction of Renouard's own vision of this supposed Venus:

The sickly white light of dawn showed him the head of a statue. Its marble hair was done in the bold lines of a helmet, on its lips the chisel had left a faint smile, and it resembled Miss Moorsom. While he was staring at it fixedly, the head began to grow light in his fingers, to diminish and crumble to pieces, and at last turned into a handful of dust, which was blown away by a puff of wind so chilly that he woke up with a desperate shiver and leaped headlong out of his bed-place. (Pp. 31–32)

The emphasis on Renouard's sensitivity to the import of faces and heads exists primarily to justify two vital identifications: Renouard as Athena and Miss Moorsom as a peculiar Venus. Renouard of course cannot notice his own resemblance to Minerva (similar to Athena, and identified with her by the Romans). Conrad must first hint awkwardly at the resemblance ("recalled vaguely a Minerva's head"), and then declare it for all to remember ("brought out startlingly the resemblance to antique bronze, the profile of Pallas"). Renouard himself, though, first notes Miss Moorsom's resemblance to a helmeted statue, and then strikes her principal identification as a Venus:

And indeed on stealing a glance he would see her dazzling and perfect, her eyes vague, staring in mournful immobility [always this insistence on immobility], with a drooping head that made him think of a tragic Venus arising before him, not from the foam of the sea, but from a distant, still more formless, mysterious, and potent immensity of mankind. (P. 36)

Renouard slowly begins to see that the Venus before him is no goddess of Spring and Love (not even a tragic one) but rather a deity of peculiarly empty egoism. She seems to rise from those affluent levels of society which neither Renouard nor Lingard knows; the word "formless" appears for the first time in the story and becomes associated in Renouard's mind with the formlessness of foam and froth, an idea which is again introduced only a few pages after Felicia has been associated with Venus and Renouard with Pallas Athena. The professor has just shocked Renouard with the suggestion that Felicia's "sentimental pilgrimage" may not be genuine, that she searches for her disgraced young man out of some motive other than love (he is inadvertently suggesting, of course, that she is no legitimate Venus). Renouard resents these remarks, and the professor counters:

"Ah! you don't understand. Yes, she's clever, open minded, popular, and — well, charming. But you don't know what it is to have moved, breathed, existed, and even triumphed in the mere smother and froth of life — the brilliant froth. There thoughts, sentiments, opinions, feelings, actions too [Renouard is a man of action], are nothing but agitation in empty space — to amuse life — a sort of superior debauchery, exciting and fatiguing, meaning nothing, leading nowhere. She is the creature of that circle." (Pp. 40–41)

Conrad is playing on the Venus image he had used a few pages earlier. The froth of her birth from the waves here assumes a social and moral importance, so that the foam, by a verbal sleight of hand, becomes "smother." We are moving imperceptibly from a traditional image to the final vision of Miss Moorsom as a goddess of absurdity. After all, the emphasis in the passage just quoted is on the emptiness of the society from which Felicia has come and of which she is the apotheosis.

It does not take long for Renouard to see that the professor (who at dinner one evening discourses on the "Impermanency of Measurable," on formlessness) is more of an only slightly different froth. He reminds one of Virginia Woolf's Mr. Ramsay in *To the Lighthouse*. Renouard thinks, "Yes! Intellectual debauchery in the froth of existence! Froth and fraud!" (p. 45) and indicts the old man for the sin he has been warned of but cannot yet affirm in the daughter. She still seems highly sculptured, ingeniously worked and arranged, almost herself an Athena—the very opposite of formlessness. Her appearance throughout as an artifact is no more than the perfect deception for an underlying void.

Earlier, Renouard had been warned of Miss Moorsom's meaning in his dream. There, as we have seen, her sculptured head suddenly turns to dust while he holds it in his hands. But Conrad is developing Renouard's awareness on the conscious level until it matches his immediate unconscious intuition that this statue is really a goddess of absurdity. He is as yet in no position to understand the dream; we presumably are.

Renouard as Athena is undoubtedly intended to suggest the power of form and craft usually associated with that goddess. Representing wisdom (her sign is the owl) and various crafts, she was also a warrior-goddess and goddess of the arts of peace and prudent intelligence. Of course neither Renouard nor Lingard is notable for his intellect—especially not for anything we might call wisdom. Conrad, insofar as he wants the Athena allusion, surely implies only the purposefulness of a Lingard, and the consequent decisive action that Lingard is ordinarily so good at. When either man becomes introspective and begins to question his own self-conception, he languishes, and action becomes indecisive, almost a parody of earlier schemes. (The perfect example is Renouard's childish attempt to get Felicia on his island and keep her there for a time: his sole strategy consists of telling her his assistant has gone on a trip.)

In making Felicia resemble Venus, Conrad had in mind primarily the ironies inherent in the birth of Venus from foam, from formlessness. He seems not to be interested in the source of that foam in the birth story (it rises from the genitals thrown into the sea after the emasculation of Uranus by Saturn), nor in the striking conclusion that it must be the traditionally chaste and "heavenly" Aphrodite reiterated by Plato in the *Symposium* who rises from that unmanning, that sexual violence. Yet clearly Felicia ironically suggests the chaste Venus, rather than the vulgar, erotic Aphrodite born of Zeus and Dione.

Miss Moorsom's role has several dimensions. Her origins in Western society make "The Planter" something of a *Waste Land* in its moral orientation, and Conrad probably intends the same criticism of the upper classes that he offers elsewhere in his work, especially in the person of Mr. and Mrs. Travers in *The Rescue*. There is certainly an empty intellectualism (the "Impermanency of the Measurable") which goes along with these empty people. Finally — and this Conrad seems to have been entirely aware of — her formlessness is sexually unapproachable, like Edith Travers's in *The Rescue*.

Conrad is compulsively insistent on these identifications. Miss Moorsom is the first to say that she stands "for truth here," suggesting that she is the goddess who must prevail (p. 47). Later, just after Conrad has confirmed the resemblance of Renouard to Pallas Athena, Renouard says to Miss Moorsom, "Oh! If you could only understand the truth that is in me!" She replies, "It's I who stand for truth here!" (p. 75). That phrase "stand for" is a bit uncomfortable for the critic who feels that too many things in this story "stand for" other things. Their confrontation, awkwardly enough, occurs on the highest point of Malata, an ersatz Olympus where one has a "view of reefs and broken water without end, and of great wheeling clouds of seabirds" (p. 72).

As Renouard reveals his deception, his attempt to hide the death of the assistant, Felicia warms to the battle and declares (as befits a goddess) that "anything less than the shaping of a man's destiny" is beneath her (p. 76). Renouard at this point is close to the subconscious knowledge revealed so much earlier in his dream. He accuses her of being meaningless foam in a speech which sounds like a denunciation of the decadent upper classes:

"You are one of these aristocrats . . . Oh! I don't mean that you are like the men and women of the time of armours, castles, and great deeds. Oh no! They stood on the naked soil, had traditions to be faithful to, had their feet on this earth of passions and death which is not a hothouse. They would have been too plebeian for you since they had to lead, to suffer with, to understand the commonest humanity. No, you are merely of the topmost layer, disdainful and superior, *the mere pure froth and bubble on the inscrutable depths which some day will toss you out of existence. But you are you! You are You! You are the eternal love itself — only, O Divinity, it isn't your body, it is your soul that is made of foam.*" (Pp. 76–77; emphasis mine)

This speech occurs at the moment when Renouard's waking mind supplies the equivalent of the head's falling to dust in his dream: "it is your soul that is made of foam." It is the final variation of the Venus image, loaded this time with a rococo array of political, moral, and metaphysical meanings. That "mere pure froth and bubble on the inscrutable depths which some day will toss you out of existence" sounds ominously and surprisingly (for the author of the *The Secret Agent* and *Under Western Eyes*) like Conrad's version of social revolution. More important, the passage unmistakably argues that this scene, for all its commentary on Western society, is a conflict of two gods: Felicia is "O Divinity." The overriding quality of the speech, of the whole conflict, is crudely metaphysical.

Miss Moorsom's emptiness is largely defined by her penultimate conversation with Renouard. (Her last remarks to him as she goes down to the boat the following morning are, like the rest of that scene, not in the manuscript of the story.[4]) All her tremendous energy of ego is directed toward fulfilling the sentimental expectations of society. Hearing of her fiancé's death, she mourns, we are told, "for herself." She lives to shape "a man's destiny," but only in the eyes and forms of her own unique level of society: "Don't you see that in the eyes of the world nothing could have rehabilitated him so completely as his marriage with me. No word of evil could be whispered of him after I had given him my hand" (p. 76). Though she is under no illusion that such a marriage could redeem him from whatever depths he had sunk to in his own estimation or even from his original mediocrity, the fact that he has been innocent places her under a "fine duty" that she must fulfill for her own vanity.

In the section Conrad apparently added in typescript (eleven), Renouard says more than he perhaps ought to by way of clarifying the nature of her emptiness: "I had nothing to offer her vanity" (p. 80). She devotes all her ego to pursuing an empty, ritualistic gesture quite apart from any real effect it may have on the man involved. The duty is "fine" in the sense that used to be associated with the Man of Feeling, the sentimentalist who savored emotions for the fineness of their aesthetic quality rather than for any moral reality. Just as Mackenzie's *The Man of Feeling* is in its last episode the decadence of sensibility, a noble tradition which began in the search for moral sanctions and ethical immediacy (and, it is interesting to note in this context, with an appreciation of the powers of imaginative sympathy), so Miss Moorsom's "fine duty" is a decadence in which only the empty shell of human solidarity remains. There is plenty of ego and energy in these people, but it all comes to "agitation in empty space," as the professor says.

Renouard seizes her in his arms and at once finds himself nearly drained of desire, not I think because of any sexual twists in Conrad's unconscious attitude toward such passion, but because of what Renouard's passion confronts in this apparition: "And she was so used to the forms of repression enveloping, softening the crude impulses of old humanity that she no longer believed in their existence as if it were an exploded legend. She did not recognize what had happened to her. She came safe out of his arms, without a struggle, not even having felt afraid" (p. 77). His experience is to be understood symbolically as well as dramatically in this moment; Renouard has confronted not only a particular sort of woman who rejects his passion but a gorgon whose ugliness may be apprehended only by the spirit and particularly by a man who still bears the spirit of "old humanity." Renouard has admired Miss Moorsom throughout the story as a sensuously physical and aesthetic object, a fine statue of the milkiest Parian marble; and considering the way she turns human emotions into a cheap imitation of aesthetic experience, Renouard's awakening perhaps comes to him as poetic justice for his gross dependence on sight, an unnatural preoccupation with faces that the newspaper editor attributes to his isolation on Malata. He loves before he knows her more than visually: love at first sight in an ominous sense.

When he understands more than the surface, he recognizes that her soul is made of foam, but cannot thereby alter his love one bit. The attraction is fatal, irrevocable, and significantly above morality. Renouard is unable to sustain in the face of this charisma his "crude impulses of old humanity," his taste for action and an avoidance of the "forms of repression." Though Renouard is not from the lower classes (he is English and has attended the same school as Professor Moorsom's son), he thoroughly despises what the upper classes have done to this magnificent woman. In the scene Conrad added after the manuscript had been finished on December 24, 1913 (the date is on the manuscript), he has Felicia suggest to Renouard that she is "not perhaps the extraordinary being you think I am," and then finally intimate that she is sexually frigid: Renouard protests that were she "steeped to the lips in vice, in crime, in mud," he would cherish her, and Felicia answers his romantic intensity with the deliberately ambiguous "Assez! J'ai horreur de tout cela" (p. 78).

The point is not only that Renouard is a man of action who is disarmed, puzzled, and then crushed by the discovery of unfamiliar passion in his own heart, not only the cliché that the man who can handle incredibly dangerous expeditions cannot handle love for a woman. (His conversation on the ersatz Olympus is described as follows: "This walk up the hill and down again like the supreme effort of an explorer trying to penetrate the interior of an unexplored country [!], the secret of which is too well defended by its cruel and barren nature" [p. 79]). More than this, Renouard is an intelligent man, ordinarily unreflective but — as he describes the professor — "sub-ironic" (p. 29) about life and capable of regarding his encounter with Miss Moorsom as a more than personal defeat. Miss Moorsom raises the whole question of justification that bedevils Heyst. Hers is a decadent but impressive sterility that undercuts all sense of purpose in Renouard, that — despite his clear moral judgment of it — seems to be the essence of beauty. He is overcome not only by his irrational passion for Miss Moorsom but by the irrational appeal of her emptiness — which seems to him the end of authenticity, purpose, action, surely the end of his life in favor of "peace."

There are similarities between *Victory* and "The Planter of Malata," but they constitute what may have been Conrad's intention to reverse many of the details of the novel. Instead of a woman drawing a man toward life, there is another sort of woman drawing a man out of it. Lena is a lower-class victim, Miss Moorsom an elegant totem. Like Heyst, however, Renouard is a solitary whose instinctive aid to a distressed human being plunges him into life and, at least superficially, causes his destruction. Renouard employs Mr. Walter (the assumed name of Miss Moorsom's fiancé) from motives that are virtually Heyst's in aiding Morrison; and it is the death of Walter on Malata and Renouard's initially concealing this fact that touches off Miss Moorsom's wrath. I suspect that Renouard is really intended to resemble Heyst despite superficial differences; though Renouard is allegedly a man who "doesn't count the cost" (p. 28) to himself or others, most of his alleged ruthlessness is merely local gossip and some of his adventures resemble Heyst's. The basic difference between the two men disappears upon close examination. Renouard is a leader of men while Heyst remains on the sidelines of even his Borneo exploration collecting "facts" and never becoming involved. For all his aggressiveness and leadership, however, Renouard is isolated as well: "The Editor noted it [an air of weariness in Renouard] as a further proof of that immoral detachment from mankind, of that callous-

ness of sentiment fostered by the unhealthy conditions of solitude
— according to his [the Editor's] own favorite theory" (p. 26).

We need not accept the Editor's confusion of effect with cause:
Renouard has strong intimations of absurdity before he meets Miss
Moorsom and feels its embodied charisma. Like Heyst he is im-
morally detached from mankind (and yet like Heyst he feels an
irrational tug in its direction — Morrison, Lena, and Walter are all
aided). But Renouard has chosen his isolation; it is not, as the Editor apparently thinks, accidental and the *cause* of his spiritual detachment from mankind. Quite the contrary, these intimations of
absurdity have induced Renouard's purely formal — albeit dirty
and strenuous — relations with agents, exploring parties, and plan-
tation crews. His seemingly active involvement with life is more
action than involvement and comes very close to Heyst's more obvious detachment. For reasons that Conrad does not dramatize,
Renouard has been touched by absurdity and ennui in the midst of
his adventures; the signs if not the causes are seen everywhere in his
life. Between him and Felicia there are, then, as many affinities as
contrasts: she draws out the sense of absurdity and detachment already implicit in him. It is even possible to consider his passion as
love not so much for Miss Moorsom as for the dream image of himself that leads him to see Felicia's marble head becoming dust: "In
this startling image of himself he recognized somebody he had to
follow — the frightened guide of his dream" (p. 31). In the manuscript "frightened" reads "fraternal," suggesting all we know of
Conrad's taste for the doppelgänger and secret sharers. It is this
other fraternal self that leads to the symbolic crumbling of the
marble head and suggests thereby its own complicity in what the
head means. That other self strongly resembles Miss Moorsom and
is finally dominant and suicidal at the end of the story. After all,
Felicia's head has always seemed Athena-like to Renouard, with
her hair shaped like a helmet. It has long been intimated that Felicia
is an aspect of Renouard.

Thus Renouard's passion is loaded with metaphysical implications that have less to do with sexual and romantic love — or with
its psychoanalytic significance in Conrad's life — than Moser has

supposed. Renouard's love for Felicia is equally love for that "fraternal guide" and for the peace of absurdity that Conrad had so long resisted within himself. We have the testimony of the 1888 crisis in Bangkok to this effect, amid other unmistakable evidence throughout his life. Mrs. Hay speculates that in "The Rescuer" Conrad intended an attack on the "civilized" English claims to moral authority but deleted one important character and blurred his criticism of that life in order not to spoil the appeal of hypercivilized, English Mrs. Travers.[5] If Mrs. Travers was to be credibly appealing for the sake of the love story, the attack on civilized England could not be so intense. But it seems to me that Conrad felt the appeal of Mrs. Travers as of Miss Moorsom in the very pulse of his mind; it was a fundamental attraction, one that we need not talk about as though it had been preserved largely because Conrad had promised his publishers a love story. That a particular kind of woman serves to trigger this surrender to absurdity is, while clearly not accidental, also not necessarily the result of an unconscious attitude toward sexual passion.

What in *The Shadow Line* is called the menace of emptiness can, it appears, seem anything but a menace under the right conditions. The search for justification can go on too long, require too much heroic effort, and leave its mark on author and character.

Like Felicia Moorsom, Edith Travers moves brilliantly in the empty ritual dance of high society; but unlike Miss Moorsom, she is profoundly dissatisfied with that life and has married Mr. Travers only because her dreams, "where the sincerity of a great passion appeared like the ideal fulfillment and the only truth of life," had been frustrated "because the world is too prudent to be sincere" (p. 151).

Mr. Travers's name was on men's lips; he seemed capable of enthusiasm and of devotion; he impressed her imagination by his impenetrability. She married him, found him enthusiastically devoted to the nursing of his own career, and had nothing to hope for now. (Pp. 151–52)

In the appearance of the native princess Immada on board the yacht in section three, Edith sees the "naked truth of things; the naked truth of life and passion buried under the growth of centuries" (p. 153).

Nothing stood between that girl and the truth of her sensations. She could be sincerely courageous, and tender and passionate and — well — ferocious. Why not ferocious? She could know the truth of terror — and of affection, absolutely without artificial trammels, without the pain of restraint. (P. 153)

What Miss Moorsom finds so unbelievable and unappealing in Renouard — the loss of these "forms of repression" — is, then, precisely what attracts Mrs. Travers to Immada, Hassim, Lingard, and the whole display of unrepressed humanity she sees so unexpectedly before her. She is to elicit from Lingard a true passion of the sort never found in her artificial society, and that passion is obviously meant to be contrasted even with the only partially repressed and rather touching disappointment in love impelling d'Alcacer around the world.

But the entire issue of regaining contact with the truth of one's sensations, with the "truth of life and passion buried under the growth of centuries" is quite ambiguous in *The Rescue*. Conrad does not simply present the process as an unqualified good which nonetheless requires, because of conflicting loyalties, the tragic separation of these two lovers who seem fundamentally so similar. As in "The Planter of Malata," it is not simply the hero's passion which destroys his ego and beckons toward the annihilation that so interests Moser and Guerard. The taste of absurdity, although not inherent in Lingard as it has been in the Heyst-figure of Renouard, is imposed on him by the important fact that this story was finished by a Conrad who had already executed *Under Western Eyes* and *Victory* and who could not sustain the imaginative egoist in the way he might have, and did, twenty years earlier. The significance of Mrs. Travers is deliberately metaphysical in passages such as the following, some of them written by 1898 but many added later as her character unfolds during the last half of the book. This one is from section three, "The Capture," and is part of the portentous 1898 style that was often purged in Conrad's 1918 revision of this beginning. It occurs the night after her first meeting with Immada, Hassim, and Lingard — after the contrast between her and Immada has been expressed as "the beginning and the end, the flower and the leaf, the phrase and the cry" (p. 148).

After a time this absolute silence which she almost could feel pressing upon her on all sides induced in Mrs. Travers a state of hallucination. She saw herself standing alone, at the end of time, on the brink of days. All was unmoving as if the dawn would never come, the stars would never fade, the sun would never rise any more; all was mute, still, dead — as if the shadow of the outer darkness, the shadow of the uninterrupted, of the everlasting night that fills the universe, the shadow of the night so profound and so vast that the blazing suns lost in it are only like sparks, like pinpoints of fire, the restless shadow that like a suspicion of an evil truth darkens everything upon the earth on its passage, had enveloped her, had stood arrested as if to remain with her forever.

And there was such a finality in that illusion, such an accord with the trend of her thought that when she murmured into the darkness a faint "so be it" she seemed to have spoken one of those sentences that resume and close a life. (P. 151)

We have seen Conrad in moods like this before, haunted by the image of interstellar space and by the crushing weight of the "long view" of man's meaninglessness in the universe. Perhaps the creation of Miss Moorsom had refreshed — for the task of finishing *The Rescue* — Conrad's sense of the metaphysical significance inhering substantially and metaphorically in the ritual forms of high society. But that metaphysical implication had always been there in Felicia; it could easily be emphasized by slight manipulations of these last two hundred or so pages.

We are led to believe in observations made by d'Alcacer, Mr. Travers, Lingard, and even Mrs. Travers herself that she and Lingard are genuinely similar, as Felicia is made to look like Renouard. D'Alcacer says that Mrs. Travers looks as though she is suited to a life of action, made for the "moral beauty of a fearless expression," and intrinsically unlike the role society has given her (p. 139); he further believes that she is dealing cleverly with Lingard for his own and her husband's lives. Though recognizing that she is in

love with an aspect of Lingard, and that there are similarities between them that may make this a form of self-love, d'Alcacer cannot believe, however, that these affinities run deep enough at this
late date to nourish any permanent changes. Despite good reasons
for discounting d'Alcacer's view not only of Mrs. Travers but of
his life in general, his humane skepticism continually reminds us
that her reaction to the unrepressed reality of Lingard's natives
and his enterprise is in many ways quite artificial. Until after Carter has blasted holes in the two Illanum war praus and genuinely
put the fat in the fire, Mrs. Travers persistently sees the reality she
has sought in Lingard and his world as a kind of operatic spectacle.
Even after Carter's action she occasionally behaves as though her
enthusiasm were not for Lingard's passionate reality so much as
for the fulfillment of her own aesthetic expectations.

Compared to the mindless class prejudices of her husband and
the Decoud-like resignation of d'Alcacer, Mrs. Traver's willingness to fulfill Lingard's honor — to encourage the return to Belarab
of her husband and d'Alcacer after Carter's attack — seems like
wholehearted commitment to Lingard's romantic idealism; and it
further appears that her willingness to go finally to Lingard in the
stockade confirms this solid participation and belief in the moral
authority of his exotic reality. Yet the morning before she leaves
on this torch-lit mission, she stands looking out from the muni-
tions-and-stores ship toward the native settlement:

> She saw, she imagined, she even admitted now the reality of
> those things no longer a mere pageant marshalled for her vision
> with barbarous splendour and savage emphasis. She questioned it
> no longer — but she did not feel it in her soul any more than one
> feels the depth of the sea under its peaceful glitter or the turmoil
> of its grey fury. (P. 367)

Even the signs on board ship that her husband and d'Alcacer have
been returned as hostages ("the camp bedsteads not taken away, a
pillow lying on the deck") and Jörgenson's deadly timing of the
fuses strike her as "idle phantasy," "fantastic" (p. 367). But she is
never to reach the sterility of Felicia Moorsom, who has emptied
the forms of her emotion of all content and savors her "fine duty"

aesthetically, as all feeling for its own sake tends to become a kind of pseudo aesthetic. Mrs. Travers wants to feel the substance of Lingard's honor as well as its form. She strives to avoid entirely the separation of form and content that characterizes Miss Moorsom, but on the whole fails for a variety of reasons. The sympathy necessary for more than simply understanding Lingard must come from sources not apparently available to Mrs. Travers, who possesses, d'Alcacer says, a "latent capacity for sympathy developed in those who are disenchanted with life or death." How deeply she is disenchanted he does not know and believes that even she herself "would never know" (p. 124).

We must, of course, decide early in the novel how seriously we are to take d'Alcacer's pronouncements about Mrs. Travers. There is enough ambiguity in her thoughts and actions to make us read the remarks of other characters with interest if not conviction as to their accuracy about her soul. But even so it is interesting that Conrad makes a man such as d'Alcacer play the role of ironic chorus to Mrs. Travers's fleeting intimations that she has begun to feel as Lingard feels, and to Lingard's conviction that she is intrinsically with him in opposition to all that Mr. Travers stands for. D'Alcacer is apparently intended to remind us that Mrs. Travers's concern for his and her husband's lives is not only a point of honor and the natural compassion for two human beings innocent of any guilt in this exotic political maneuver. She is also, in ways that will never be clear to Lingard, closer to both of these men than to her ideal self-image. Apart from d'Alcacer's warnings about the extent to which her identity depends on that ritual dance (pp. 412–13), Conrad treats her own thoughts on the subject ironically and thus suggests that she is a long way from finding her path out of that artificial existence. After hearing Lingard's appeal for help and the narration of his life story the night of their first meeting, Conrad says of her:

Mrs. Travers found that Lingard was touching, because he could be understood. How simple was life, she reflected. She was frank with herself. She considered him apart from social organization. She discovered he had no place in it. How delightful! Here was a human being and the naked truth of things was not so very far from her notwithstanding the growth of centuries. Then it occurred to her that this man by his action stripped her at once of her position, of her wealth, of her rank, of her past. "I am helpless. What remains?" she asked herself. Nothing! Anybody there might have suggested: "Your presence." She was too artificial yet to think of her beauty; and yet the power of personality is part of the naked truth of things. (P. 167)

Although this analysis occurs early in the novel, Mrs. Travers does not greatly improve her sense that nothing remains of her identity "apart from social organization." She does, of course, discover that her power of personality is more than enough to move Lingard, but she can never really enter the world that he thrives in.

Especially does she fail to appreciate the sense in which nobody, least of all Lingard, can really have "no place" in social organization. Lingard is immured in the niceties of Malayan social intrigue; though apparently above it, he is really entirely dependent on the delicate relations among legitimate ruler, upstart aspirant, and third force — between Belarab, Tengga, and Daman. And this is not merely political involvement but just as thoroughly social as Lingard's dependence on the social position of his noble prince and princess of Wajo. To Mrs. Travers it is the society of an opera stage, but it is for the time being Lingard's social context just as surely as the yacht and the London season are hers. One of the important ideas that emerges in the second half of the novel is not that Mrs. Travers progresses toward the passionate, unrepressed humanity of Lingard, but that this image of romance and adventure — basic human feelings in asocial, unrepressed contact with each other — is imaginary. Certainly — and this is a very important point — it is antithetical to everything Conrad had suggested in *Under Western Eyes*.

At one point after Mr. Travers and d'Alcacer have been returned from their first captivity, Mr. Travers accuses his wife of not having "feelings appropriate to your origin, social position, and the ideas of the class to which you belong" (p. 267). Had she been a man, he says, she "would have led a most irregular life. You would

have been a frank adventurer" (p. 268). Responding to his conclusion that she is at heart "perfectly primitive," Edith suggests
that if so she has nonetheless had to discipline herself if only to
keep from committing suicide. "It sounds like something a bar-
barian, hating the delicate complexities and restraints of a nobler
life, might have said," responds Mr. Travers. But of course Edith's
taste for the primitive does not automatically make her Lingard's
companion in an Eden where two people love one another with unrepressed purity. Edith romanticizes the primitive state as Conrad
characteristically did not, and Lingard himself is not far behind
her in attributing to at least Hassim and Immada an idealism that
actually depends for its imaginative intensity almost entirely on
himself. The novel becomes unintentionally comic in its use of the
ring, which Hassim first sends as a sign that he is about to die and
that Lingard should not foolishly try to rescue him, but which Lingard seizes as a challenge to rush in where natives fear to tread.
Such is the natives' actual pragmatism and Lingard's contrasting
romanticism.

Though Conrad is careful to indicate that Edith, bothered as she
is by images of interstellar night, cannot reach the stage of early
mankind described as the leaf, the cry, the beginning, cannot join
Lingard in the unrepressed authenticity of feeling and expression,
the larger issue posed by the novel is whether Conrad seriously intends us to believe two things: that such a state really exists, and
that had Edith been capable of such immediacy she might have
joined Lingard in "Paradise."

The character of Mrs. Travers does not change a great deal from
the 1898 work to that of 1918, except that in the last half of the
novel she is made to perform a function in the plot conceived in
1898 but irrelevant to the Conrad of 1918. Lingard's dilemma is
supposed to be an inevitably unsatisfactory choice between his passion for Mrs. Travers (which also means refusing to deliver her
husband and d'Alcacer to the rapacious Daman) and his pledges to
Hassim and Immada. In order to salvage any of his plans for the re-
capture of Wajo, he must decide at once after Carter's attack to
deliver Mr. Travers and d'Alcacer to Daman, as Belarab belatedly

suggests, and hope thereby to disrupt the alliance of Tengga and Daman. (The details of this strategy have, of course, become ludicrously complex at this late point in the novel, and few readers want to follow them.) Most readers detect, however, that Conrad has lost all ability to give this dilemma the emotional force and validity he claims for it in Lingard. We are told at various times in the last half of the novel that this knight who can handle any opposition from without cannot grasp the division within his own mind (p. 210), but surely this observation about the unreflective man of action was a cliché long before Conrad used it. Lingard's will (he is accustomed to seeing the "visible surface of life open in the sun to the conquering tread of an unfettered will" [p. 210]) is paralyzed; whether one wants to believe that the paralysis comes from the simple fact that he is impaled on the horns of a dilemma or from the peculiar nature of his passion (as Moser supposes), Conrad is more or less committed by the original scheme of the novel to make a great thing out of the paralysis of will, a disposition he had long since abandoned in his work. It further seems to me that he would not have retained this motif had he not been dealing with at least a shadow of the imaginative egoist common to his work through *Nostromo*.

Why is it so difficult to get interested in the paralysis of this once decisive will? One explanation seems to me quite simple: whatever Lingard does or does not do can have little effect on the questions raised by the character of Edith Travers. Conrad had always planned that she and Lingard would never tread the paths of paradise together; but, more important, her sense of what constitutes paradise will have no more or less authority under any circumstances. Conrad consciously arranges the plot to relieve her of any direct responsibility for Lingard's paralysis by pointing out that in withholding Hassim's ring she is not the only one keeping from Lingard word of his friends' capture. Belarab knows that the prince and princess are being held by Daman but fears Lingard's "fierce energy" (p. 434) should he be told; and d'Alcacer hears enough from Edith to wonder whether he ought to tell Lingard that she comes with a message from Jörgenson. As many critics have pointed out, Lingard later says he would not in any event have chosen Hassim and Immada over his passion for Edith (and would not have demonstrated the choice by returning Mr. Travers and d'Alcacer to Daman). Thus we are rather awkwardly led to see that only his passion for Edith and not any flaw on her part has induced this paralysis.

It is not, however, that Conrad now accepts along with his hero the infinite desirability of this ominous love for Edith, this "profound indifference, this strange contempt for what his eyes could see, this distaste for words, this unbelief in the importance of things and men" (pp. 431–32). Conrad has, rather, lost faith in the value of either term of the dilemma and consequently in the whole matter of choosing or failing to choose. He has, as Moser argues, taken the moral initiative away from Lingard. True, Lingard's willingness to take the disillusioned Jörgenson into the adventure makes the explosion of the stores ship more than chance; Lingard has chosen Jörgenson and might have expected some sort of last-ditch expression of contempt for something Conrad had earlier called "what is intrinsically great and profound within the forms of human folly" (p. 162). But for the most part Lingard's paralysis is systematically plundered of the moral significance inhering in the root metaphor of will and passion that the novel overtly suggests. The surrender to "love" for Mrs. Travers is not shared by author and character as the "greatest good," but is an expression of the truth that Conrad is no longer interested in the moral-psychological rubric characteristic of his first two novels, "The Lagoon," and "Karain," and imposed on "The Rescuer" as early as 1896. There is some feeling of loss when the romantic, idealistic restoration of Hassim and Immada to Wajo goes up in a single blast, but there is no sense of lost opportunities when Mrs. Travers and Lingard inevitably part company on the ruins of Lingard's honor, and literally before the grave of the fleet-footed, faithful cliché of a messenger who has carried the ridiculous ring back and forth throughout the novel.

The longest description of the night-long surrender Lingard makes to his passion for Mrs. Travers is full of the exhausted-swimmer-and-statue imagery familiar to readers of "The Planter of Malata" (p. 432). Like Renouard Lingard seems to be surrendering not to love for a woman but to complete metaphysical failure, to intimations of absurdity in the midst of protestations that this love is the supreme value; but unlike Renouard, no such signs have been apparent in Lingard's career — and he has not, as it were, his own fraternal guide. What we have, it seems to me, is the superimposition of late Conradian preoccupations on a rubric that is not suited to their fulfillment or exploration. Having robbed Lingard's paralyzed will — that psychological and moral metaphor so common in *Almayer's Folly* and *An Outcast* — of all moral significance by in large part exonerating Lingard of responsibility for either the broken love affair or the destruction of the Wajo political romance, there is not the means within the novel to explore even old issues. The 1898 plan may have included the explosion of the stores ship, but I doubt that had the novel been completed in 1898 Conrad would have so emptied Lingard's paralysis of moral significance or so loaded his description of the passion for Edith with unique echoes of "The Planter of Malata" and, hence, of *Victory*. His original idea, as a letter to *Blackwood's Magazine* suggests, called for Lingard to sacrifice his plans for the "necessary conditions of her happiness," and thereby to face "his reward — an inevitable separation." [6] In such a plot Lingard would have been responsible for a good many things, and we should have felt him genuinely confronted with a dilemma.

Conrad in 1898 may have intended to locate a good part of the moral interest of the novel in Edith's discovery of the primitive virtues. As Mrs. Hay points out in her discussion of the character Wyndham, Conrad may have contemplated using many of the natives as a wellspring of masculine virtue that has been lost to the decadent civilization suggested by both Mr. and Mrs. Travers and by d'Alcacer. But Wyndham was deleted from the manuscript, and the second half of the novel beyond doubt loses whatever faith the first half may in manuscript have shown in the value of Lingard's imaginative egotism or of his participation in the unrepressed reality of the native. The pristine qualities that Mrs. Travers admires in Immada, immediately upon seeing her, and then in Lingard ("Oh! This is truth—this is anger—something real at last." [p. 132]) are practically meaningless to the Conrad who had spent twenty years undercutting any such a priori virtues. I suspect that Conrad in subjecting Mrs. Travers to Lingard's and the natives' reality may in 1898 have been working with the preoccupation of *The Nigger* and "Falk": the idea that a full awareness of ego, of the Schopenhauerian vision, is therapeutic for decadent modern society. In 1918, however, Conrad was no longer vitally interested in that formulation. He had capped his use of the native mind with a subtly metaphysical view of their innocence, of qualities he had attributed to them in his first two novels; and apparently, if the deletion of Wyndham means anything, he drew back in 1918 from attributing to them pristine virtues that his use of natives in at least three other novels (*Almayer's Folly*, *An Outcast*, and *Heart of Darkness*) had severely qualified. Had he allowed Wyndham to remain, with all his praise for the masculine virtues of the native world, we should have wondered along with Conrad how much more masculine virtue the world of 1918 could stand.

Mrs. Travers seems now and again in both halves of the novel to share the author's deepest awareness that the problem is not how to make contact with more than the form of Lingard's unrepressed reality, but how to justify a sense of value at all. Her consciousness penetrates beyond the myth of decadent humanity refreshed and possibly saved by contact with its origins, the myth that Wyndham suggests so strongly. As a character she was from the outset hard for Conrad to handle not only because she was a Western woman and elicited the difficulties he had always had with the language and rhetoric of passion, but because even in 1898 she must have looked ahead to the existential vision Conrad was to see first in *Heart of Darkness*.

Let there be no doubt that *The Rescue* provides one of the most illuminating insights into the process of artistic creation to be found anywhere in literature. How few moments there are in the history of any art when we may observe the artist returning after incredibly mature successes to a project conceived in the assumptions of the beginning of his career. The whole effect might be like watching Jackson Pollock complete, a few years before his death, a landscape begun in the 1930s. The confrontation of early with late in style, root metaphors, and major motifs (whatever their relative merit) might well destroy the entire effort. It is surprising that Conrad felt he could finish *The Rescue* at all, and that so many critics are not astonished he felt this way. Only Moser has offered a lively suggestion as to how the early and late could have been reconciled in the finished novel, and of course his theory pivots on the suggestion that Conrad had given up his own and his characters' formerly heavy burden of moral responsibility in favor of a grotesque quest for peace. This abdication is allegedly a large part of Conrad's "decline," and I have no desire to call it anything else. Conrad is thought to have disarmed the original fragment of any motifs that might make emotional trouble for him.

Moser detects in the late Conrad a death wish that supposedly overwhelms the complex moral considerations originally attaching to the character of Lingard, as indeed to Lord Jim and other "imaginative egoists." If, however, we simply make a naïve observation of these earlier characters, of Lord Jim for instance, they will not finally seem so different from the Lingard of *The Rescue*. My view of Lord Jim, as I have sufficiently indicated, is that he seeks the death of man so that God might be born, seeks to be the self-founded, in-itself conscious of itself. He is the "useless passion" that Sartre discusses in a way which clearly suggests that he and Conrad are using similar models of the human mind. The similarity between Sartre's description of his own life in *The Words* and Lord Jim's sense of ordination are remarkable but not unexpected by anyone who had read *Being and Nothingness*. Young Jean-Paul's feeling that every incident in his life is, in a sense, already part of "The Biography of Sartre, the Famous Writer," that the essence of any of these events precedes their existence, is closer to Lord Jim's state of mind than to that of any other fictional character I can think of. Although we do not think of Jim, Charles Gould, Decoud, or Nostromo as men who seek the peace so notoriously

associated with Felicia Moorsom or Mrs. Travers, they do in fact
seek to emulate the condition of in-itself. They seek to abdicate
the radical freedom and responsibility that both Sartre and Conrad
believe constitutes man's true godliness.

Though Lingard in *The Rescue* pursues his stasis, immobility,
peace, impenetrability (the precise quality is hard to pin down) by
relinquishing for the moment his life of willful action in favor of
his love for Mrs. Travers, on the contrary Lord Jim, Gould, and
Nostromo seek many of the same qualities (often suggested by the
silver) through continued or even intensified activity, will, and
dedication. The means to the end appear quite different in these
two instances (Lingard on the one hand; Jim, Gould, and Nostromo on the other). The appearance, however, is deceptive, since
both kinds of project are designed by the characters to divest
themselves of those unique qualities of human consciousness that
by contrast make their goal so ominously unconscious (or contradictory in the desire to be consciously unconscious, like in-itself
observing itself). In short, the root projects of all these characters
are remarkably similar despite superficial differences. Nostromo
desiring to "absorb" the silver does not seem unlike Lingard em-
bracing the "immortality" of Mrs. Travers or admiring her "inde-
structibility." The language Lingard uses to describe Mrs. Travers
might almost without alteration be applied by Charles Gould to
the silver or even to "material interests." Gould's passion for the
mine is treated as though it were love for another woman, and if
for another woman then one very much like Lingard's image of
Mrs. Travers. As Lingard succumbs to Mrs. Travers, we are told
he

was seduced away by the tense feeling of existence far superior to
the mere consciousness of life, and which in its immensity of contradictions, delight, dread, exultation and despair could not be
faced and yet not to be evaded. There was no peace in it. But
who wanted peace? Surrender was better, the dreadful ease of
slack limbs in the sweep of an enormous tide and in a divine emptiness of mind. If this was existence he knew that he existed. And he
knew that the woman existed too, in the sweep of the tide, without

speech, without movement, without heat! Indestructible — and, perhaps, immortal! (P. 432)

Words have almost failed Conrad in this incantation; denotative qualities slip out of place and contradict one another. There is peace but no peace, contradiction with unity, tension and release simultaneously. All we can be sure of is that Lingard envisions a sense of "existence far superior to the mere consciousness of life." To call this a death wish or annihilation is grossly to ignore Conrad's awkward attempt to suggest a unique mode of existence, a mode adequately though ornately conveyed by Sartre's phrase "in-itself-for-itself." Lingard wants, above all, to relinquish his freedom and responsibility; he wants simultaneously to revoke the very nature of consciousness and yet to enter its simulacrum. If this is not closely akin to the fundamental projects of Lord Jim, Charles Gould, and Nostromo, then I have seriously misunderstood one or all of these novels.

Of course I have not intended to explain why Conrad reads all this into love for a woman — that is essentially a psychoanalytic task, whether existential or Freudian. It is not, however, simply death or annihilation or even peace that is found in this woman. The imagery of surrender to an immense tide is unmistakably an echo of Renouard's swimming to his death in "The Planter of Malata." Though introduced in 1898 or even earlier, this type of metaphysically pregnant woman is not and probably could not have been given her full significance in Conrad's work until quite late, until the existential vision had been explored. If only sexual fears and anxieties were involved in her creation, presumably she might have appeared and have worked her effect on Lingard at any time in Conrad's career and have borne little or no relation to Conrad's developing conceptions of mind.

But the effect of Mrs. Travers on Lingard eludes any grip the root conceptions of 1898 might have given us on these final scenes. Because, however, this Lingard had been conceived early in Conrad's career, *The Rescue* sometimes suggests that we are watching a paralysis of the will, a man seduced by erotic passion, when in fact, had *The Rescue* not come equipped with its embarrassingly naïve inheritance from 1896–98, we should have been more readily aware that in the final scenes no metaphor but those of *Lord Jim*, *Nostromo*, and *Victory* were really adequate. In short, the final significance of *The Rescue* has very little to do with the psychological model ostensibly given us for its understanding, though to say so does not mean that *The Rescue* is in my eyes greatly improved as a novel. What happens to Lingard happens in terms of the awarenesses achieved from *Heart of Darkness* through *Victory* and cannot really be fathomed as erotic passion subverting a characteristically powerful will. Effective responsibility for what happens is thus removed from Lingard's shoulders as an instinctive sign from the author, it seems to me, that we are to look elsewhere than in Lingard's will for the moral significance of the novel — that we may well search among the labored descriptions of Lingard's surrender for echoes (albeit pathetically weak ones) of Jim, Nostromo, and Charles Gould.

# 11

# Conclusion: Responsibility and the Existential Metaphor

The revolution that Conrad more than any other of his contemporary novelists had helped create is, despite the ultimate affinities with Kipling, Pascal, Shakespeare, and Sartre, nevertheless so deeply involved with Schopenhauer and subsequently with Freud that the three names should be inseparable in the history of the period. It is always the name of Schopenhauer that surprises people when a claim of this sort is made, largely because we do not today remember that by the 1890s he was better known than "any other modern Continental metaphysician, except Kant" [1] and had influenced subtly the principal current of awareness culminating in the philosophical and clinical discoveries of Freud. To Descartes, Schopenhauer attributed the idea that will is "an act of thought and to be identified with the judgement," [2] that human wishes are not only clear to the reason but largely under its direction. As one of the best recent students of Schopenhauer has somewhat overcautiously said, "possibly some philosophers, when discussing human action, have shown a regrettable tendency to introduce references to obscure psychic faculties and quasi-mechanical agencies, or have played fast and loose with various highly indeterminate terms of which 'volitions' is the most notorious . . ." [3]

Even if we grant that all philosophic language lies open to the same risks, this is surely what the psychology that Conrad inherited did, and indeed Conrad carries on a good many of its quasi-mechanical agencies while discovering in his own imaginatively powerful work the truth that Schopenhauer had already announced: that will is largely an unconscious force which nonetheless "chooses" just as surely as we had been used to thinking of the will-as-thought-and-judgment choosing. Thus Schopenhauer's will is not equivalent to the passion of the Platonic and Christian volition-and-passion metaphor; unlike that allegedly animal force which we did not choose, but which overcame our willful thought and judgment, the will Schopenhauer describes is just as authentically a choice as any product of the conscious, rational mind. Schopenhauer prepares the way for talking about such unconscious acts of will not as a merely "lower" nature that we do not really "want" to fulfill, but as part of our humanity that is just as definitively human as reason and judgment or other godlike attributes. If he paired rational judgment and unrational will as a lame, seeing man seated on the shoulders of a blind giant, and speculated that the giant would only occasionally listen to the directions of the lame man, it is nonetheless vital to remember that both agents in this metaphor are human.

Furthermore, the Cartesian will-and-passion model usually postulated that the rational judgment was aware of and could describe lower passions even if it could not control them; Schopenhauer and Freud, in a discovery that was to shape much of the twentieth century, established the truth that we often do not know what our will is until we have done it, that our will is not merely on occasion a charted if brutish passion but a mystery only inadequately characterized by the disdainful language and in the categories of rational judgment.

Schopenhauer and Conrad both knew how self-image became important in this description of will:

We may, for instance, "entertain a desire for years without even confessing it to ourselves, or even allowing it to come to clear consciousness; for the intellect must know nothing about it, because the good opinion we have of ourselves would thereby suffer. But if it is fulfilled, we learn from our joy, not without shame, that we have wanted this — for example the death of a near relation whose heir we are." [4]

From a similar insight follow so many of what appear to be night journeys in Conrad's work; and it is interesting that neither Conrad nor Schopenhauer limits this process to discoveries of dark ego, self-love, or even what Freud called id; both men include anything that must be withheld from our quasi-rational self-image. Conrad especially was not inclined to dwell on the content of that will but to examine its effect on self-image, since the drama of self-image was in many ways the focus of his art and provided him with a model much more flexible than the categories of classical psychology. The ultimate desires of man were at best a mystery that even the idea of self-love crudely oversimplified.

Part of the failure of *The Rescue* is that it requires Conrad to deal with a hero who denies Conrad's own Schopenhauerian and Pascalian changes in the Cartesian will-and-passion model, changes so disturbingly achieved and almost simultaneously surpassed (shortly after the original manuscript of "The Rescuer" had been begun) in *Heart of Darkness*. Kurtz is the archetype of the hero who, in nearly the manner Schopenhauer described, discovers that he had wanted something beyond all the powers of his conscious judgment to conceive, something that eludes all attempts to describe it as the victory over his rational will of an animal passion he had not chosen. Kurtz has chosen his degradation, and the faculty which has made these choices is not, as for centuries it had so conveniently been described, his animal nature overcoming his godlike or at least uniquely human attributes, but as much part of his uniquely human reality as his reason. The fiction of dividing the whole man into an animal part and a godlike part is broken in *Heart of Darkness*; Kurtz's wishes are distinctly human, for no animal could do or choose to do what he has relished. Similarly, his own self-judgment comes not from the godlike attributes viewing the animal part of his nature run rampant, but from the *whole* man — presumably (and this is a vital point) from the same will that has chosen everything else and that might, conceivably, have chosen not to live at all, or to live as Heyst does. Lingard of *The Rescue* can, for a multitude of reasons, see none of this.

Once the venerable Greek and Christian and Cartesian model has been shattered, Conrad moves away from Schopenhauer's thought and even Freud's, guided as only a creative artist can be by the sensual power of his own imagination to envision not even Schopenhauer's rich panoply of willful possibilities — most of which nonetheless revolve about self-love — but what today would be called the existential freedom of the will. The will, as Schopenhauer never quite saw, can deny itself or can feel no justification for its existence, and can produce thereby the peculiar late-Victorian disease often inadequately called *mal du siècle*. The tension in Conrad's late work is, if we are talking about will and justification, between the implications of Razumov, who makes a compelling choice of human solidarity as his only justification, and Heyst, whose metaphysical pessimism permits him only to offer his life as expiation for a failure to make a similar choice.

The only imperative Conrad finally recognizes, after a lifetime imagining the possible claims of innumerable sanctions upon the human spirit, is not even human solidarity (not even the sense of our common tragic predicament) but a personal responsibility approaching the meaning of the existential term "authenticity." To recognize the humanity and infinite scope of man's wishes and not to call the choices unacceptable to reason or morality "animal," to recognize even in Heyst's conviction that he has the truth about life and about man's position in the cosmos a *choice* and a responsibility for that choice — this is man's highest moral achievement. There are innumerable ways to deny our responsibility for what we are, not the least of them being a taste for metaphysical skepticism founded in the awareness of our absurd place in nature. The affirmation in Conrad's work, however, lies not intrinsically in any "enthroned" imperatives but in his passionate sense that man is *responsible* for those values and others, or for the absence of all value. The idea of free choice, originally bearing vaguely Christian but largely Cartesian assumptions, altered by Conrad with Schopenhauerian and Pascalian perceptions, and finally vital with Conrad's own insights, is resurgent in his work—by implication even in *The Rescue*, where an earlier and, for Conrad, impoverished conception of it is simply allowed to die a natural death. Conrad felt the necessity for a new sense of responsibility, for a way of seeing even the all-important ideal of human solidarity not as some sort of Platonic form emanating its innate authority, but as the fragile child of human volition. Such, after all, is the true victory of Axel Heyst and a large part of the immorality of Villiers's Axël: Heyst is finally willing to affirm not the innate authority of commitment to life (as so many readers assume), but his own responsibility for, most immediately, Lena's death and ultimately for the attitudes that throughout most of the story he had offered as though they were the inevitably rational consequence of cosmic truth. If Heyst cannot really choose life as his victory, he nonetheless recognizes that it is his responsibility to do so or not, and that there is no appeal from this choice. He reaffirms in relatively plain language what Marlow in *Heart of Darkness* had earlier found almost unutterable.

The kind of responsibility that Conrad imagines is not easily understood, either by those characters directly involved or by the reader. Conrad's redefinition of will lies open to a criticism often directed against Schopenhauer's conception of our willing as a largely unconscious activity. Patrick Gardiner summarizes it:

For if in the last resort I have to *discover* what my will is by observing what I do, the ways in which I respond to considerations and circumstances, can I any longer feel in the full sense responsible for my will, regard it as being truly mine? It seems to have become in a fashion cut off from me, in the way in which the will of another is separate from me: why, then, should I feel any more answerable for what I will and do than for what somebody else wills and does?

To defend Schopenhauer against all of these objections would certainly not be easy . . .[5]

Willems and Lord Jim (to select only prime early examples) have both developed rationalizations for their behavior—for their betrayal of moral standards — which are similar to the argument Gardiner sketches: Willems's metaphor of Aïssa's theft of his white soul and Jim's "I had jumped . . . It seems," both dodge the fact of their betrayals by shifting responsibility onto another person or an allegedly will-less moment. Conrad knows how painful it is to accept the burden of these acts that do seem almost to have been done by another person, but that difficulty is precisely the measure of the responsibility demanded by the final self-knowledge of a Razumov, Heyst, or Kurtz. Lingard's acceptance of responsibility in his three novels is never of the same quality as Kurtz's. Never once in the final scenes of *The Rescue* does he feel responsible for having willed his passion for Mrs. Travers; like Lord Jim, whose aesthetic parent he was, he tries to adapt the Cartesian volitions in the only way possible, by speaking not of new discoveries about his wishes (as Schopenhauer would) but of an unexplained paralysis of the will. Of course in some of the late work, in *Under Western Eyes* and in *Victory*, the act for which responsibility must be accepted is not the criminal transgression of Willems, Lord Jim, or Kurtz. But both Razumov and Heyst do commit what for Conrad's last years was a more resonant betrayal of human solidarity, and both men are for a large part of their stories perfectly capable of avoiding a sense of responsibility with rationalizations far more subtle than Willems's or Lord Jim's.

Thus the true sense of freedom can only develop in Conrad's characters under the awareness of this peculiar responsibility for acts and attitudes whose source we may never really understand with the rational powers of the mind. Kurtz is "free" after his acknowledgment of responsibility, after his "victory," as no other character in the work preceding *Heart of Darkness* had been — free not in the sense of being able to change his character, but clearly free as Thomas Mann develops the conception in his short story, "Mario and the Magician." There the hypnotist Cipolla does not — as the usual misunderstanding of the story has it — make people act against their will; on the contrary, he ordinarily allows them to fulfill wishes they have suppressed or imperfectly understood. The signora whom Cipolla attracts despite the futile supplications of her husband has, we are told a number of times, been living in the past glory of her service and — indeed — love for a famous actress; she has in spirit been separated from her husband from the outset of their marriage, and Cipolla has done nothing against her will (just as, one supposes Mann to suggest, Mussolini had really done little against the will of Italy). As the hypnotist says, there is freedom and there is will, but there is no freedom of the will in the abstract: the will must wish *something*, not negatively its own freedom.

Thomas Mann has, in this story, imaginatively explored the psychological-moral metaphor of will with a boldness and sympathy that matches Richardson's in *Clarissa* and the best of Conrad. And he has suggested what Conrad believes, that the principal bondage lies in not recognizing our own wishes, in, say, attributing them to something or somebody else, to the will of a dictator, of a Cipolla or Mussolini, to the "eyes of a savage" or to a mysterious paralysis of the will. The spirit to combat the kind of dictatorship that so disturbed Mann in 1929 comes not entirely from our love of freedom but also from our willingess to recognize the dictator as a catalyst to the wishes in all of us. We are free to recognize the enormous potential of human wishes — not usually to change those wishes, though that may occasionally happen, but to achieve a self-image that allows our responsibility for the whole man rather than simply for the conscious mind.

Conrad, however, in the subtlety of some of his late work suggests that it is not only the criminal act for which we must accept responsibility, not only the dark impulse that Guerard envisions as the heart of the night journey, but Heyst rescuing Morrison and Lena. Heyst considers both those acts of sympathy as much a violation of his self-image (and no less impregnated with untoward consequences) as Jim does his leap from the *Patna*. Like Jim, he cannot acknowledge the implications for his self-image of those — to him — incredible breaches in his conscious will. But his death is not Jim's, and his final state of mind is not Jim's: he has at least won through to a sense of his responsibility, not only for his attempted disengagement from life but for his love of Lena. The night journey will not do as a metaphor of self-discovery in Conrad at least in part because he has discovered that these unconscious wishes cannot readily be described as dark ego; for some men, for Heyst and Razumov, they have more to do with love for others than with self-love. What is conscious and acceptable to one man may be unconscious and unacceptable to another: it is the drama of self-image challenged by unacknowledged wishes, or more precisely by the fact that no man is ever one with his self-image, rather than any universal portrait of *all* such wishes that interests Conrad. That Heyst should feel his self-image shattered by a compassion and love that another man might accept as a most desirable and conscious wish is, I suppose, pathetic; but is it any more so than Lord Jim's persistent refusal to accept responsibility (despite his return for trial) for behavior that he cannot explain within the self-image that dictates his every conscious move?

Proust, D. H. Lawrence, Ford Madox Ford, Lawrence Durrell, and Conrad have all announced the breakdown of old conceptions of monolithic character and have all adopted a rather impressionistic bias. But like Swann in *Remembrance of Things Past* and Darley in *Justine*, some of these writers accept the theory of the multi-faceted self without really being able to imagine life according to the theory. Darley, though he very early asserts that there are many "truths," is continually satisfied with the single image in *Justine*, the single angle of vision, and is terribly upset when Justine goes about living the theory, shedding truths like clothes. Of the writers mentioned, only Conrad explores impressively the *moral* implications of such a new impressionistic metaphor for human character: what does it mean morally to suggest not only that, as Einstein — Durrell's favorite authority — and Schopenhauer said, the "fact" is relative to the observer, but that each man is in a powerful sense an observer of himself, that the self is multiple and elusive, disappearing as we close our hands on it? Conrad more than any other of these writers has pursued the ancient sense of moral responsibility into the elaborately mirrored, even prismatic labyrinth of the new metaphor. Like the existentialist, but distinctly unlike the characters in that impressionistic tour de force *The*

*Good Soldier*, Conrad's characters are sometimes made to face the existential nature of identity — that is, they are required to sense their responsibility for identity, as even the relatively inarticulate Meursault is made to in Camus's *The Stranger*. Dowell in *The Good Soldier* raises all the impressionist's questions (most of them similar to Justine's "You know I never tell a story the same way twice. Does that mean that I am lying?"); but nowhere in that novel does Ford offer us anything comparable to Meursault's rejection of all the ready-made identities that society offers him (the mourning son, the distraught and betrayed lover, and so on). Society in effect tries to seduce his freedom by offering a series of identities containing ready-made explanations of the crime, inviting him to say he is one with one or another of them. He refuses and establishes himself as the absurd man, subsumed by no identity but responsible for choosing his mode of existence. Though we are invited to infer from Dowell's unreliability the distinct possibility that, for example, Florence, his wife, may not be only the vulgar opportunist he portrays, and the far more interesting and subtler conclusion that there is nonetheless "reality" in appearance (this is of course Durrell's point), the novel does not conduct us from the questions of impressionism to those of existential responsibility. There is a highroad between these two kinds of perceptions, but of the so-called Impressionists only Conrad travels it. Even Durrell, writing, as it were, surrounded by existential thought, either rejects the connections between his impressionism and some of Sartre's or Camus's implications, or — as seems more likely to me — cannot see them.

I want, then, to suggest carefully the sense in which Conrad is existential, for there are many sides to contemporary existentialism that he would have rejected out of hand. To recognize that the self is multiple and elusive, not only in its appearance to others but inherently, this is impressionistic; and to suggest further that the kind of reality we usually have inheres in the impression, this is equally impressionistic. But to go on from these bench marks to a profound moral dissatisfaction with the man who cannot see or will not admit that he is not at one with and defined by an "identity," this is

distinctly to invoke the existential sense of responsibility and, simultaneously, an existential sense of freedom. Undoubtedly we
inherit dispositions, psychological and physiological, and Conrad
would have been the first to acknowledge them. But the use we
make of these predispositions is always in some sense and to some
degree our responsibility. We are free especially in the sense that
there is no option not to be free, and our freedom is the measure of
our responsibility. It is always useful to remember Lord Jim when
discussing the connection between freedom and identity. Jim believes he *is* a selfless hero, despite certain allegedly unfair situations
that might indicate to the unfaithful either that he *is* a coward (a
conclusion that would be as monolithic and as false as Jim's) or
that he is not one with any identity. My point is that although he
can deny his freedom to be something other than a selfless hero, in
Conrad's eyes he cannot escape his responsibility for having done
so. In cleaving to an identity as though it had been ordained, he
denies his freedom but has not lost it. He has *chosen* to deny it and
for that must bear a responsibility fully as great and as significant
as the one he ought to bear for leaving the *Patna*. Lord Jim, however, owes a great deal to the character of Lingard in the manuscript of "The Rescuer," and as Conrad even twenty years later is
confused about whether Lingard's acute sense of honor outweighs
his tacit denial of freedom, so is he ambivalent with Lord Jim. Jim's
love affair with this particular self-image commands our respect,
and it is tempting to say — as Mrs. Hay does — that Jim's behavior
confirms our belief and Marlow's in the authority of a fixed standard of conduct — not this standard in particular, but the whole idea
of standards. What Conrad had begun to see, however, was that in
order to so inspire us with his faith in the power of an abstraction,
Jim had as a character become involved in a more resonant, seminal
transgression: he had to believe in the ordained self, to remain unaware of his responsibility for choosing an ideal, unaware of his
responsibility as a free man. He goes to Patusan not to expiate guilt
but to redeem reputation ("You-shall-hear-of-me."), if not in the
eyes of other white men at least in his own. It is the often slight but
immensely important distance between the free human spirit and

identity or self (including the values, the idealism of that self) that Conrad begins to see in Lord Jim and, only months before, has suggested in the victory of Kurtz. Henceforth Conrad's most compelling moral awareness lies always in the exploration of this precious interior distance, though the root conceptions of his art must be changed for its sake.

What finally persuades me that Conrad has occasionally been imagining the human mind by means of metaphors, or in the mode of metaphor, is the fundamental role that this interior distance, or, better, nothingness, plays in his work. From the moment that Willems accuses Aïssa of assaulting him with her empty eyes, on through the hollowness of Kurtz and continuing through *Nostromo* and *Under Western Eyes*, Conrad has been haunted by the seemingly unthinkable notion that the mind is somehow involved with nothingness. On the face of it such a comparison is ridiculous: how can something as tangible to us as consciousness be like nothing? One feels that he may simply be playing with words in discussing these matters at all. Yet there it is — in or just behind the text again and again. And what is so remarkable is Conrad's willingness to entertain the metaphor at all, much less give it its head in such drama as Razumov with his problems of identity. Had he not approached the problem of mind and consciousness in the spirit I have suggested, he could not have approached this nothingness. It is the state of mind characteristic of metaphor that allows the logically paradoxical doubleness which both protects the author from some of the more intimidating aspects of such nothingness and yet allows him to move dangerously near. I do not use the word "dangerously" lightly. Conrad was perfectly capable of neurotic symptoms in which one feels nearly disembodied, totally self-alienated — not only the routine morning question to the mirror, "Is this really me?" but the more disturbing, "Is there a me?" He takes a passionate interest in stripping characters of their names: Nostromo, Razumov, Lena, to cite only conspicuous examples.

Without metaphor the idea of an affinity between consciousness and nothingness is literally unthinkable. Nothingness may have a great many characteristics, not all or even most of which suggest qualities of consciousness. A glass empty of its water, a city square empty of its people, the space between stars — all these are in some sense different kinds of emptiness and yet even these share the quality of having been negatively stated. Conrad's nothingness, as is Sartre's, is a positive quality, a tangible presence, almost with its own taste. Analogy and metaphor allow him to explore some of its characteristics without needing to affirm them as ideas, much less beliefs. As in a poem by Dylan Thomas the "hanging man" may be both Christ and the embryo of Thomas himself, so Conrad's nothingness is often an exercise in doubleness and even contradiction.

Without allowing metaphor to ply its natural trade, its capacity for eluding the mode of logical proposition, Conrad would never have discovered some of the qualities that define his total vision. He would not have developed the special sense of freedom that goes with these intimations of nothingness — a sense that is, if anything, their redeeming quality. And, finally, he would not have cultivated that special sense of responsibility that seems to me the very timbre of his voice.

# NOTES

# Notes

## Introduction

1. M. H. Abrams, *The Mirror and the Lamp: Romantic Theory and the Critical Tradition* (New York: Norton, 1958).
2. Abrams, *Mirror and the Lamp*, pp. 34–35.
3. Colin Murray Turbayne, *The Myth of Metaphor* (New Haven: Yale University Press, 1962).
4. Gilbert Ryle, *The Concept of Mind* (London and New York: Hutchinson's University Library, 1949).
5. Turbayne, *Myth of Metaphor*, p. 63.
6. Turbayne, quoting Max Black, in *Myth of Metaphor*, p. 12.

## Chapter 1. The Paralysis of Will:
### *Almayer's Folly* and *An Outcast of the Islands*

1. Ian Watt, *The Rise of the Novel: Studies in Defoe, Richardson and Fielding* (Berkeley: University of California Press, 1964).
2. Mark Spilka, *Dickens and Kafka: A Mutual Interpretation* (Bloomington: Indiana University Press, 1963).
3. Paul L. Wiley, *Conrad's Measure of Man* (Madison: University of Wisconsin Press, 1954), p. 52. Comments on this basic model will be found throughout Wiley's introduction and second chapter.
4. See George Ross Ridge, *The Hero in Decadent French Literature* (Athens: University of Georgia Press, 1961), pp. 31–32, for an explanation that involves the effect of "megalopolis."
5. See Jocelyn Baines, *Joseph Conrad: A Critical Biography* (London: Weidenfeld and Nicolson, 1960), p. 399, on an article by Katherine Haynes Gatch, "Conrad's Axel."
6. Edmund Wilson, *Axel's Castle* (New York: Scribner's, 1931), pp. 265–66.

7. Gerard Jean-Aubry, *Joseph Conrad: Life and Letters* (Garden City, N.Y.: Doubleday, Page, 1927), 2:289.

8. Wiley, *Conrad's Measure of Man*, p. 41.

9. *Ibid.*, pp. 80–81.

10. *Ibid.*, p. 31.

11. John Galsworthy, *Castles in Spain* (New York: Scribner's, 1927), p. 121. See also A. Baillot, *Influence de la philosophie de Schopenhauer en France* (Paris, 1927). Before Conrad ever read Schopenhauer, he must have been thoroughly exposed to Schopenhauerian ideas.

## Chapter 2. Ego and Sympathy: *The Nigger of the Narcissus*

1. Thomas Moser, *Joseph Conrad: Achievement and Decline* (Cambridge, Mass.: Harvard University Press, 1957); Bernard C. Meyer, *Joseph Conrad: A Psychoanalytic Biography* (Princeton: Princeton University Press, 1967).

2. Vernon Young, "Trial by Water: Joseph Conrad's *The Nigger of the 'Narcissus,'*" *Accent*, 12 (Spring 1952):67–81.

3. Lawrence Graver, *Conrad's Short Fiction* (Berkeley and Los Angeles: University of California Press, 1969).

4. Morton Dauwen Zabel, "Conrad," in *Craft and Character in Modern Fiction* (New York: Viking, 1957); Albert J. Guerard, *Conrad the Novelist* (Cambridge, Mass.: Harvard University Press, 1958).

5. Guerard, *Conrad the Novelist*, p. 104.

## Chapter 3. A Source for the Ego-Sympathy Model: Schopenhauer

1. As Edward W. Said has suggested, Conrad may have first known Schopenhauer by way of Brunetière's essays, especially his "La Philosophie de Schopenhauer et les conséquences du pessimisme," in *Essais sur la litterature contemporaine*, but its date of publication, 1892, suggests that it could not have been his first encounter with Schopenhauerian ideas. See Edward W. Said, *Joseph Conrad and the Fiction of Autobiography* (Cambridge, Mass.: Harvard University Press, 1966), p. 102.

2. Frederick Copleston, *Arthur Schopenhauer, Philosopher of Pessimism* (London: Burns, Oates and Washbourne, 1946), pp. 29–30.

3. William Bisshe Stein, "The Lotus Posture and *Heart of Darkness*," *Modern Fiction Studies*, 2 (Winter 1956–57):235–37.

4. *The Basis of Morality*, trans. Arthur Bullock (London: Allen & Unwin, 1915).

5. *Basis of Morality*, pp. 174–75.

6. *Basis of Morality*, p. xxv.

7. Jean-Aubry, *Life and Letters*, 1:83–85.

8. Copleston, *Arthur Schopenhauer*, p. 28.

9. Quoted from *Die Welt als Wille und Vorstellung*, in Israel Knox, *The Aesthetic Theories of Kant, Hegel, and Schopenhauer* (New York: Columbia University Press, 1963), pp. 132–33.

10. Knox, *Aesthetic Theories of Kant, Hegel, and Schopenhauer*, p. 133.

11. *Ibid.*, p. 136.

12. John Wilcox, "The Beginnings of *L'Art pour L'Art*," *Journal of Aesthetics and Art Criticism*, 11 (June 1953):360–77.

## Chapter 4. The Psychology of Self-Image: *Lord Jim*

1. Eloise Knapp Hay, *The Political Novels of Joseph Conrad* (Chicago: University of Chicago Press, 1963), pp. 64–65, 66.

## Chapter 5. Existential
## Models: *Heart of Darkness* and *Lord Jim*

1. James Guetti, *The Limits of Metaphor: A Study of Melville, Conrad, and Faulkner* (Ithaca: Cornell University Press, 1967), pp. 46–68.

2. Jean-Paul Sartre, *Being and Nothingness: An Essay on Phenomenological Ontology*, trans. Hazel E. Barnes (New York: Philosophical Library, 1956), pp. 557–74.

3. "Key to Special Terminology," *ibid.*, p. 630.

4. *Ibid.*, p. 566.

5. *The Phantom Rickshaw and Other Tales* (London, 1890). Subsequent page references are to the 1898 Scribner's edition published in New York.

6. See the very interesting *White Man in the Tropics: Two Moral Tales*, ed. with introductions by David Daiches (New York: Harcourt, Brace and World, 1962). The book represents the first important comparison of *Heart of Darkness* with another tale from the genre, "The Beach of Falesá," although Daiches invariably uses Stevenson's work to point out Conrad's infinite superiority.

7. Graver, *Conrad's Short Fiction*, p. 12.

8. Jean-Aubry, *Life and Letters*, 1:264.

9. *Ibid.*, 1:209.

10. *Ibid.*, 1:208.

11. Elliot L. Gilbert, "What Happens in 'Mrs. Bathurst,'" *PMLA*, 77 (September 1962):450–58.

12. See the reproduction of this manuscript letter in Hay, *Political Novels of Joseph Conrad*, p. 77.

13. *Pensées*, trans. W. F. Trotter (New York: Dutton, 1931).

14. J. Hillis Miller, *The Disappearance of God* (Cambridge, Mass.: Harvard University Press, Belknap Press, 1963).

15. Sartre, *Being and Nothingness*, pp. 609–11.

16. *Ibid.*, p. 615.

## Chapter 6. The Psychology of Self-Image: *Nostromo*

1. Irving Howe, *Politics and the Novel* (New York: Horizon Press and Meridian Books, 1957), pp. 76–113; Hay, *Political Novels of Joseph Conrad*, chap. 5.

2. Claire Rosenfield, *Paradise of Snakes: An Archetypal Analysis of Conrad's Political Novels* (Chicago: University of Chicago Press, 1967), p. 58.

3. Robert H. Knapp, "The Psychology of Personality," in *The Behavioral Sciences Today*, ed. Bernard Berelson (New York: Harper Torchbooks, 1963), pp. 158, 164.

## Chapter 7. The Whole Man: "The Secret Sharer"

1. "Henry James: An Appreciation," in Conrad, *Notes on Life and Letters* (London: Dent Collected Edition), p. 15.

2. Baines, *Joseph Conrad*, p. 356.

3. Bruce M. Johnson, "Conrad's 'Falk': Manuscript and Meaning," *Modern Language Quarterly*, 26 (June 1965):272. The "Falk" manuscript is now at Yale University. Permission to quote has been granted by the Trustees of the Joseph Conrad Estate.

4. Royal A. Gettman and Bruce Harkness, "Morality and Psychology in 'The Secret Sharer,'" in *Conrad's "Secret Sharer" and the Critics*, ed. Bruce Harkness (Belmont, Calif.: Wadsworth Publishing Co., 1962), pp. 131–32.

5. Carl Benson, "Conrad's Two Stories of Initiation," *PMLA*, 69 (March 1954):46–56; reprinted in Harkness, *Conrad's "Secret Sharer" and the Critics*.

6. Benson, in Harkness, *Conrad's "Secret Sharer" and the Critics*, p. 84.

7. Walter Wright, *Romance and Tragedy in Joseph Conrad* (Lincoln: University of Nebraska Press, 1949), p. 49.

## Chapter 8. The Psychology of Self-Image: *Under Western Eyes*

1. Hay, *Political Novels of Joseph Conrad*, pp. 25–26.

2. Gerard Jean-Aubry, *The Sea Dreamer: A Definitive Biography of Joseph Conrad*, trans. Helen Sibba (London: George Allen and Unwin, 1957), pp. 255–56.

3. Leo Gurko, *Joseph Conrad: Giant in Exile* (New York: Macmillan, 1962), p. 186.

4. Gurko, *Conrad*, p. 190; Hay, *Political Novels of Joseph Conrad*, p. 309.

5. Frederick R. Karl, *A Reader's Guide to Joseph Conrad* (New York: Farrar, Straus; Noonday Press, 1960), p. 223.

6. *Ibid.*, p. 217.

7. Both letters are in *Letters from Joseph Conrad*, ed. Edward Garnett (New York: Bobbs Merrill, Charter Books, 1962), pp. 232–35.

## Chapter 9. Renewed Existential Models: *Victory*

1. Baines, *Joseph Conrad*, p. 372.

2. Both this quotation and that above are from Howe, *Politics and the Novel*, p. 80.

3. Quoted in Richard Ellmann, *Yeats: The Man and the Masks* (New York: Dutton, paperback ed., 1958), p. 89.

4. Moser, *Joseph Conrad*, pp. 117–18.

## Chapter 10. The Exhaustion of a Model: "The Planter of Malata" and *The Rescue*

1. Moser, *Joseph Conrad*, pp. 146, 148, 150.

2. Hay, *Political Novels of Joseph Conrad*, p. 97.

3. Wiley, *Conrad's Measure of Man*, pp. 158–62.

4. The manuscript of "The Planter of Malata" is now in the Harvard University Library, which kindly provided me with a microfilm.

5. Hay, *Political Novels of Joseph Conrad*, pp. 99–102, including footnote 34.
6. Joseph Conrad, *Letters to William Blackwood and David S. Meldrum*, ed. William Blackburn (Durham, N.C.: Duke University Press, 1958), p. 10.

## Chapter 11. Conclusion: Responsibility and the Existential Metaphor

1. Josiah Royce, quoted in Patrick Gardiner, *Schopenhauer* (Penguin Books, 1963), p. 21.
2. Quoted in *ibid.*, p. 159.
3. *Ibid.*, pp. 159–60.
4. Schopenhauer, quoted in *ibid.*, p. 162.
5. *Ibid.*, p. 168.

INDEX

# Index